First World War
and Army of Occupation
War Diary
France, Belgium and Germany

51 DIVISION
Divisional Troops
256 Brigade Royal Field Artillery
2 May 1915 - 25 March 1919

WO95/2854/4

The Naval & Military Press Ltd
www.nmarchive.com
Published in association with The National Archives

Published by

The Naval & Military Press Ltd

Unit 10 Ridgewood Industrial Park,

Uckfield, East Sussex,

TN22 5QE England

Tel: +44 (0) 1825 749494

www.naval-military-press.com

www.nmarchive.com

This diary has been reprinted in facsimile from the original. Any imperfections are inevitably reproduced and the quality may fall short of modern type and cartographic standards.

© **Crown Copyright**
Images reproduced by permission of The National Archives, London, England, 2015.

Contents

Document type	Place/Title	Date From	Date To
Heading	WO95/2854/4 256 Brig. Royal Field Arty 1915 May-1919 March		
Heading	256th (Highland) Bde RFA May 1915-Mar 1919		
Miscellaneous	1/2nd Highland Bde RFA Vol I 2-30.5.15		
War Diary	Bedford	02/05/1915	02/05/1915
War Diary	Havre	03/05/1915	30/05/1915
Diagram etc			
Heading	2nd Highland Bde RFA. Vol II 1-30.6.15		
Heading	War Diary Of 1/2nd Highland Field Artillery Brigade From 1 June 1915 To 30 June 1915		
War Diary	Le Touret	01/06/1915	30/06/1915
Heading	1/2nd Highland Bde R.F.A. Vol III From 3rd To 30th July 1915		
War Diary	Laventie	03/07/1915	30/07/1915
Heading	1/2 Highland Bde RFA. Vol IV 4-28 Aug 15		
War Diary	Mericourt L'Abbe	04/08/1915	28/08/1915
Heading	1/2nd Highland Bde RFA. Vol V Sept 15		
War Diary		03/09/1915	30/09/1915
Heading	2nd Highland Bde RFA Vol VI Oct 15		
War Diary		01/10/1915	29/10/1915
Heading	1/2 Highland R.F.A. Bde Nov Vol VII		
War Diary	The Field	01/11/1915	27/11/1915
Heading	1/2 Highland Bde R.F.A. Jan 1916 Vol IX		
War Diary	In The Field	08/01/1916	29/02/1916
War Diary	Field	01/03/1916	29/04/1916
War Diary	In The Field	08/05/1916	30/06/1916
Heading	War Diary Of 256th Brigade RFA From 1st July 1916 To 31st July 1916 (Volume)		
War Diary	In The Field	01/07/1916	14/07/1916
War Diary	Field	15/07/1916	31/07/1916
Heading	256th Brigade Royal Field Artillery. August 1916		
War Diary	Field	01/08/1916	31/08/1916
Heading	War Diary of 256th Brigade R.F.A. from 1st September 1916 to 30th September 1916		
War Diary	Field	01/09/1916	30/09/1916
Heading	War Diary. of 256th Brigade Royal Field Artillery From 1st October 1916 To. 31st October 1916		
War Diary	Field	01/10/1916	31/10/1916
Heading	War Diary Nov. 13th To 16th 1916 Appendix B.		
Miscellaneous	Report On Operations From 13th To 16th November Inclusive.		
Heading	War Diary 13th To 16th Nov. 1916 Appendix A.		
Heading	War Diary of 256th Bde R.F.A. Nov. 1st To Nov 30th 1916		
War Diary	Field	01/11/1916	16/11/1916
Heading	War Diary of 256th Brigade R.F.A. From 1st December 1916 To 31st December 1916 Vol 20		
War Diary	Field	01/12/1916	31/12/1916
Miscellaneous			
Operation(al) Order(s)	51st Divisional Artillery. Operation Order No. 59	10/11/1916	10/11/1916

Type	Description	From	To
Miscellaneous	255 Bde R.F.A	11/11/1916	11/11/1916
Miscellaneous	51st Divisional Artillery Table A.		
Miscellaneous	51st D.A. No. BM 304/38	11/11/1918	11/11/1918
Operation(al) Order(s)	51st Divisional Artillery. Operation Order No. 60	14/11/1916	14/11/1916
Miscellaneous	A Form. Messages And Signals.	14/11/1916	14/11/1916
Miscellaneous	A Form. Messages And Signals.	15/11/1916	15/11/1916
Miscellaneous	A Form. Messages And Signals.		
Miscellaneous	Headquarters. No. 2 Group.	15/11/1916	15/11/1916
Miscellaneous	A Form. Messages And Signals.	15/11/1916	15/11/1916
Miscellaneous	A Form. Messages And Signals.	16/11/1916	16/11/1916
Map			
Miscellaneous	Add 30 M.R.		
Heading	War Diary Of 256th Brigade R.F.A. From 1st Jan 1917 To 31st Jan 1917		
War Diary	Field	01/01/1917	31/01/1917
Heading	War Diary Of 256th Brigade R.F.A. From 1st February 1917 To 28th February 1917 Vol 22		
War Diary	Field	01/02/1919	28/02/1919
Heading	War Diary Of 256th Bde R.F.A. From 1st March 1917 To 31st March 1917 Vol 23		
War Diary	Field	01/03/1917	31/03/1917
Heading	War Diary Of 256th Brigade R.F.A. From 1st April 1917 To 30th April 1917 Vol 24		
War Diary	Field	02/04/1917	30/04/1917
Heading	War Diary Of 256th Brigade R.F.A. From 1st May 1917 To 31st May 1917 Vol 25		
War Diary	Field	01/05/1917	31/05/1917
Heading	War Diary From June 1 1917 To June 30 1917 256th Bde R.F.A.		
War Diary	Field	01/06/1917	23/06/1917
Miscellaneous	No Diaries for Period Between June and December 1917		
Heading	War Diary Of 256th Bde R.F.A. From 1st To 31st Dec 1917 Vol 32		
War Diary		01/12/1917	28/12/1917
War Diary	Field	28/12/1917	28/12/1917
Heading	War Diary Of 256th Bde. R.F.A. From 1st To 31st January 1918 Vol 33		
War Diary	Field	01/01/1918	31/01/1918
Heading	War Diary Of 256 Brigade R.F.A. (T.F.) From 1st February 1918-To 28th February 1918 Vol 34		
War Diary	Field	01/02/1918	28/02/1918
Heading	256th Brigade Royal Field Artillery March 1918		
Heading	War Diary Of 256 Brigade. R.F.A. (TF) From 1st March 1918 To 31st March 1918 Vol 35		
War Diary	Field	01/03/1918	31/03/1918
Heading	256th Brigade Royal Field Artillery April 1918		
Heading	War Diary Of 256 Brigade R.F.A (T.F.) Fro 1st April 1915 To 30th April 1918 Vol 36		
War Diary	Field	01/04/1918	30/04/1918
Heading	War Diary Of 256 Bde. R.F.A. (T.F.) From 1st May 1918 To 31st May 1918 Vol 37		
War Diary	Field	01/05/1918	31/05/1918
Heading	War Diary Of 256 Bde. R.F.A. (T.F.) From 1st June 1918 To 30th June 1918 Vol 38		
War Diary	Field	01/06/1918	30/06/1918

Heading	256th Brigade R.F.A. July 1918		
Heading	War Diary Of 256 Bde. R.F.A. (T.F.) From 1st July 1918 To 31st July 1918 Vol 39		
War Diary	Field	01/07/1918	31/07/1918
Heading	War Diary Of 256 Bde. R.F.A. (T.F.) From 1st August 1918 To 31st August 1918 Vol 40		
War Diary	Field	01/08/1918	31/08/1918
Heading	War Diary Of 256 Bde. R.F.A. (T.F.) From 1st September 1918 To 30th Sept 1918 Vol 41		
War Diary	Field	01/09/1918	30/09/1918
Heading	War Diary Of 256 Brigade R.F.A. (T.F.) From 1st October 1918 To 31st October 1918 Vol 42		
War Diary	Field.	01/10/1918	30/11/1918
Heading	War Diary Of 256 Highland Brigade R.F.A. T.F. From 1st November 1918 To 30th November 1918 Vol 43		
Heading	War Diary Of 256 Bde R.F.A. (T.F.) From 1st December 1918 To 31st December 1918 Vol 44		
War Diary	Field	01/12/1918	01/12/1918
Heading	War Diary Of 256 Highland Brigade R.F.A. T.F. From 1st January 1919 To 31st January 1919 Vol 45		
War Diary	France	01/01/1919	01/01/1919
Heading	War Diary Of 256 (Highland) Bde. R.F.A. T.F. From 1st February 1919 To 28th February 1919 Vol 46		
War Diary	France	01/02/1919	01/02/1919
Heading	War Diary Of 256 (Highland) Brigade R.F.A. T. From 1st March 1919 To 31st March 1919 Vol 47		
War Diary	France	01/03/1919	25/03/1919

WO 95 2854/4

256 Brig. Royal Field Art'y
1915 May – 1919 March

51ST DIVISION

256TH (HIGHLAND) BDE RFA
MAY 1915 - MAR 1919

121/5502

51st Division.

1/2nd Highland Bde RFA.

Vol. 2 — 30.5.15.

a2
a56

17.

WAR DIARY
or
~~INTELLIGENCE~~ SUMMARY
(Erase heading not required.)

Army Form C. 2118.

Hour, Date, Place	Summary of Events and Information	Remarks and References to Appendices
Bedford 2/5/15	SOUTHAMPTON SOUTH: The Brigade left for ~~Southampton~~ embarking at ~~Southampton~~ HAVRE ~~Southampton for Havre~~ in the evening of this date. SOUTHAMPTON The following officers of the Brigade embarked at Southampton:- Headquarters Lieut. Col. R.A. Mudie, Officer Commanding. 2/Lieut H.A. Ollett, Adjutant. Capt. A.R. Gill, Orderly Officer. Lieut G.R.E.J. Mackay R.A.M.C. Medical Officer Lieut B.H. Benson A.V.C. Veterinary Officer. Forfarshire Battery Major H. Fraser, Capt. S.E. Wilson, Lieut J.B. Mudie, Lieut James Bruce. Fifeshire Battery Major W.K.O Shepherd, Capt J.O. Shepherd, Lieut R.R. Wall, 2/Lieut F.L. Jack City of Dundee Battery Major K.S. Malcolm, Capt J.G. Lawrie, Lieut H. Fawther, 2/Lieut R.B. Alexander. Ammunition Column Capt. J.H. Bowman, Lieut G.A.D. McDonell, Lieut A.A. Wightman, 2/Lieut G.C. Caird.	Alex R. Gill Alex R. Gill

Army Form C. 2118.

1/2ND HIGHLAND BDE. R.F.A.

WAR DIARY
or
INTELLIGENCE SUMMARY
(Erase heading not required.)

Hour, Date, Place	Summary of Events and Information	Remarks and References to Appendices
Havre 3/5/15 4/5/15	The Brigade entrained at HAVRE HAZEBROUCK proceeding to Hazebrouck, thereafter proceeding to MERVILLE and thence where they detrained and went into billets at BERGUET HAMET RIGHET near ST VENANT.	
6/5/15	The Brigade moved to RIEZ DU VENAGE	
12/5/15	The Brigade returned to HAMET BILLETS	
14/5/15	The Brigade moved to BORRE HAZEBROUCK	
18/5/15	The Brigade moved to LA GORGUE	
19/5/15	The Brigade moved to PARADIS	
20/5/15	A section of each of the batteries took up positions at a point between RUE DES CHAVATIES RUE DES BORCEAUX LACOUTURE and Rue des Vaches and Rue La Bassee near and proceeded to register various points	
21/5/15 22/5/15	The remaining sections of the batteries joined the sections already in action. The headquarters being billeted at LE TOURET The Ammunition Column moved to a point between LOCON and HINGES (Vide? map attached shewing various points registered.)	

31/5/15

Army Form C. 2118.

WAR DIARY
INTELLIGENCE SUMMARY
(Erase heading not required.)

Instructions regarding War Diaries and Intelligence Summaries are contained in F. S. Regs., Part II. and the Staff Manual respectively. Title pages will be prepared in manuscript.

Hour, Date, Place	Summary of Events and Information	Remarks and References to Appendices
22/5/15 to 23/5/15	The batteries registered numerous points on zones allotted to them	
24/5/15 & 25/5/15	The batteries took part from 11 p.m. to 1 a.m. in a bombardment in support of an attack by the Canadians. Yoker battery fired at working parties on new trench and redoubt between P.16 and N.14	
	City of Dundee battery shelled trench 21/2° right of Q 9	
25/5/15	The batteries fired at working parties which appeared at various points	
26/5/15	Fifeshire Battery fired at working party in neighbourhood of P.12. City of Dundee Bhy. shelled Mound between Q.10 & Q.12 and Q.9. Enemy reported to be massing opposite P.10 and trenches were shelled and diggers party near P.14 also fired at	
27/5/15	Fifeshire Bhy. shelled suspected German Bhy. position on line to N.18. Earthwork on battery position at N.16 was shelled by Yoker Bhy. and also middle house at P.13 apparently an observation post	
29/5/15		
30/5/15	City of Dundee Bhy. shelled front west of P.16 where there appeared to be some movement	

Reference - Trench Map 1/5000

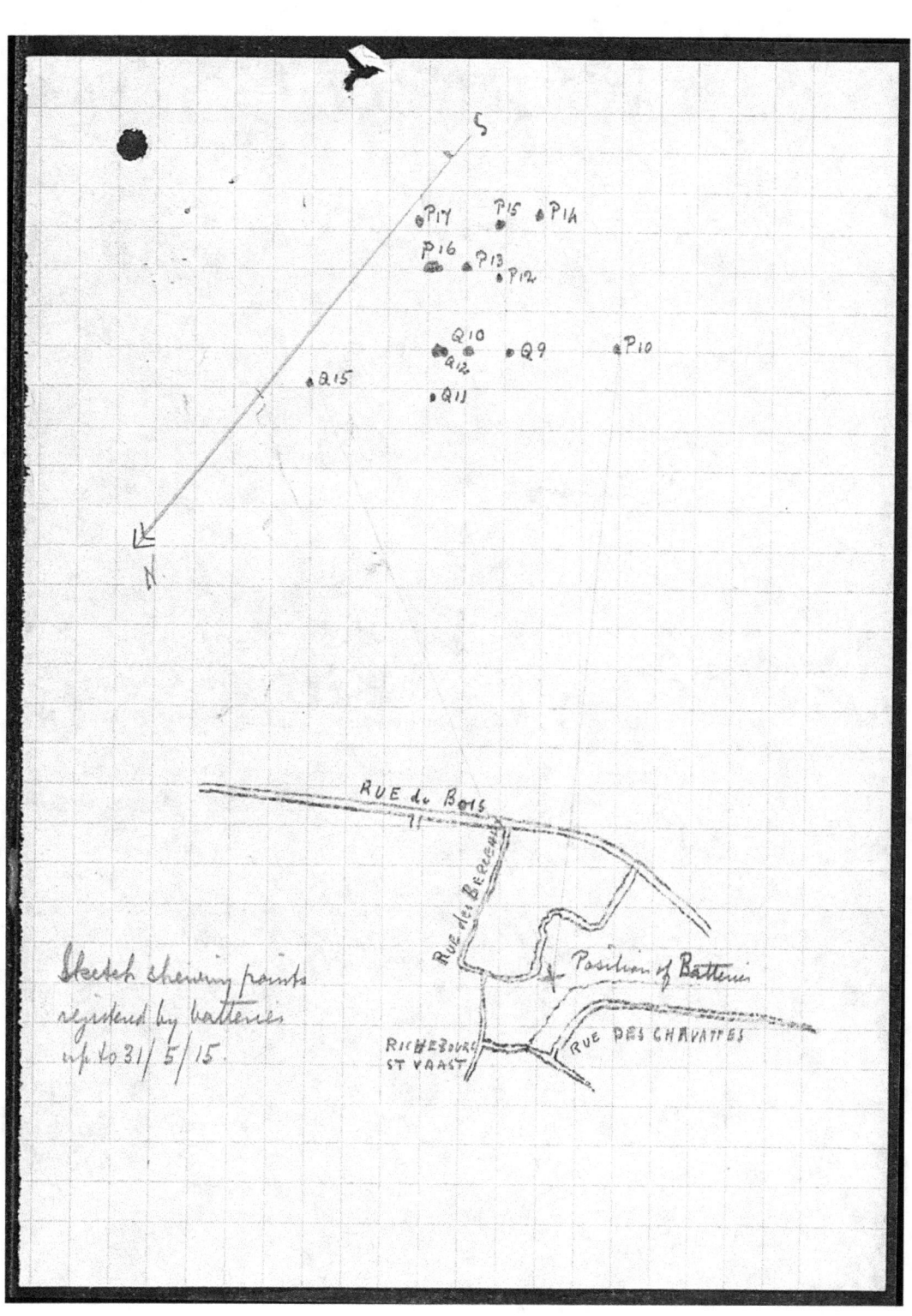

a2
a96.

137/5914

51st Division

2nd Highland Bde R.F.A.

Vol II   1 — 30.6.15

Confidential.

War Diary
of
1/2nd Highland Field Ar-
:tillery Brigade

From 1 June 1915
To 30 June 1915

Army Form C. 2118.
20.

WAR DIARY

INTELLIGENCE SUMMARY.

(Erase heading not required.)

Instructions regarding War Diaries and Intelligence Summaries are contained in F. S. Regs., Part II. and the Staff Manual respectively. Title pages will be prepared in manuscript.

Place	Date	Hour	Summary of Events and Information	Remarks and references to Appendices
Le Touret	1/6/15	9.30 a.m	Forfar Bty. fired at M18 with object of registering same but though observing from Brewery at FESTUBERT rounds could not be observed	a.r.g.
	"	4.30 p.m	Forfar Bty. fired on trench west of P.11 where working parties were seen	a.r.g.
	"	—	Fifeshire and bty of Dundee Bhys. registered on M11 and M15 respectively with view to firing on German horse-Iimit reported to pass along RUE DU MARAIS each evening.	a.r.g.
	3/6/15	3.40 p.m	Forfar Bty. fired on working party observed near P.12	a.r.g.
		9.30 p.m	The Three Btys. fired on RUE DU MARAIS where transport reported to be passing	a.r.g.
	4/6/15	2.10 p.m	Fifeshire Bty. observing from FESTUBERT registered on M16 on RUE DU MARAIS	a.r.g.
		6.35 p.m	Forfar Bty. fired on working party at trench in front of P.12	a.r.g.
	4/6/15	8 p.m / 8.40 p.m }	Forfar Bty. fired on transport reported to be passing along RUE DU MARAIS	a.r.g.
			Batteries continued registration of various points.	a.r.g.
	5/6/15	4.30 p.m / 4.35 p.m }	Batteries fired on transport reported passing along RUE DU MARAIS	a.r.g.
			Batteries continued registration of various points.	a.r.g.
	6/6/15	3.50 a.m	Forfar Bty. fired on transport reported on RUE DU MARAIS.	a.r.g.
		11.30 a.m	Do – fired on working party on trench near N15	a.r.g.

Army Form C. 2118.

21.

WAR DIARY
INTELLIGENCE SUMMARY.
(Erase heading not required.)

Instructions regarding War Diaries and Intelligence Summaries are contained in F. S. Regs., Part II. and the Staff Manual respectively. Title pages will be prepared in manuscript.

Place	Date	Hour	Summary of Events and Information	Remarks and references to Appendices
LE TOURET	6/6/15	2.25 p.m.	Forfar Bty. fired on trenches in neighbourhood of N14 and N15 and on trench between M9 and M16 for regis: tration and effect and at 6.5 p.m. fired on same trenches in conjunction with a 9.2 in gun "Mother"	apg.
		5 p.m. 5.45 p.m. 8.30 p.m. 10.30 p.m.	Batteries fired on RUE DU MARAIS and trench near N15	apg.
	7/6/15	12.40 p.m.	Forfar Bty. fired on trench near N14	apg.
		5 p.m.	Fifeshire Bty. fired on party of trench between M9 and M16	apg.
		8.25 p.m. 10 p.m.	Transport on RUE DU MARAIS fired on by Dundee Bty. registered on redoubt near N15 and trench between M16 and M9	apg. apg.
	8/6/15		Transport on RUE DU MARAIS fired on at various times	apg.
		11.30 a.m. 2.15 p.m.	Trench between M9 and M16 fired on	apg.
	9/6/15	8.30 a.m.	Forfar Bty. were observed by German aeroplane and three shell fired at it, two men being hit by splinter but no damage done to guns.	apg.
	10/6/15		During the night the Forfar Bty. took up new position about half a mile to E of former position. Forfar Bty. registered from new position on known points previously registered but owing to mist registration could not be completed.	apg. apg. apg.

1577 Wt. W10791/1773 500,000 1/15 D.D. & L. A.D.S.S./Forms/C. 2118.

Army Form C. 2118.

WAR DIARY

~~INTELLIGENCE SUMMARY.~~

(Erase heading not required.)

Instructions regarding War Diaries and Intelligence Summaries are contained in F. S. Regs., Part II. and the Staff Manual respectively. Title pages will be prepared in manuscript.

22/

Place	Date	Hour	Summary of Events and Information	Remarks and references to Appendices
Le Touret	11/6/15		During forenoon and afternoon the batteries fired on the RUE DU MARAIS and trench between N15 and N17 and also registered further points.	A.R.J.
	12/6/15	1.15 p.m.	Forfar Bty fired on trench M9 to M16 & at 4.10 p.m. on new S.W. of Q.12 movements of the enemy having been seen there & many same apparently as an observing station.	A.R.J.
		6.40 p.m.	Transport on RUE DU MARAIS fired on	A.R.J.
	13/6/15	2 a.m.	Forfar and 6th of Dundee Btys fired on RUE DU MARAIS, trench east of N15 and Redoubt near N15	A.R.J.
	14/6/15 15/6/15 16/6/15		In connection with a projected attack on part of the German line opposite FESTUBERT misrepresentation was carried out by the Artillery on the front and the batteries of this Brigade kept up a steady slow during the nights to prevent them being repaired	A.R.J.
	16/6/15	3.30 p.m. 8.45 a.m.	Brigade took part in attack on German line opposite Festubert which at first resulted in our gaining the first line trench. In face of a counter attack we had to give up this trench & fall back to our original line. During the night the British guns attacked but failed to make any progress. Batteries fired at intervals on RUE DU MARAIS and trench M9 to M16	A.R.J. A.R.J.
	17/6/15		During the above bombardment one of the Fifeshire Btys guns developed defects & had to be sent out of action	A.R.J.

1577 Wt. W10791/1773 500,000 1/15 D. D. & L. A.D.S.S./Forms/C. 2118.

Army Form C. 2118.
23

WAR DIARY
INTELLIGENCE SUMMARY
(Erase heading not required.)

Instructions regarding War Diaries and Intelligence Summaries are contained in F. S. Regs., Part II. and the Staff Manual respectively. Title pages will be prepared in manuscript.

Place	Date	Hour	Summary of Events and Information	Remarks and references to Appendices
LE TOURET	18/6/15	5.15 p.m. 7.30 p.m.	The Fifeshire Bty after being observed by a hostile aeroplane was heavily shelled by the enemy one man being wounded. No damage was however done to the guns the range being very slightly over.	A.R.S.
	19/6/15 to 24/6/15		The Batteries continued registration of various points and from time to time fired on Rue Du MARAIS. Our transport reported to be passing along same.	A.R.S.
	25/6/15	9 p.m.	The Brigade moved to RUE DE LA LYS near ESTAIRES	A.R.S.
	26/6/15		The Battery moved into position FIFESHIRE Bty at M6 a 5.5 FORFAR Bty at M12 a 2.8 and CITY OF DUNDEE at M11 c 8.4. The HEADQUARTERS of the Brigade were established at M6 a 5.6. Rifle Shots 30/20,000	A.R.S.
	27/6/15		The Batteries proceeded to registration of various points.	A.R.S.
	30/6/15	3 a.m.	In connection with explosion of British mine at Point 326 Forfar Bty fired on communication trenches to left of this point after explosion	A.R.S.

Alex. R. Sokel Capt. R.F.A.

30 June 1915.

121/6410

as a,6

51st Division

1/2nd Highland -Bde R. F. A.

Vol III

From 3rd to 30 July 1915.

Army Form C. 2118.

WAR DIARY
INTELLIGENCE SUMMARY
(Erase heading not required.)

Instructions regarding War Diaries and Intelligence Summaries are contained in F. S. Regs., Part II and the Staff Manual respectively. Title pages will be prepared in manuscript.

Place	Date	Hour	Summary of Events and Information	Remarks and references to Appendices
LAVENTIE	3/7/15	2.20 a.m.	Germans opened with heavy rifle and machine gun fire and then shelled RUE TILLELOY heavily with hig grenades and howitzers and our Batteries replied each firing about 70 rounds	
"	4/7/15	8.30 to 11 a.m.	Germans fired over 100 howitzer shells on RUE VERTE the bulk of them landing in an orchard close to the 4 johnne Bty position and Brigade headquarters but no damage was done to either personnel or material at either of these places	
"	6/7/15	4.25 a.m. to 1.15 p.m.	The Batteries of the Brigade kept up a steady fire in retaliation for enemy shelling and trenches at F3	
"	8/7/15	1.45 p.m.	Forfar Battery fired 32 rounds in retaliation for enemy shelling our trenches at F2 and F5.	
"	9/7/15		The 1st body of Aberdeen Bty was of this date transferred to this Brigade temporarily for tactical purposes, the body of Dundee Bty being transferred temporarily to the 18th Brigade for same purpose. The 9th Battery R.F.A (18th Brigade) was also of this date transferred temporarily to this Brigade for tactical purposes	
"	11/7/15		The 9th Battery fired on trench mortar but owing to stormy weather failed to obtain a hit	

Alex R. Fith Capt. R.F.A

WAR DIARY

INTELLIGENCE SUMMARY

Army Form C. 2118.

25.

Place	Date	Hour	Summary of Events and Information	Remarks and references to Appendices
Laventie	19/4/15		Forfarshire and Fifeshire Batteries came out of action and moved to new billets at NEUF BERQUIN by ESTAIRES	
	21/4/15		Body of Dundee Bty came out of action and with Headquarters of Brigade joined Forfarshire and Fifeshire Batteries at new billet at NEUF BERQUIN. The 1st City of Aberdeen and 94th Batteries returned to their own Brigade.	
	27/4/15		The Brigade moved by road to MERICOURT L'ABBÉ Department SOMME	
	28/4/15		The Ammunition Column joined the Brigade at MERICOURT L'ABBÉ	
	30/4/15		Forfarshire and 6thy of Dundee Batteries moved one section each into new positions previously occupied by French batteries near MESNIL	

Alex R. Sylch Capt. R.F.A.
2nd Highland F.A. Brigade.

121/6874

51st Division

1/2 Highland Bde R.F.A.

Petrie

4 – 28 Aug 15

Army Form C. 2118
26.

WAR DIARY
INTELLIGENCE SUMMARY
(Erase heading not required.)

Place	Date	Hour	Summary of Events and Information	Remarks and references to Appendices
MERICOURT L'ABBE	6/8/15		Headquarters of Brigade moved from MERICOURT L'ABBE to MARTINSART and established Headquarters at Villa La Hirondelle there. Remaining sections of batteries already in position near MESNIL. A/82nd Battery under command of Capt. Noakes came under command of Brigade for tactical purposes and took up a position near MARTINSART. D/83rd Battery under command of Capt. Hewlett also came under command of Brigade for tactical purposes and took up a position midway between MARTINSART and AVELUY. The batteries proceeded to register various points in German line from ST PIERRE-DIVION to point opposite AUTHUILLE	
	9/8/15		The Brigade Ammunition Column moved from MERICOURT L'ABBE to WARLOY	
	9/8/15		Infantry Battery moved from MERICOURT L'ABBE to WARLOY	
	10/8/15		Infantry Battery moved from WARLOY to billets in BEHENCOURT	
	16/8/15		Headquarters of Brigade along with Infantry and Battery of Dundee Batteries came out of action and moved to join Infantry Battery in billets at BEHENCOURT.	
	17/8/15		The Brigade Ammunition Column moved from WARLOY to BEHENCOURT.	
	19/8/15		Lieut. R.R. Will, Lieut. Frank McBain and 2/Lieut. R.M. Lindsay joined the Brigade from Scotland for instructional purposes. Lieut. Will was posted to Infantry Battery	

Army Form C. 2118.

WAR DIARY
or
INTELLIGENCE SUMMARY.
(Erase heading not required.)

Instructions regarding War Diaries and Intelligence Summaries are contained in F. S. Regs., Part II. and the Staff Manual respectively. Title pages will be prepared in manuscript.

Place	Date	Hour	Summary of Events and Information	Remarks and references to Appendices
19/8/15 (contd)		—	and Lieut. McBain & 2/Lieut Lindsay to the Brigade Ammunition Column. Lieut. McDowell and Lieut Bould were transferred from the Brigade Ammunition Column; the former to the Btty of Dundee and the latter to Fortarline Batteries.	
	28/8/15	—	The three batteries of the Brigade got delivery of new 18 pr. Q.F. guns & equipment in place of the 15 pr. B.L.C. guns so far previously used by them. The Brigade Ammunition Column at same time got delivery of the new enemy 18 pr. Ammunition Wagons	

Alex. R. Gill. Capt. R.F.A.
2nd Highland H.A. Brigade

12/7341

51st Division

O.C. 1/2nd Highland Bde R.F.A.

9thV

Sept. 15.

Army Form C. 2118.
28.

WAR DIARY
INTELLIGENCE SUMMARY.

Place	Date	Hour	Summary of Events and Information	Remarks and references to Appendices
	3/9/15		One section of FIFESHIRE Battery left BEHENCOURT to take up position occupied by D/82nd Battery referred to in Brigade War Diary under date 4/8/15.	
	4/9/15		Remaining section of FIFESHIRE Battery joined the first section at above position, the battery passing to command of "1st Highland F.A. Bde for tactical purposes, and proceeding to register various points in German lines.	
	14/9/15		One section of Brigade Ammunition Column under 2/Lieut R.C. Macpherson moved from BEHENCOURT to WARLOY. The remaining section of Brigade Ammunition Column moved from BEHENCOURT to WARLOY	
	16/9/15		Headquarters of Brigade moved from BEHENCOURT to MARTINSART and established themselves at Villa des Hirondelles there, previously occupied by them. One section each of FORFARSHIRE and CITY of DUNDEE batteries took up position, the former the position previously occupied by them near MESNIL (see Bde War Diary under date 4/8/15) and the latter the position near MARTINSART previously occupied by A/82nd Battery (see Bde War Diary under date 4/8/15)	
	17/9/15			

Army Form C. 2118.

29.

WAR DIARY
INTELLIGENCE SUMMARY.

Place	Date	Hour	Summary of Events and Information	Remarks and references to Appendices
	17/9/15		The remaining sections of Foizelue and Bty of Dundee batteries joined the sections of their batteries already in action as above and proceeded to register various points in German line.	
	18/9/15		The Brigade Ammunition Column moved from WARLOY to CONTAY. D/85 (How) Battery R.F.A. under command of Major J Gawthen and occupying a position midway between MESNIL and MARTINSART came under command of the Brigade for tactical purposes and Foizelue Battery returned to their own Brigade.	
	18/9/15 to 30/9/15		The Batteries of the Brigade along with D/85 Bty, registered various points in German line and on hostile working parties and transport at various points	
	23/9/15 & 24/9/15		The Batteries of the Brigade carried out a systematic bombardment of wire in front of enemy's trenches with a view to cutting same. This was in the nature of an ex:periment and the experience gained showed that for this purpose the 18 pr guns would have to be brought up to a shorter range than they are at present to be usefully effective	
	25/9/15			

Army Form C. 2118.

WAR DIARY
INTELLIGENCE SUMMARY.
(Erase heading not required.)

Instructions regarding War Diaries and Intelligence Summaries are contained in F. S. Regs., Part II. and the Staff Manual respectively. Title pages will be prepared in manuscript.

Place	Date	Hour	Summary of Events and Information	Remarks and references to Appendices
30.	30/9/15		A hostile AVIATIK biplane passed over our lines this morning and was attacked and brought down near SENLIS by an VICKERS biplane, both occupants of German plane being killed. Alex. R. Lyth Capt. R.F.A. 2nd Highland Field Artillery Brigade	

51st Brown

121/7429

2nd Highland Bde. R.F.A.

Vol VI.

Oct 15

WAR DIARY
or
INTELLIGENCE SUMMARY

Army Form C. 2118.

31

Place	Date	Hour	Summary of Events and Information	Remarks and references to Appendices
	1/10/15 to 31/10/15		The Batteries of the Brigade, along with D/85 Bty, remained in positions previously occupied by them and carried through quotidian registration of points in German lines, and when necessary retaliated for enemy trench mortar and shell fire and also when necessary fired on hostile working parties and transport.	
	20/10/15		On coming out of the trenches on this date the C.O. of the 6th Batt. Black Watch, who held the right subsector of line covered by the Brigade sent the following message to the C.O. of this Brigade: — "The C.O. 6th Black Watch wishes to convey to you his high appreciation of the Artillery support his Battalion has received while in the trenches. He considers it has always been quick, satisfactory and all over the best artillery co-operation he has yet had and that this message be conveyed to Lott Field, Lyon and Hardige batteries." (Respective Btys, 3rd High. (How.) Bde. ¼) the Forfarshire Bty of Dundee D/85 and a section of 15th Siege Battery under command of Capt Hart, had part in instituted Ohio Scheme was, drawn up by G.S. of 51st (High) Division which was carried out successfully	

Alex. R. Gold Capt. R.F.A.

for O.C. 2nd Highland Field Artillery Bde.

2/11/15

51 S/5 Brown

1/2/Highland R? A. Boe

Ans V

Vol VII

12/7779

WAR DIARY
INTELLIGENCE SUMMARY
(Erase heading not required.)

Army Form C. 2118
32.

Place	Date	Hour	Summary of Events and Information	Remarks and references to Appendices
The Field	1/11/15 to 30/11/15		The Batteries of the Brigade along with D/65 Battery remained in position previously occupied by them. Further registration of points in German lines was carried out. A good deal of firing took place on enemy working parties and transport reported front line trenches. Retaliation was also given for enemy trench mortar and shell fire when necessary. Several bombardments were carried through by Brigade in conjunction with Howitzer batteries. During the month the weather was very unsettled and there was much mist which made observation difficult.	
	15/11/15		Enemy bombarded left subsection (G3) of front covered by this Brigade during afternoon, firing about probably 1500 shells. Guns were ranged from 4 p.m. to 4.2 p.m. Some damage was done to our parapet but casualties were practically nil. We retaliated during after- noon and evening and their reply to our fire in the evening was very slight.	
	17/11/15 24/11/15		2/Lieut J.M. Bonifer joined the Brigade & was posted to Brigade Ammunition Column. The Midlothian Battery, R.F.A. (M.J.) (1st Lowland Bde R.F.A.) under command of Major Anderson took up position alongside of and immediately N of that occupied by Forfarshire Bty and came under command of this Brigade for tactical purposes & proceeded to register various points in zone allotted to them.	
	25/12/15			

Alex R. Gold Capt. R.F.A.
for O.C. 2nd ~~Highland~~ F.A. Brigade

1/2 Highland Bde R.F.A.
Jan 1916
Vol IX

Army Form C. 2118.
35

WAR DIARY
or
INTELLIGENCE SUMMARY.
(Erase heading not required.)

Place	Date	Hour	Summary of Events and Information	Remarks and references to Appendices
In the field	1916 JAN 8th/9th		The remaining sections & mark of the batteries came out of action and proceeded to WARLOY	
	9th	9am	Brigade marched to billets in ARGOEUVES and there went into rest. From this date until the end of the month Brigade training was carried out, and reveilling, and interior economy looked into.	
	26th		CAPT. A.R. GIBB was posted to C Bty 2 Dundee Battery VICE CAPT. J.B. TAWSE invalided home. LIEUT. R.C. COULL was posted to Bde HQrs. VICE CAPT. A.R. GIBB to City of Dundee Battery.	
	19/2/16			GCCoull Lieut R.F.A. for O.C. 2nd Highland F.A. Bde.

Army Form C. 2118.
36

WAR DIARY
INTELLIGENCE SUMMARY.
(Erase heading not required.)

Instructions regarding War Diaries and Intelligence Summaries are contained in F.S. Regs., Part II. and the Staff Manual respectively. Title pages will be prepared in manuscript.

Hour, Date, Place	Summary of Events and Information	Remarks and references to Appendices

1916
February 1. The Brigade remained in training at ARGOEUVES
" 4. LT-COL. R.A. MUDIE relinquished command of Brigade.
" 7. Brigade moved to BUSSY-LES-DAOURS, and there continued with Brigade training.
" 15th 11.40am. An explosion occurred accidentally which killed armourer artificer No 608 Staff Sgt. S.E DAVIS and seriously wounded No 697 Wheeler Sgt. J. FORSYTH.
Major L.M.DYSON R.F.A. joined the brigade and took command from this date.
" 20th. The 2nd Battery 3rd Highd F.A. (How) Brigade came under command of this Brigade for tactical purposes.
The CO Major DYSON and the OC of the FORFAR, FIFE, and DUNDEE BATTS, Major FRASER, May SHEPHERD, and CAPT. WILSON and OC Bde. Ac Capt BOWMAN horsed to BRAY & Supt HdQrs and from there went to their respective units to see the new positions.
" 21st. One section 1/FORFAR BATT and one section of 3rd (How) Batt of 3nd Highland Brigade went into Action in front of BRAY.

(73989) W4141—463. 400,000. 9/14. H.&J.Ltd. Forms/C. 2118/10.

Army Form C. 2118.

37

WAR DIARY
INTELLIGENCE SUMMARY.
(Erase heading not required.)

Hour, Date, Place	Summary of Events and Information	Remarks and references to Appendices
1916. February 23rd	One section of FIFE BATT. and one section of DUNDEE BATT. went into action in front of BRAY; DUNDEE in centre, and FIFE on left of group.	
" 25th	Bde HdQrs and remaining sections of the four batteries in this Bde moved up into action.	
" 26th 10 a.m.	Major L.M. DYSON took over command of left group consisting of FORFAR, FIFE, DUNDEE, D148, 18ldr batteries, D150 and 3rd Bde. 3rd Highland F.A. Bde, howitzer batteries.	
" 27th	Bde A.C. moved up to new position in BOIS de TAILLES, behind BRAY.	
" 28th	Brigade moved out of action, and proceeded first to BUSSY-LES-DAOURS.	
" 29th	Brigade moved to VILLERS-BOCAGE.	

GCMcKent
for Commanding, 2nd High F.A. Bde.

2/3/16.

Army Form C. 2118.

38

WAR DIARY
INTELLIGENCE SUMMARY.
(Erase heading not required.)

Place	Date	Hour	Summary of Events and Information	Remarks and references to Appendices
Field	1916 March 1st		The Brigade remained at VILLERS-BOCAGE	
	6th		Brigade moved to OUTREBOIS	
	8th		Brigade proceeded to REBREUVIETTE	
	9/10th		One section of the FORFAR, FIFE and DUNDEE Batteries took over from the French in a new part of the line and went into action about due South of the village of ROCLINCOURT.	
	10/11th		The remaining returns of the batteries proceeded into action and Colonel Ryan took over command of the Right Group of the 51st Division. The 51st Division being on the right, and the 46th Division being on the left of the 51st Division.	
	12th		Registering carried on by the batteries.	
	12/13th		The 3rd 306" Battery of the Bde High (How) Bde proceeded into action and came under the command of this group for tactical purposes.	
	13th		All batteries continued registering prominent points and trenches. Until the 30th March nothing unusual occurred on this front	

Place	Date	Hour	Summary of Events and Information	Remarks and references to Appendices
Julu	March 14th to 30 & 31st		The batteries fired on working parties, and traffic on the roads. Work was carried on during the month, strengthening the positions. At 3.37 am the officer at the O.P. heard an explosion, and saw two red rockets go up. Immediately the batteries received S.O.S. They opened fire on the trenches behind the German front line. At 4 am the order to cease fire was given by the Liaison officer of the left battalion. GCevill Lieut for Officer commanding 2nd High F.A. Bde	

Army Form C. 2118.

40.

WAR DIARY
INTELLIGENCE SUMMARY.
(Erase heading not required.)

Instructions regarding War Diaries and Intelligence Summaries are contained in F. S. Regs., Part II. and the Staff Manual respectively. Title pages will be prepared in manuscript.

Place	Date	Hour	Summary of Events and Information	Remarks and references to Appendices
Field	1916 April		The Brigade to which is attached "R" battery, 3rd Highland (How) Bde R.F.A. remained in action in the positions previously occupied by them	
	3		2/Lieut. P.D. FISHER joined the Bde and was posted to Fife Amm Coln 19th March 1916 and again posted to FIFE Battery on 8th April	
	3		2/LIEUT. E C BATCHELOR joined Bde and was posted to Dundee Battery 3rd April	
	3		" " J.M. FAIRLIE " " " " Fife Battery 3rd April
	3		" " J.S. ANDERSON " " " " Bde Amm Coln 3rd April
	8		" " G.J. MEIKLE " " " " Forfar Battery, 8th April
	8		" " D.B. REEKIE " " " " "D" Battery 8th April
	8		" " P.W. JOHNSTON " " " " "D" Battery 8th April
	15		" " E.F. BOYD " " " " Fife Battery 15th April
	15		" " W. HAY " " " " Dundee Battery 15th April
	15		" " D. NICOLL " " " " "D" Battery 15th April
	15		" " J.H. THORNE " " " " "D" Battery 15th April
	9		LIEUT R.R. ALEXANDER " " " attached Dundee Battery 9th April
	9		2/LIEUT G.H. LORD " " " attached Forfar Battery 9th April

WAR DIARY
INTELLIGENCE SUMMARY
(Erase heading not required.)

Army Form C. 2118.

4-1

Place	Date	Hour	Summary of Events and Information	Remarks and references to Appendices
Field	1916 April 4th			
	17th		"D" Battery, 2nd Hgh. F.A. Bde was formed.	
			Combined shoot with Divisional Artillery, Trench Mortars and Machine Guns.	
	26th		Combined shoot. "R" (Hen) Battery during registration had a premature at the muzzle of the gun, resulting in one man being killed, and knbs, two being wounded.	
	28th/29 2.15 am		Lyff and Trundle batteries opened on their barrage lines on receiving a message from the infantry that the enemy had blown a mine; firing was continued until 3.15 am, and then gradually quietened down.	
	29th	9.35 am	One ambulance seen behind enemy lines.	
		10 to 11.30 am	Three other ambulances were seen behind enemy lines.	
		2 to 2.30 pm	Another two ambulances were observed. All these ambulances were seen to be full of wounded, and looked as if they had just collected them from an advanced aid post. It seems probable from this observation that we caused considerable casualties

Army Form C. 2118.

WAR DIARY
or
INTELLIGENCE SUMMARY.
(Erase heading not required.)

Place	Date	Hour	Summary of Events and Information	Remarks and references to Appendices
Field	April 29th		to the enemy as a result of the previous night firing. Gillnell Lieut. fr. O.C. 2nd Highland F.A. Bde.	
	23/May. 1916.			

Instructions regarding War Diaries and Intelligence Summaries are contained in F. S. Regs., Part II. and the Staff Manual respectively. Title pages will be prepared in manuscript.

WAR DIARY
INTELLIGENCE SUMMARY.
(Erase heading not required.)

Army Form C. 2118.

46(A)

Place	Date	Hour	Summary of Events and Information	Remarks and references to Appendices
			A nominal roll of Officers in the brigade as it now stands is here given.	

Headquarters.
Lt.Col L.M. DYSON
Lieut H.A. OLLETT Adjutant
Lieut G.C. COULL Orderly Officer.

A Battery.
Major H. FRASER
Lieut. J. BRUCE
2/Lieut. J.M. ANDREW
2/Lieut. J.M. COUPER
2/Lieut T.J. MEIKLE
2/Lieut G.H. LORD

B. Battery.
Major W.K.O. SHEPHERD
Lieut R.R. WILL
Lieut A.A. WIGHTON
Lieut F.C. JACK
2/Lieut D. NICOLL
2/Lieut P.D. FISHER
2/Lieut E.F. BOYD
2/Lieut J.M. FAIRLIE

C Battery
Capt. S.C. WILSON
Capt. A.R. GIBB
Lieut. H. LOWTHER
Lieut R.R. ALEXANDER
2/Lieut R.C. MACPHERSON
2/Lieut E.C. BATCHELOR
2/Lieut W. HAY

D Battery
Capt. A.F.S. NAPIER
Lieut. C.C. WELSH
2/Lieut P. WHITE
2/Lieut G.R. WILLISON
2/Lieut A. BAILLIE

Gerrill Lieut
for O.C. Cavalry 256th Bde R.F.A.

256 Bde R.F.A
51
43

Army Form C. 2118.

WAR DIARY
or
INTELLIGENCE SUMMARY.
(Erase heading not required.)

Oct 1/2 High ... 13

Place	Date	Hour	Summary of Events and Information	Remarks and references to Appendices
Richebourg	1916 May			
		6.30 p.m.	The Brigade to which is attached "R" Battery, 3rd High. (Hrs) Bde, remained in action in the positions formerly occupied by it. An artillery shoot was carried out by the Divisional Artillery, assisted by the Trench Mortar Batteries; considerable damage was done to the Enemy's front line.	
	8th.		During the next few days there was considerable Trench Mortar activity on the part of the enemy and the Batteries in the Brigade were called upon frequently for retaliation. During the whole afternoon the O.P's were shelled intermittently with 77 m.m. and 4.2" guns	
	17th	8.5-8.30 p.m.	The infantry of the Brigade on our left had a cutting out expedition and t.c. Sirdee, his "R"(Hrs) batteries put up barrages behind the enemy front line. Our infantry returned safely to their own trenches and the whole scheme proved to be successful.	
	19th		On this date the 2nd Highland Brigade R.F.A. was reorganised. A 4.5"(Hrs) battery being added, and an 18 pdr battery and the Belle Vrun. Coln.	

WAR DIARY
or
INTELLIGENCE SUMMARY.

Army Form C. 2118.

44

Place	Date	Hour	Summary of Events and Information	Remarks and references to Appendices
In Field	1916 May 19th		being taken away. The Brigade was also renamed, being in future to be known as the 256th Bde. R.F.A., The batteries now constituting the brigade were renamed as follows:- The Tozer Battery became A/256 "Fife" " B/256 "Dundee" " C/256 "B"(Hry)battery from the 3rd Highland (Hry) Bde. R.F.A. became D/256. The 18/Lair "D" battery formerly in the Bde was transferred to the 256th Bde R.F.A. and was named B/258. The Ammunition Column was transferred to the Div. Ammunition Column to form the nucleus of that unit as reconstituted.	
	22nd			
	23rd		During the evening the enemy put up a heavy barrage with lachrymatory shells, and delayed all transport coming to batteries. C/256 was called upon by balloon to register on a position where a gun flashes were seen. Owing to the haze in which arose the shoot was not completed.	

WAR DIARY or INTELLIGENCE SUMMARY

Army Form C. 2118.

45

Place	Date	Hour	Summary of Events and Information	Remarks and references to Appendices
In the field	1916 May 23rd	10//m	B/256 fired on enemy's trenches assisting the 5th Div. by putting up a barrage. The infantry of the 5th Division had a cutting out expedition which was successful, but not so good as was desired.	
	26th		C/256 and D/256 fired on trenches to do as much damage as possible. The scheme was arranged by the C.R.A., the centre and left groups of the Division also assisting.	
	28th		D/256 knocked out a trench mortar emplacement.	
	29th	1.10 am	The enemy exploded a mine on the extreme left of the brigade of infantry covered by this brigade. S.O.S. was immediately sent down to the Bde, and all batteries opened fire at as slow rate on their barrage. At 1.30 fire was concentrated immediately behind the crater formed by the explosion, and kept up till 2.13 am, when the fire was again slowed down. At 2.30 am everything was reported quiet by the infantry.	
	30th	8.30//m	There was a continuous artillery shoot on enemy front trenches. Considerable damage was done.	

WAR DIARY
or
INTELLIGENCE SUMMARY.

Army Form C. 2118.

Place	Date	Hour	Summary of Events and Information	Remarks and references to Appendices
In the field	1916 May		During the month the sniping guns fired on points where movement was usually seen, ruined or the road, and crossroads leading into forward targets on many occasions. Towards the end of the month movement had greatly decreased, the enemy being compelled to seek the shelter of a trench whenever he showed himself.	
	1/6/16		Duckipoo Lt. Col. Comdg. 256th Bde. R.F.A.	

WAR DIARY
INTELLIGENCE SUMMARY.

(Erase heading not required.)

Army Form C. 2118.

256 Bde R.F.A.

Vol 14

Place	Date	Hour	Summary of Events and Information	Remarks and references to Appendices
In the Field	1916 June 1		The Brigade to which is attached B/258th Bde R.F.A. are now in action in the position previously occupied by it. C/256 got a direct hit on a tent which exploded it.	
		8.45 p.m	There was a bombrick shoot on the enemy's front line; much damage being done to same.	
	3rd	8.46 p.m.	The infantry raided the enemy's trenches. Owing to phosphorous 8.46 p.m. to 8.55 p.m. the field batteries barrages the enemy's front line at 8.55 we exploded two mines and the infantry advanced with bombs. This phase the guns lifted and barrages behind points where infantry attacked. The signal that the infantry had returned was given at 10.15 p.m. the guns keeping on their barrage all the time. Three prisoners were brought back and a great deal of damage was done to enemy's trenches, several dugouts being also bombed.	
	4th		Congratulatory messages were received from G.O.C. Div. and G.O.C. 154 Inf. Bde. on the successful cooperation of the artillery in the previous night's operation.	

WAR DIARY
INTELLIGENCE SUMMARY
(Erase heading not required.)

Army Form C. 2118.
7-8.

Instructions regarding War Diaries and Intelligence Summaries are contained in F. S. Regs., Part II. and the Staff Manual respectively. Title pages will be prepared in manuscript.

Place	Date	Hour	Summary of Events and Information	Remarks and references to Appendices
	5th	8.45 am 1.00 12.1 am	All the batteries in this group fired a/c salvos intervals on important trench junctions, also the enemy	
	7th		was suspected of having a relief on. The hostile trench mortars were very active today and the infantry called for retaliation of fire at various times between 8 am. and 6.30 pm.	
	9th	9/hr to 12.1 am	A, B, & C batteries fires salvos at various intervals on trench junctions, as it was suspected that an enemy infantry relief was taking place.	
	10th 11th 12th 13th		Enemy fired frequently with T.M.s and field guns. And M.guns retaliated. Enemy very active with field guns. Be replied. Heavy trench mortar engaged a shrub which silenced T.M. A good deal of M.G. activity to which we replied with field guns and howitzers.	
	14th 15th		Many working parties were put on. Enemy T.M.s and field guns active; we bombarded	

Army Form C. 2118.

WAR DIARY
or
INTELLIGENCE SUMMARY.
(Erase heading not required.)

Instructions regarding War Diaries and Intelligence Summaries are contained in F. S. Regs., Part II. and the Staff Manual respectively. Title pages will be prepared in manuscript.

Place	Date	Hour	Summary of Events and Information	Remarks and references to Appendices
	17th		Enemy aeroplane flew over in direction of AUBIGNY.	
	18th	3.30	9 German planes crossed our lines.	
		4.40 pm	Allied aeroplane fell between enemy front and support lines.	
		8 pm	7 German planes crossed our lines again; they were attacked by our fighters, and all compelled to return to their own lines. Just as German planes were crossing the line the enemy opened very heavy fire on our battery position, probably hoping to get men who would be watching the aeroplanes.	
	19th 20th 21st		Agns dead quiet. Enemy T.M. activity, especially in evening. Of 12.1 trm. started a few days scheme for the artillery. This group being assisted by batteries on left. A battery cuts gaps in wire by 13/256, D/256, C/121, and A/121, also fired in accordance with the scheme. A/121 keeping the enemy long repair damage by firing at irregular intervals during the night. Hostile retaliation been very feeble.	

1577 Wt.W10791/1773 500,000 1/15 D. D. & L. A.D.S.S./Forms/C. 2118.

Place	Date	Hour	Summary of Events and Information	Remarks and references to Appendices
	(cont'd) 25th - 26th -		During afternoon fokker planes were very active. A/256 again cut two gaps 25 yds wide for the Invalid? gun battery parties B/256, C/256, B/258 D/256 C/121 again fired on hunks as per scheme A/121 again firing during night to prevent enemy repairing wire. The days shooting was very effective in spite of difficult observation owing to smoke. Hostile retaliation quite feeble	
	27th -		The scheme was again carried out today. A/256 extended the gap in the wire B/256, C/256, D/256 B/258, A/121 again firing on trenches. C/121 fired on BOIS CARRÉ to prevent hostile observation when Anti-aircraft dump. Aeroplane observation preventing enemy repairing damage. Enemys retaliation was again feeble. Trench guns were firing in. He used only field guns and small trench-mortars. Observation today was still harder, and bombardment was reported generally successful. While forward guns were cutting wire heavy fire in them and got a direct hit on one emplacement but no damage has done.	
	27/28th 28th		A/121 was relieved by B/300 + C/121 by A/303. The guns remaining in position today handed over. On this day the ammunition allotment was curtailed	

Place	Date	Hour	Summary of Events and Information	Remarks and references to Appendices
	28th		scheme was proceeded with. The enemy retaliation was again very feeble, he only using 3 field batteries and possibly 1 battery of [heavier]. This afternoon we were to fire off a smoke cloud if wind was suitable, but as the weather conditions were unsuitable it was postponed.	51.
	29th	3.50 a.m.	During the first days bombardment, the enemy retaliated very feebly, it was reported that he has only three field batteries and one howitzer battery in addition to his T.M's. Enemy fire was concentrated fire on or near the T.M. field [guns] small trenches & T.M's; our batteries replies difficulty as enemy stopped firing at 4.45 a.m. In addition this days scheme was started at 10.30 a.m. C/256, B/256, B/256, D/256 and A/256 taking part.	
	3/vii		As conditions were favorable, the previous days scheme which was postponed was carried out, the smoke cloud was very successful, hostile retaliation was a little stronger.	

WAR DIARY
or
INTELLIGENCE SUMMARY.

(Erase heading not required.)

Army Form C. 2118.

Place	Date	Hour	Summary of Events and Information	Remarks and references to Appendices
	30th	3.22 a.m.	Germans opened a mine on left of our right sector. At	
		3.32.3 a.m.	our batteries opened fire and kept up a steady rate until the enemy ceased firing. No damage was done to our trenches except by shell fire; firing ceased at 4 a.m.	
		2.10 p.m.	Carried out 13/258 before us 4/258 scheme. During the month much work was done by the batteries in alternate positions, also wire cutting & trench 073, shepherding of bayonets, and forward gun positions for wire cutting.	

4-7-16.

[signature]
Lieut. Colonel.
Comdg. 256th Bde R.F.A.

CONFIDENTIAL.
No 309/A
HIGHLAND DIVISION.

Vol 15

Confidential

War Diary

of

256th Brigade R.F.A.

from 1st July 1916 to 31st July 1916

(Volume)

CONFIDENTIAL
No
HIGHLAND DIVISION

Army Form C. 2118.
53

WAR DIARY
INTELLIGENCE SUMMARY.
(Erase heading not required.)

Place	Date	Hour	Summary of Events and Information	Remarks and references to Appendices
In the Field	1916 July 1		The Brigade to which is attached B/258, A/300 and B/300 field batteries remained in the positions previously occupied by them.	
	5		Very quiet, and very little firing up to this date	See
	6		Single heavy enemy Trench mortar very active.	See
	8	9.30 p.m.	Artillery scheme carried out in conjunction with heavy mortars.	See
	9		Enemy's artillery a little more active; air hostile balloons up.	See
	10 to 12		Very quiet.	See
	13th	4.25 p.m.	Mine reported having gone up on right of Sussex battalion.	See
		9.50 p.m.	All again reported quiet; no enemy attack in ms.	
		10 p.m.	Artillery Bombardment of front trenches carried out. Considerable damage was done. C/256 Battery one gun put out of action by an H.E. shell by enemy in the bore. Lt Patterson was wounded.	See
	14th		256th Bde was relieved by the 301st Bde. 160th Division. The guns were handed over in the gun pits. Relief was completed at 11.40 p.m. Batteries of Brigade marched independently to horse lines at LARISSET	See

WAR DIARY
or
INTELLIGENCE SUMMARY.

Army Form C. 2118.

3-4

Place	Date	Hour	Summary of Events and Information	Remarks and references to Appendices
Ailly	July 1916 15th	6 am	Bde started from LARESSET and proceeded to GROUCHES and stayed there one night.	See.
	16th	9.30 am	Bde marched to OUTREBOIS arriving there at 12.30 pm. There it was found that the Division was in the Reserve having	See.
	19th	9 pm	Bde moved to HAVERNAS arriving at 3.30 am in morning of 20th.	See.
	20th	7.30 am	Brigade marched to DERMANCOURT. There it was ascertained that the division was in the XV Corps 4th Army, and was no longer in the XIII Corps 3rd Army, being fresh troops of XV.	See.
	23rd	6 pm	Bde having received orders, proceeded into action and took on positions previously occupied by the 79th Bde, 17th Division. The relief was completed at 10.30 pm. The positions taken up were A, C, (& D) batteries about 300 yds S.W. of MAMETZ WOOD, and B battery about 250 yards N.E. of extreme East corner of MAMETZ WOOD. The 2 were allotted to the Brigade was covering HIGH WOOD. The Bde was under orders from the Corps and not acting as Divisional Artillery covering infantry.	See.

WAR DIARY
or
INTELLIGENCE SUMMARY.
(Erase heading not required.)

Army Form C. 2118.
55

Place	Date	Hour	Summary of Events and Information	Remarks and references to Appendices
Field	1916 July 24th		51st Division took over that front from 5th Div. and extended its line to the right (24/6th Wood).	See
	25th		Bn. Robertson Jas. B/256 was wounded. During the afternoon the enemy barraged the valleys leading to the guns very heavily and the Brigade suffered several casualties.	
			817 Cpl. Lawson R.T. HQrs. Staff Killed	
			4420 Gnr. Chishti Jr. A/256 Wounded	
			4289 Br. Skea Q.B. A/256 Wounded	
			6313 Cpl. Johnston D. B/256 Wounded	
			6324 Pt. Inglington J. B/256 Wounded	
			6349 D. Kirkcaldy W. B/256 Wounded	
			462 Sgt. Macdonald W.F. D/256 Wounded	
			4399 Gr. Cobb D/256 Wounded	
			956 Gr. Edmans E. D/256 Wounded	
			L/18846 Gr. Jones H. D/256 Wounded	
			4/18770 Br. Blackford D/256 Wounded	
			C battery had gun put out of action by an enemy shell.	See

Army Form C. 2118.

WAR DIARY
or
INTELLIGENCE SUMMARY.
(Erase heading not required.)

Place	Date	Hour	Summary of Events and Information	Remarks and references to Appendices
Field	1916 July 25th	12 pm	The divisional artillery ceased to be Corps artillery and became divisional artillery covering its own infantry.	
		9.20 pm	154th Inf Bde attacked. The artillery prepared the ground for attack starting 15 min before the assault. A little ground was gained from L/137/c & L/131/d/c. Davis CH D/256 was sent to hospital suffering from shell shock.	SGG
	26.			SGG
	27.	7.10 am	There was no action in front of Bde. Very important LONGUEVAL and DELVILLE WOOD were attacked from the South by the XIII + XV Corps. The 67th Divisional artillery assisted by shelling SWITCH TRENCH and the northerly approaches to same. There was another small advance. 4526 & White H. A/256 and L/13632 Gnr Rushworth D/256 were wounded.	SGG
	28.	10 pm	Not very much shelling by enemy during the day. S.O.S. was received from the division front and the batteries immediately opened on intense barrage on the front attacked.	SGG

WAR DIARY
or
INTELLIGENCE SUMMARY.
(Erase heading not required.)

Army Form C. 2118.

57

Place	Date	Hour	Summary of Events and Information	Remarks and references to Appendices
Field	1916 July 28		Information was received from O.P's and from LIAISON Officer with the left Infantry Battalion. Evidently the enemy did not make a very strong attack at 11:14 p.m. All was again normal.	
	29th	9 a.m.	B/256 relieved from position occupied by it and sent over section to A battery, had one section to B battery, thus forming two 6" gun batteries instead of three four-gun batteries. 4337 Bn. John W. A/256 and 2/Bn. Liddell G. A/256 were wounded. A/256 had one gun put out of action by enemy fire. C/256 received	See
	30th	3 p.m. 12:20 a.m.	orders to replace one battery and to rest when ordered of enemy's intended f/attack on night of 13th. Heavy shelling was reported on known front out to the left, all batteries at one found intense barrage on our lines.	See
		12:53	17. 1/B/256 reported that enemy troops had lifted and batteries again fired very intensely. No enemy attack took place. On the left of Division the enemy attacked and were driven back, we took	
		1:35 a.m.	various some ground. Everything was again normal.	

WAR DIARY
INTELLIGENCE SUMMARY.
(Erase heading not required.)

Army Form C. 2118.

58

Place	Date	Hour	Summary of Events and Information	Remarks and references to Appendices
Field	1916 July 30		Throughout the morning everything was normal. In early part of the afternoon the enemy barrage through the valleys where ammunition was being brought up.	
		4.45 p.m.	Bombardment started for attack on N.W. and E. of HIGH WOOD. The 18 pdr batteries of this brigade bombarded the trench to be attacked, and at the time of attack lifted and search back by fifties to 200 yds.	
		5.55 p.m.	About 200 Germans left their support trench, and upon suffering fairly heavy fire from our 6/236 O.P. reported the infantry not in front of the trenches	
		6 p.m.		
		6/236 O.P.		
		6 p.m.	Very heavy machine-gun fire from snipers from the left flank K.	
		6.10 p.m.	The infantry attacked, and the Germans put up an intense barrage behind our men.	
		6.16 p.m.	O/156 O.P. reported fighting very fierce and our men getting on well.	
		6.21 p.m.	Observation from the O.P. became impossible owing to smoke.	
		6.30 p.m. to 7.10 p.m.	The enemy barrage on our support trenches very heavily.	
		7.52 p.m.	The barrage eases.	

WAR DIARY
or
INTELLIGENCE SUMMARY.

(Erase heading not required.)

Army Form C. 2118.

59

Place	Date	Hour	Summary of Events and Information	Remarks and references to Appendices
			Information from the liaison officer had to be sent by runner, as the wires were cut by shell fire. The information from the infantry was that the right battalion had advanced and the left and centre battalions were held up by very heavy enfilade fire from machine guns from the Right and left of HIGH WOOD. During the trench attack very valuable information was provided by LIEUT. LOWTHER from the O.Ps. N Cases were being obtained, were in use all the time. Visual signalling from the O.P. proved successful owing to smoke and dust. The following casualties were reported. Major H. FRASER wounded slight – at duty. The following NCOs & men were wounded:- 4366 Sgt. RILEY T.J. ——— No 34 Sgt. LAWMAN J.C. – at duty; 665- Br. MUIR J.C.? 115 Cpl. HICKS, F.H.D – at duty; 4/10865 Br. BROCKBANK, J.D. – at duty. The day was very quiet; the ♯Enemy had one observation balloon up for a short time during the forenoon	
	2/8/16			
	3[?]			

Cuthrie, 256 th ptte R.F.A.
Lui Dyton.
Lt. Col. R.F.A.
256 th ptte R.F.A

51st Divisional Artillery.

256th BRIGADE

ROYAL FIELD ARTILLERY.

AUGUST 1916 :::::

WAR DIARY
or
INTELLIGENCE SUMMARY.
(Erase heading not required.)

Army Form C. 2118.

No 51(A)
HIGHLAND DIVISION

Place	Date	Hour	Summary of Events and Information	Remarks and references to Appendices
Field	1916 August 1		The Brigade remained in the position occupied by it last month. The day was quiet. No incident of any importance was reported. The morning was quiet.	Peg.
	2.	4.15 to 5.15 pm	The divisional artillery bombarded HIGH WOOD and trenches leading to same. At the same time the enemy bombarded the strong point at the East corner of HIGH WOOD. The rest of the night was quiet.	Peg.
	3.	9.50 am to 10.10 am	The divisional artillery carried out a systematic bombardment of the trenches to the right of HIGH WOOD. During the rest of the day the situation was normal. During the evening the enemy shelling was a little more than normal. Gr. SHORE T. D battery was killed by a premature.	Peg.
	4.	10.25 to 11.35 am	The divisional artillery carried out another bombardment scheme, on "WOOD LANE" sending back to the "SWITCH TRENCH." The enemy had five balloons up.	Peg.
	5.	7-4.30 am	The bombardment of the 4. Ins. gun carried out	Peg.

Army Form C. 2118.

61

WAR DIARY
or
INTELLIGENCE SUMMARY.
(Erase heading not required.)

Instructions regarding War Diaries and Intelligence Summaries are contained in F. S. Regs., Part II. and the Staff Manual respectively. Title pages will be prepared in manuscript.

Place	Date	Hour	Summary of Events and Information	Remarks and references to Appendices
Sully	1916 July 5	4.30 to 5.10 p.m.	The bombardment was again carried out. The rest of the day was quiet.	ecg.
	6.	9.5 to 10 a.m. but 3.20 - 3.25 p.m.	A systematic bombardment of the German support and front trenches was carried out. Cpl Hicks & H.D. battery were wounded.	ecg.
	7.	5.30 to 6.30 p.m.	A bombardment of the German trenches between HIGH WOOD and DELVILLE WOOD was carried out. The 57th Divisional artillery firing at to left.	ecg.
	8.	9.45 p.m. till about midnight	The staffs were heavily shelled by 8" and 11" H.E.s and machine guns were turned out.	ecg.
	9.	4 a.m.	The rest of the day was normal.	ecg.
			The day was quiet and normal, only the normal day and night firing taking place.	ecg.
	9/10		I school of all the field batteries of 15th D.A. was relieved by the 14th Div arty and all the How. battery were relieved. The artine and battery proceeded to their wagon lines at MEAULTE.	ecg.
	10th		Quiet.	ecg.

1577 Wt. W10791/1773 500,000 1/15 D. D. & L.   A.D.S.S./Forms/C. 2118.

WAR DIARY
INTELLIGENCE SUMMARY.

Army Form C. 2118.

65

Place	Date	Hour	Summary of Events and Information	Remarks and references to Appendices
	10/4/17		Section of 115th Battery were relieved.	See.
	11th	6 a.m.	Command of brigade was handed over to 14th Div.	See.
		8.30 a.m.	The brigade moved off from tryou line at MEAULTE, and proceeded to BONNAY.	
	13th	5.30 p.m.	At intervals of an hour the units of the brigade moved off and proceeded to LONGEAU, in the order A, B, C, D, & HQ Qrs; Here the brigade entrained and proceeded to THIENNES, detraining there.	
	14th		The units marched independently to SERCUS. Brigade commander and Battery commanders proceeded by first train.	See.
		2.30 p.m.	Brigade commander and B.C's proceeded to front area to see positions to be taken over.	See.
	15th	10 a.m.	Orderly officer, and 1 officer per battery went to front area, and in afternoon one section of each battery, and the staffs staff relieved the 1st Bde. of the New Zealand Division in position east of ARMENTIERES.	See.

WAR DIARY
INTELLIGENCE SUMMARY

Army Form C. 2118.

Place	Date	Hour	Summary of Events and Information	Remarks and references to Appendices
Field	1916 Aug. 16.		Section in action proceeded to register fronts on their zones.	See.
	16/17		Second section of batteries relieved the New Zealand Bde F.A.	See.
	17. 7-8pm		Brigade command was taken over by C.L. DYSON.	See.
	18.		The batteries of the Brigade continued registration	See.
	19.		759 Gnr WILLIAM SUDDERS C battery and 699 Br CHARLES CROCKETT C battery were awarded military medals for gallantry in the field during the recent operations on the SOMME.	See. See. See.
	20.		The batteries retaliated on the German trenches for enemy shelling.	
	21.		Very little firing was done.	
	23.		Capt G.R.E. Q. MACKAY R.A.M.C. was attached 256th Bde R.F.A. was awarded the military cross for gallantry during the operations on the SOMME.	
		12.4 p.m.	The Divisional artillery was again reorganised. B battery 258th Bde and half of C/258th Bde was absorbed into 256th Bde R.F.A. making this brigade consist of three (six gun) 18-pdr batteries and one four gun 4.5" (How) battery	See.

WAR DIARY
INTELLIGENCE SUMMARY
(Erase heading not required.)

Army Form C. 2118.

65.

Place	Date	Hour	Summary of Events and Information	Remarks and references to Appendices
Field	1916 Aug 29th		The 2nd Army Commander, Sir H.C.O. PLUMER G.C.M.G., K.C.B., presented Medal ribbons to the Officers and men of the 57th (H.G.W.)	See
	30th		Division, for gallantry during the recent operations near SOMME.	See
	31st		Very quiet; the batteries retaliated for occasional trench mortars and also for shelling of our trenches.	See

Rudyton
Lieut-Col. R.A.
Comdg. 256th Bde R.F.A.

CONFIDENTIAL.
No 21/A
HIGHLAND DIVISION.

CONFIDENTIAL

WAR DIARY

of

256th BRIGADE R.F.A.

from 1st SEPTEMBER, 1916 to 30th SEPTEMBER, 1916.

Army Form C. 2118.

65

WAR DIARY
or
INTELLIGENCE SUMMARY.

(Erase heading not required.)

Instructions regarding War Diaries and Intelligence Summaries are contained in F. S. Regs., Part II. and the Staff Manual respectively. Title pages will be prepared in manuscript.

Place	Date	Hour	Summary of Events and Information	Remarks and references to Appendices
Zulu	1916 Sept. 1.		The Brigade remained in the position occupied by it last month. The brigade remained split up between the Right and Left Groups of the divisional artillery.	
	2.		Very quiet day.	see
	3.	4 p.m.	C battery cut wire on the German front line. The shooting was very satisfactory and steady, but great damage was done. The artillery in conjunction with the medium trench mortars bombarded enemy front system. The enemy's retaliation was very weak. Aeroplanes in the sky in large nos. & planes being seen flying into the air. Very little artillery activity. ARMENTIERES was shelled during evening.	see
	4.			see
	5.			see see
	6.		Very quiet. Hostile artillery very quiet until evening when they shelled ARMENTIERES. The day was dull and misty; there was very little firing.	see see
	7.			see
	8.		Very quiet day again.	see
	9.			see
	10.	10 a.m.	Lt.Col. L.M. DYSON handed over command of Right Group of artillery and took over command of Left Group, relieving Lt.Col. OLDHAM.	

Army Form C. 2118.

66

WAR DIARY
INTELLIGENCE SUMMARY.
(Erase heading not required.)

Instructions regarding War Diaries and Intelligence Summaries are contained in F. S. Regs., Part II. and the Staff Manual respectively. Title pages will be prepared in manuscript.

Place	Date	Hour	Summary of Events and Information	Remarks and references to Appendices
Toll	1916 Sept			
	10th		The H.Q. staff of the 336th Bde also moved to H.Q. of Left grp.	See
	11th		The day was quiet; observation was difficult at times, owing to the mist.	
	12th		Very quiet. An enemy heavy trench mortar fired occasionally and was successfully pieced by the batteries.	
	13th		A his left a series of two minute internal bombardments was started. At stated times all the field batteries in the group concentrated on a certain part of the enemy's line, and bombarded intensively for two minutes.	
		7 a.m	Intense bombardment	
		9.10 a.m	" "	
		12.25 p.m	" "	
		6.5 p.m	" "	
		9.15 p.m	" "	
			A great deal of damage was done, and the enemy retaliated very feebly.	

1577 Wt.W10791/1773 500,000 1/15 D.D.&L. A.D.S.S./Forms/C. 2118.

WAR DIARY

INTELLIGENCE SUMMARY.

(Erase heading not required.)

Army Form C. 2118.

Place	Date	Hour	Summary of Events and Information	Remarks and references to Appendices
"Field"	Sept 14th	8.20am	Intense bombardments lasting two minutes were carried out at these times. A considerable amount of damage was done. The enemy retaliated with a few rounds from a heavy T.M. which ceased firing immediately it was fired on by a field battery.	P.g.
		11. am		
		3.35 pm		
		6.30 pm		
	15th	6.30 am	Again intense bombardments were carried out, and much damage was done. The enemy's retaliation was very feeble.	P.g.
		2.5 pm		
		5.40 pm		
		8.55 pm	A raid was carried out by the infantry covered by the artillery & the left groups. This raid was quite successful, the infantry bringing back a prisoner.	P.g.
	16th	9.30 am	Again intense bombardments were carried out; the enemy's retaliation being particularly nil. Another raid was carried out by the Enemy; a great deal of damage was done, and a prisoner was captured.	P.g.
		10.45 am		
		8.30 pm		
	17th		The day was quiet; during the afternoon observation was very difficult owing to haze.	P.g.

Army Form C. 2118.

68

WAR DIARY

INTELLIGENCE SUMMARY.

(Erase heading not required.)

Instructions regarding War Diaries and Intelligence Summaries are contained in F. S. Regs., Part II. and the Staff Manual respectively. Title pages will be prepared in manuscript.

Place	Date	Hour	Summary of Events and Information	Remarks and references to Appendices
Field	1916 Sept. 19th	12.30	The C.R.A. Brig-Gen. L.O. OLDFIELD, D.S.O., presented cards for Gallantry to LIEUT. M. LOWTHER. No. 759 Cpl. W. SLIDDERS and No. 699 Sr. CHARLES CROCKETT.	Egg Egg
	20th to 22nd		The front was very quiet.	
	20th		20 Lt-Col. OLDHAM took command of the left group and Lieut-Col. L.M. DYSON with the HdQrs staff of the 256th Bde., went into rest billets near STEENWERCK.	Egg
	22/23		One section of B,/C and D batteries were relieved and proceeded to the wagon lines.	Egg
	23rd		Bde HdQrs moved to VERTE RUE near VIEUX BERQUIN, accompanied by the section of the batteries which was relieved.	Egg
	23rd/24th		The remainder of the batteries, and the whole J/B battery came out of action and proceeded independently to VERTE RUE.	Egg
	25th		The Bde proceeded to BURBURE and stayed there for one night.	Egg
	26th		The Bde marched to HEUCHIN.	Egg
	27th		The Bde proceeded to LIGNY-SUR-CANCHE.	Egg
	28th		The Bde proceeded to BUS-LES-ARTOIS.	Egg

Army Form C. 2118.

69.

WAR DIARY
INTELLIGENCE SUMMARY.
(Erase heading not required.)

Instructions regarding War Diaries and Intelligence Summaries are contained in F. S. Regs., Part II. and the Staff Manual respectively. Title pages will be prepared in manuscript.

Place	Date	Hour	Summary of Events and Information	Remarks and references to Appendices
Field	1916 Sept 29th		The Bde marched to PUCHEVILLERS. The O.C. Bde went forward to reconnoitre battery positions.	
	30th		This Division joined the 2nd Corps Reserve Army. One section of each of the 104th batteries and D battery completed moved into a station opposite THIEPVAL. The O.C's batteries, Major FRASER A battery, Major SHEPHERD, Capt SHEPHERD, C battery and Capt NAPIER D battery, went into action with the first sections.	ECS

SES |
| | 1/10/16 | | | |

Mulyton
Lieut-Col. R.A.
Comdg. 251st Bde R.F.A.

CONFIDENTIAL.
No. 21/A.
HIGHLAND DIVISION.

Vol 15

CONFIDENTIAL.

W A R   D I A R Y.

-*- of -*-

_____, 256th BRIGADE, ROYAL FIELD ARTILLERY,

From   To.
1st OCTOBER 1916.   31st OCTOBER 1916.

WAR DIARY

Army Form C. 2118.

Place	Date	Hour	Summary of Events and Information	Remarks and references to Appendices
Field	1916 Oct 1		The Headquarters, and the remaining two sections of each 18 pdr battery proceeded into action; The Headquarters being in the valley about 800 yds north of CRUCIFIX CORNER. The following casualties occurred. 6047 B.Q.M.S. T. LEITCH, 6380 Gr. DICK, J., wounded; 1373 Gr. RATTRAY, J. killed. On the whole the rest of battery positions was quiet.	B/battery C/Battery O.C.
	2nd	8:30 to 9:30 am	All six guns of B battery, and one gun of A battery were put out of action by direct hits from enemy shells. The following casualties occurred. 6350 Sgt. BUIST, J.; 4326 Gr. MAXWELL, H.; 6428 A/Bdr. ADAMSON, A.J.; 6405 Gr. McLEAN A.; 6419 Gr. GRIEVE, J.; 6605 Gr. GORDON, A.; 1571 Gr. McINTOSH, A.; all B battery, all wounded.	640.5 O.C.
	3rd		During the early morning and forenoon the howitzers of 77 and 573 batteries were heavily shelled. There was desultory firing all night. The 51st Div. arty. came directly under the 18 Div. arty.; the 41st Bde. R.F.A. 2nd Div. went out of action, and the groups of artillery were evacuated of the 256th Bde R.F.A. only. During the day the batteries carried out their normal day and night firing.	O.C. O.C.

Army Form C. 2118.

WAR DIARY

~~Intelligence Summary~~

(Erase heading not required.)

Instructions regarding War Diaries and Intelligence Summaries are contained in F. S. Regs., Part II. and the Staff Manual respectively. Title pages will be prepared in manuscript.

Place	Date	Hour	Summary of Events and Information	Remarks and references to Appendices
Field	Oct 1916 4th		During the afternoon B/Battery having received two of its guns from the I.O.M. moved them into action about 200 yds N.W. of C battery's position.	G.C.C.
	5th	9am to 10am	On the whole the day was quiet, weather was bad, and observation impossible, only intermittent shelling taking place. 4/355 Gr. ROSCOE, J.W., and 778 Ftr. PETRIE, H., D/battery, were wounded. The Brigade moved out of action and proceeded to the bivouac lines at SENLIS.	G.C.C.
	6th		The Brigade moved to LOUVENCOURT and stayed there for one night, the bivouac lines being established there. A battery of D/battery moved into action about 500 yds east the I.O.M. Lt-Col. M.M. DUNCAN, commanding 255th Bde. R.F.A. came under the command of 170th Bde. The Bde took up the battery positions being in front of COLIN CHAMPS.	G.C.C.
	7th		Moved to COURCELLES.	G.C.C.
	8th		The two batteries proceeded to register and cut wire. The batteries proceeded to dig new gun positions, the entire out of action sending up working parties to dig their new positions.	G.C.C.

1577 Wt.W10791/1773 500,000 1/15 D.D.&L.   A.D.S.S./Forms/C. 2118.

WAR DIARY
or
INTELLIGENCE SUMMARY.
(Erase heading not required.)

Army Form C. 2118.

72

Place	Date	Hour	Summary of Events and Information	Remarks and references to Appendices
Field	1916 Oct. 9th		Work was proceeded with at the gun positions, which consisted mainly of camouflage netting. The Huns also started digging a forward S.A.A. to be used for an attack.	ecg
	10th 10/11th		The digging of gun emplacements for enemies with. The other two Batteries C and B of this brigade moved into action.	ecg ecg
	11th		All batteries proceeded to register their new zones, and the brigade then came under the command of Lieut-Col. L.M. Dyson. Wire cutting done.	ecg
	12th	2.5 p.m.	Bombardment accompanied by discharge of smoke took place, and was very successful. Wire cutting not very successful; bad light.	ecg
	13th	8.30 p.m. to 10.30 p.m.	A noise demonstration has given.	ecg
	14th		C & D batteries fired on enemy wire and although no distinct lanes was cut, the wire was very badly damaged. Orders received to stop all work on battery positions.	ecg
	15th 16th		During the afternoon B and D batteries, which were used by fire, were shelled with 8"A.P. about 200 rnds being fired. Although no direct hits were obtained on the guns, several of them were	ecg ecg

Army Form C. 2118.

73

WAR DIARY
~~INTELLIGENCE SUMMARY~~
(Erase heading not required.)

Instructions regarding War Diaries and Intelligence Summaries are contained in F. S. Regs., Part II. and the Staff Manual respectively. Title pages will be prepared in manuscript.

Place	Date	Hour	Summary of Events and Information	Remarks and references to Appendices
Toh	1916 Oct 16		No. 1633 Cpl. Hirst W. R.A.M.C. attached to this brigade was presented with the Distinguished Conduct Medal.	
		7.30 p.m.	Buried and each battery had an ammunition dump blown up. Orders were received that batteries were to move out of action at 10 p.m. and proceed to wagon lines. Batteries arrived at LOUVENCOURT about 3 a.m. on 17th.	See
	17th		Lieut. Col. L.M.Dyson reconnoitred new positions for batteries.	
			F.A.Bns arrived at Wagon Lines at LOUVENCOURT.	See
	18th	1 p.m.	One section of each battery proceeded into action and took up positions from the 39th 2nd Bde R.F.A. Artillery, the battery position here on either side of MAILLY — MAILLET — SUCRERIE road. A on the right. B C & D at the Gr. 530 HQrs and remaining sections of batteries moved into action. Batteries proceeded to register guns and howitzers. Wagon lines moved to VARENNES.	See
	19th		Batteries cut wire very successfully. C battery, D battery and SA battery got orders to move into new positions, and start cutting wire as soon as guns were registered.	
	20th		J Battery moved to A batterys position, C battery moved into an entirely	

Army Form C. 2118.

WAR DIARY
INTELLIGENCE SUMMARY
(Erase heading not required.)

Place	Date	Hour	Summary of Events and Information	Remarks and references to Appendices
Field	1916 Oct. 20		new position and proceeded to dig in. A battery also moved into a new position. Batteries cut wire very well. Light was very good all day.	
	21st	10.15 a.m.	No. 8657. BRENNAN. P. was killed. Wire cutting was proceeded with and gaps were cut. Light very good.	S.S.S.
	22nd		The enemy's retaliation was very feeble. Light again very good during afternoon, and wire cutting continued with.	S.S.S.
	23rd	5 a.m. to 6.15 a.m.	Intense bombardment of German lines carried out, to which the enemy's reply was very feeble. Light was bad for wire cutting and extent of damage could not seen from O.P.s.	S.S.S.
	24th to 25th		Morning bombardment again carried out. Light bad all day. Morning bombardment again; enemy's reply again feeble. Owing to haze all day wire cutting was practically impossible. A battery of 5 but could not tell result owing to smoke thickening haze.	S.S.S. S.S.S.
	26th		Morning bombardment. During intervals of good light, batteries cut wire	S.S.S.

WAR DIARY
INTELLIGENCE SUMMARY
(Erase heading not required.)

Army Form C. 2118.

75.

Place	Date	Hour	Summary of Events and Information	Remarks and references to Appendices
Field	1916 Oct. 26th (cont)		The wire was much damaged but it was impossible to say to what extent. Morning bombardment. A high and squally wind was against steady & extensive shooting but, on the whole, good results were obtained at wirecutting.	See.
	27th		Morning bombardment. During forenoon and up till 3 p.m. the light was good and all batteries cut wire successfully.	See.
	28th		While A battery was being shelled 2nd Lieut. J.M. COUPER was wounded. Morning bombardment. Very gusty wind and rain all day. Wire cutting was continued with but small extent of damage could not be seen. Lieut. G.A.D. MATSON EWE was wounded to hospital with 2/Lieut. F.E. BARTLETT	See.
	29th	3am		
	30th		Junior this brigade from D.A.C. Lieut. F.C. JACK Battery was present with a cast. gallantly. Morning bombardment. Base light for wire cutting. Enemy's rear systems? defence were shelled.	See.
	31st		Morning bombardment. Light good but wind to gusty for wire cutting.	See.

2/11/16

Wulyton
Lieut-Col. R.F.A.
Comdg. 256th Bde R.F.A.

APPENDIX B.
WAR DIARY Nov 13th to 16th 1916
Lessons learnt from recent operations.

Report on Operations from 13th to 16th November inclusive.

1. GUNNERY.

(a) O.P's   Observation was done from a Brigade O.P. by two Officers selected for this work.   These Officers remained at the O.P. during the whole period under review and maintained observation night and day.   The strain on these Officers was considerable and was accentuated by the discomfort attendant on the weather conditions.   The lesson learned is that it is essential to make careful provision for the comfort for the O.P. personnel, e.g. good dugouts heating arrangements, latrines, storing of water etc.   It should also be borne in mind that considerably more accomodation will be required on and after Z day – i.e. there will be 2 Officers, 2 or 3 signallers and 2 runners there instead of the usual observing Officer with one signaller.

SHOOTING.
(b)   During the earlier part of the operations the bursts were too high but this was rectified later. When observation was possible the shooting appeared to be good both for line and range but fuzes behaved erratically – i.e. in order to avoid an undue percentage of high bursts it appeared necessary to shoot with a corrector giving about 50% of gauges.   The Division on our left continued to shoot with a large percentage of very high bursts in a good many cases as high as 3° throughout the operations

OBSERVATION.
(c)   This was much hampered by thick fog and smoke during the heavier barrages but very valuable information was obtained by the Observing Officers – both by day and during the night.   Their deductions proved in the majority of cases to be correct.   The detailing of senior and very experienced Officers for this duty is thought to have been more than justified.

SERVICE OF THE GUNS.
(d)   The maximum rate of fire (4 rounds per gun per minute) adopted throughout is reported by B.C's to be a very suitable one which in no way fatigues the detachments or overheats the guns.   This rate of fire can be kept up almost indefinitely and 3 men per detachment can undertake it.

AMMUNITION SUPPLY.
(e)   This was carried out successfully but required considerable provision on the part of the B.C's and entailed very hard work on the Wagon Line personnel. This was largely due to the very great distances between Wagon Lines, Dump and Battery positions, the congested condition of the roads with consequent frequent stopping & starting. It is suggested that small dumps might have been established nearer the battery positions with ammunition so that when wagons came to battery position with ammunition they would not have required to return the whole way to the main dump to refill if further supplies were necessary.

The provision of ammunition pits at the battery position before Z day entailed a great deal of labour and very little assistance was obtained in the way of supply of material.   Weather conditions were extremely bad but not abnormal for the time of year.

COMMUNICATIONS.

(a) With Divisional Artillery.
This line worked very well and the exchange work was very efficient but great delay occured on several occasions in getting even "priority" messages through on account of congestion on the wire from exchange to H.Q. Divnl. Artillery.
Suggested. That at least two lines be provided to Artillery, from exchange or, better, a separate line from each Group with an operator for each wire at Artillery Headquarters. Written messages took a long time to transmit, the operators having difficulty in making themselves understood when dealing with unfamiliar names, words and Map References.

(b) The other lines consisted of (i) O.P. in a 6 feet trench all the way, pegged in near feet of the trench. (ii) Brigade Liaison - buried wire in charge of Signals (iii) Battalion Liaison - in a trench from Brigade Liaison pegged to feet of trench. (iv) Batteries and flank Brigades - separate wires over the open.
These lines all worked extraordinarily well except that between Brigade Liaison and Battalion Liaison which was frequently cut.✗ This freedom from trouble is attributed to the burying of the line in question and the marked absence of shelling in the back area.
Suggested that the wire to Brigade Liaison should have been continued to Battalion Liaison

✗ and the Bde Liaison wire owing to frequent + unjustifiable interference by the 2nd Div Signals who tapped in where the wire ran through one of their Dug outs

SIGNALLING.

No visual signalling was done either by the Infantry or by this Brigade. Major Fraser was strongly of opinion that lamp, flag or disc signalling could have been established between LEAVE AVENUE and the O.P. This would have had the disadvantage of entailing D.E.D.D. messages but alternatively it is suggested that a separate lamp station might have been established at some distance from O.P. and connected to it by telephone. It is considered however that any attempt at signalling with the present type of electric signalling lamps would have failed owing to the difficulty of aligning the lamps without telephone communication between the two lamp stations.

REPORTS.

O.P. Continuous information was received from the observing Officers throughout the operations and these most valuable both to the G.O.C. 152 Inf. Bde. and to myself. Not only were actual observations received but valuable &, as afterwards appeared, almost always accurate deductions from lights, sounds of rifle fire etc.

BRIGADE LIAISON.

See Colonel Dyson's report.

BATTALION LIAISON.

These were in nearly every case sent to Brigade Liaison in the first instance and then transmitted.

GENERAL

The biscuit tins used to indicate NEW MUNICH TRENCH were most useful. Major Fraser was of opinion that the flares used to indicate the position of infantry to aeroplanes should be extended to perform a similar office for OPs. By means of a simple code flares might be indicated. The contact aeroplane is thought to have missed an excellent opportunity of gaining information on the afternoon of Z day between 4 & 4.30 pm. our lamp absent.

APPENDIX A.

WAR DIARY 13th to 16th Nov. 1916.

51/8s

Vol 19

WAR DIARY
of
256th Bde R.F.A.
Nov. 1st to Nov 30th 1916

WAR DIARY
INTELLIGENCE SUMMARY

Army Form C. 2118.
No. 76

Place	Date	Hour	Summary of Events and Information	Remarks and references to Appendices
Zillebeke	1916 November 1.		The Brigade remained in the position previously occupied by it. Wire cutting was continued with.	G.S.O.
	2.	5.30 to 6.10 p.m.	A bombardment of enemy's trenches was carried out. The wire cutting today was good. During the morning a bombardment of the enemy trenches was carried out.	G.S.O.
	3.	6.40 to 6.45 a.m.	Heavy bombardment of enemy's trenches took place. Wire cutting very satisfactory owing to excellent light.	G.S.O.
	4.		The usual night firing took place, and the wire cutting was carried out from about 9 a.m. to 3 p.m. when light began to fail. The effect was good; in some places the wire was destroyed, and many gaps were made.	G.S.O.
	5. 6.		Grey day with strong drying wind. No guns for wire cutting. Showery but good light between showers; wire cutting proceeded with. Bombardment of enemy's lines carried out at 8.35 a.m.	G.S.O.
	7.		Wet all day, and wind very gusty.	

WAR DIARY
INTELLIGENCE SUMMARY

Army Form C. 2118.

77

Place	Date	Hour	Summary of Events and Information	Remarks and references to Appendices
Field	1916 Jan. 7.	5.45 pm.	Batteries opened a barrage on enemy's trenches, preparatory to an infantry raiding party going out. This barrage was kept up till infantry reached the German wire, when they found the wire manned and unms? to machine gun fire, and Lewis took cover just under the trench. Gradually the artillery fire slackened until at 6.30 p.m. firing was again normal. Bad light for observing; wire kept open by 16 pdrs.	S.C.S.
	8th		Good light and moderate wind. Hun planes very active all day	S.C.S.
	9th		Dry but hazy in morning. Wind kept strong.	S.C.S.
	10th		The Division under orders on 13th. Orders received the 13th to be known as "Z" day.	S.C.S.
	11th		A bombardment of the enemy's front trenches was carried out at 5.45 am. Very feeble retaliation. "X" day.	S.C.S.
	12th		"Y" day. Hazy during day, observation difficult. Final arrangements were made for the attack on the 13th. Lieut. Col. L. M. DYSON went to Bde 132nd Inf Bde HQrs at WHITE CITY as liaison officer for this Bde.	S.C.S.

WAR DIARY
INTELLIGENCE SUMMARY

Army Form C. 2118.

Place	Date	Hour	Summary of Events and Information	Remarks and references to Appendices
Field	1916 Nov 12th		Major H. FRASER and Lieut. C.C. WELCH manned the O.P. Lieut. R.R. ALEXANDER went to H.Q'rs 8th A. & S. Hdrs as liaison officer with the attacking battalion on left of this division. The Bde was commanded by Major N.K.O. SHEPHERD. B/battery.	See
	13th		"Z" day. Division attacked German front. BEAUMONT-HAMEL captured. Infantry reached MUNICH TRENCH. Hostile lines on FRANKFORT TRENCH. Situation somewhat obscure. Very misty all day.	See
	14th	2:45	An attack made on FRANKFORT TRENCH which was unsuccessful. Situation still obscure owing to enemy shelling and bad light for observation. Night firing. 150 yds beyond FRANKFORT TRENCH.	See
	15th		Fine afternoon. Air shell spells light was very good. Enemy shelled heavily during afternoon. Still misty. Quiet night.	See
	16th	8:35 am	Aeroplane call received that our infantry were crossing open at R 20 g 5. D battery opened fire and dispersed them.	See
		1:21 pm	Situation quiet. Lieut. Col. DYSON was relieved by Col. OLDHAM. Quiet night, and again very misty.	See

WAR DIARY
INTELLIGENCE SUMMARY
(Erase heading not required.)

Army Form C. 2118.

79

Place	Date	Hour	Summary of Events and Information	Remarks and references to Appendices
Field	1916 Nov. 17th		Our trenches consisted chiefly of consolidated positions. Very little firing by batteries.	See.
	18th		Practically no firing by batteries except for defensive purposes and bringing on receipt from S.O.S. Messages	See.
	19th	6.10am	32nd Div. attacks FRANKFORT TRENCH. This brigade barrages on its old zone on MUNICH TRENCH then lifted to FRANKFORT TR. and then lifted to 150 yards beyond FRANKFORT TR. until orders were received from the Div arty to cease firing. The attack was unsuccessful. Lieut. Col. L. M. DYSON resumed command of the brigade.	See.
	20th		Quiet day. Observation difficult. Very little firing.	See.
	21st		Handed over defence line to 32nd Div Artillery. Practically no firing by batteries. Quiet day	See.
	22nd		Very quiet; no firing.	See.

WAR DIARY
INTELLIGENCE SUMMARY
(Erase heading not required.)

Army Form C. 2118.

80

Instructions regarding War Diaries and Intelligence Summaries are contained in F. S. Regs., Part II. and the Staff Manual respectively. Title pages will be prepared in manuscript.

Place	Date	Hour	Summary of Events and Information	Remarks and references to Appendices
Field	1916 Nov 23rd		Moved out of action and proceeded to wagon lines at VARENNES. Col. L.M. DYSON and Orderly Officer reconnoitred new battery position in front of POZIERES.	G.G.G.
	24th		One section First battery proceeded into action and took new position from 4th Canadian Division. Remainder of batteries marched to new wagon lines in Brickfields North of ALBERT. Guns were exchanged	
	25th		as it was impossible to shift them owing to the mud. Remainder of batteries proceeded into action and HdQrs relieved those of 6 Canadian F.A. Bgde. Position of HdQrs	G.G.G. G.G.G.
	26th		in sunken road running N.E. into POZIERES — COURCELETTE Road. Raining in morning. Cleared up in forenoon, and continued registering. Misty in afternoon.	G.G.G.
	28th		Bgde. HdQrs moved back to 600 yds west of POZIERES. Very misty. Light firing on trenches and approaches.	G.G.G.
	29th 30th		Guns very misty, light firing on trenches and approaches. Observation very difficult and observation impossible.	G.G.G. G.G.G. G.G.G.

3/12/16

W.O. Wrighton R.F.A.
Adjg. 256th Bde 1st Cdn F.A.

A.D.S.S./Forms/C. 2118.

WAR DIARY or INTELLIGENCE SUMMARY

Army Form C. 2118.

Appendix to War Diary for November 13th 1916

Place	Date	Hour	Summary of Events and Information	Remarks and references to Appendices
Field	1916 Nov 13th		At 5.45 a.m. on 13th V Corps attacked German positions from JOHN COPSE to the ANCRE S. of BEAUMONT-HAMEL. The men of battle from N. to S. were 3rd Div, 2nd, 51st, 63rd, and 37th Div. in reserve. The tanks given to the 51st Div. were to dawn on map No 1. the green line being the intermediate and the yellow line the final objective. The frontage attacked was roughly 1700 yds. in length. The main obstacle to be overcome was the very strongly defended village of BEAUMONT-HAMEL, which the first hostile system comprised. Hill machine-guns and numerous extraordinary entrenchments all heavily wired. In addition the entire system was furnished with numerous extensive and very deep dugouts which greatly lessened the vulnerability of the garrison, and its machine guns during the preliminary bombardment. The 51st Div. attacked with two Inf. Bdes in the line, viz the 152nd on left and the 154th on right. The 153 Infantry Bde in reserve. 1 C/Bde in reserve of	

Army Form C. 2118.

Appendix to War Diary
W. 13 & 6/6.2/96.

WAR DIARY
or
INTELLIGENCE SUMMARY.
(Erase heading not required.)

Summary of Events and Information

The 152 nd Bde attacked with two battalions in the line and one in support, and one in reserve. This Bde covered Regt/152 nd Inf Bde commanded by Brig-Gen. PELHAM-BURN D.S.O.

The Bns of the 152 nd Inf Bde were arranged as follows, 5th Seaforths on right, 8th A. & S. Highrs, on left, 6th Seaforths forming next wave, 6 th Black Watch in support, and 7 th Gordons in reserve.

The enemy's entanglement had been almost entirely destroyed by our cutting. Their Front line had been very badly damaged by heavy and siege artillery. During this period, so much so that in tramping upon his artillery during this period, so much so that in tramping upon his amongst whom trophies were blocked, and all his telephoning wires cut.

The enemy field gun barrage was in covering one to shown in the map, and this barrage from the line was carried out by Major H. FRASER. A battery and Lieut. C.C. WELSH D battery; Liaison with 152 Bde by Lieut Lt L.M. DYSON and liaison with inf/ battalion by Lieut R.R. ALEXANDER. A battery.

Zero hour was before daylight and mobility was further reduced by very thick fog which limited vision to about 25 yards, even after daylight.

After the short preliminary barrage no enemy mg line was lifted and the 8 th A. & S.H. took many prisoners & took enemy front line practically without resistance.

This process was repeated on second line and live prisoners were taken.

Army Form C. 2118.

WAR DIARY
or
INTELLIGENCE SUMMARY.
(Erase heading not required.)

Appendix to War Diary
Nov. 13th to 16th 1916

Instructions regarding War Diaries and Intelligence Summaries are contained in F. S. Regs., Part II. and the Staff Manual respectively. Title pages will be prepared in manuscript.

Place	Date	Hour	Summary of Events and Information	Remarks and references to Appendices
			A more stubborn resistance was encountered in Enemy's third line, and for some time it looked as if attack might be held up. Col. DYSON decided that in the next ½ hour possibility of ascertaining progress made by the Battalions on right and left. It would have been necessary to stop the barrage by bombing on from flanks. 8th & 5th cleared this trench also. After this front the situation became completely obscure, and in absence of information it was necessary to continue the barrage as framed in Schedule. They kept the day observation was impossible on account of mist, but about 3 p.m. the enemy front line could be distinguished by exhausted missile till about. The enemy did not open till 5.52 and was then weak and badly directed. Hostile shelling being apparently without information probably their heavy barrage as a precautionary measure. Enemy artillery continued to barrage the neighborhood at intervals throughout the day but was chiefly at own new front to the situation. At 12 noon a report was received that the 5th Inf Bde on left were in MUNICH TRENCH and no report from Battn's cstrl of this and no infantry were holding STEAK LINE, and probably east of this. On report being received that 5th Inf Bde took the barrage from counter attack stopped range was then 150 yards from track at Q5d 45.45. to Q6d 80.99 at rate of 3 mins per gun for 8 mins.	
		2 p.m		
		4.30 p.m		
		5.15 p.m		
		5.30 "	Re-opened to 12 " " "	
		5.53 "	" 3 " " "	
		7.10 p.m.	132nd and 153rd Inf Bdes joined up on our flanks with 2nd Div. on left and were in touch with 2nd Div. on left and were in Green Line " "	

WAR DIARY or INTELLIGENCE SUMMARY

Army Form C. 2113.

Appendix to War Diary Nov. 13th 6/16 = 2.1.9/16

Place	Date	Hour	Summary of Events and Information	Remarks and references to Appendices
Field	Nov 13th		Right firing orders received to fire steadily rapid throughout the night on line H (see map No.1) Stuchin's trench.	
		9.31 pm	Barrage lifted 200 yards.	
		10.18 pm	Very misty.	
		11.15 pm	General desultory fire but no heavy barrage.	
	14th		152nd 2nd Bde captured 800 prisoners. Enemy appears 1200. Enemy barrage very heavy for about half an hour.	
		1.37 am	Enemy opened barrage in original no mans land. O.Ten received for batteries & fire on FRANKFORT TRENCH until broken often.	
		6.19 am		
		6.43 am	OP. reported we held MUNICH TRENCH.	
		9.18 am	Battalion in MUNICH TR. in touch with 2nd Div.	
		9.50 am		
		11.30 am	D. Division reports captured strong point and from 300 to 400 prisoners. 152nd Bde & Rifle Brigade and 58 men.	
		2.45 pm	Orders received that 152nd Bde to barrage Q6 C9050 to Q66 oo at 3 pm & passing to infantry attacking FRANKFORT TR.	
			1 gun per minute	
		2.51 pm	10 yds lift 150 yds bayonet shields	
		2.54 pm	2 rounds per gun per minute	
		2.57 pm	1 " " "	
		3 pm	and onwards 3 a min per gun fire magnifi. Attack was unsuccessful and situation was however when night fell.	

Army Form C. 2118.

WAR DIARY
or
INTELLIGENCE SUMMARY.
(Erase heading not required.)

Appendix to War Diary
Nov. 13th & Nov. 16th 1916

Place	Date	Hour	Summary of Events and Information	Remarks and references to Appendices
	15		Situation still somewhat obscure. Very misty.	
		2.28 p.m.	Light haze lifted for short period. Portion of NEW MUNICH TRENCH could not be seen clearly.	
		4.15 p.m.	Mist closing in; observation impossible. Right line on FRANKFORT TRENCH on reported area.	
		11.9 p.m.	Last report shells falling short; all batteries replied laying correct; probably they were enemy shells.	
	16.		Position of line was as shown on Map No 2.	
		8.35 am	Conference call received. Hy. & 60 infantry news rolling across them at R.2 a.95; D. battery fired on this party and infantry it.	
		1.21 p.m.	Situation quiet. Situation chiefly consists of consolidating positions now, and completing relief.	
	3/12/16			

C. W. Cuthfurand
Major R.F.A.
Comdg. 253rd Bde R.F.A.

Vol 20

WAR DIARY
of
265th BRIGADE R.F.A.

From 1st December 1916. to 31st December 1916.

WAR DIARY / INTELLIGENCE SUMMARY

Army Form C. 2118.

80

Place	Date	Hour	Summary of Events and Information	Remarks and references to Appendices
Field	1916 Sep		The brigade remained in the position previously occupied by it last month. A bombardment was carried out by the artillery of the enemy's defences and much damage was done.	see
	3-5		LIEUT. J.B. MEIKLE & battery to & eff. and 26th August 1916. LIEUT. R.R. WILL B battery to & eff. and 26th August 1916.	see
	4		2/Lieut. J. MACFARLANE was awarded the Military Cross for gallantry during operations from 13 to 16 Nov 1916.	see
			2/13400 L/Cpl C.L. GREEN was awarded the Military Medal for gallantry during operations from 13 to 16 Nov 1916.	see
			During this week the batteries carried out the enemy's front line trench system or selected points behind the enemy's front line. Many targets were engaged also by the harassing effects shoot. Many working parties dispersed.	see
	10th Nov		R.F.A. No 21145 Bomb HICKS, H. D battery was killed in action. No 2051 Sgt SCOTT, J. C battery. No 597 a/L/Bdr RATTRAY, S.J. C battery. No 703 Gnr ADAMS, H. C battery. No 426 Bdr ROBERTSON, J.C battery, were wounded.	see
	12.7		Temp. LIEUT. (Temp. CAPT.) J.S. LENNIE was posted to B battery. EXPT J.S LENNIE sick from 30/9/16 and attached to B battery on attachment on looking reinstated till was Temp. Capt. J.S Lennie was carried out several	see
	1,2,10,11		The normal day and nightly firing was carried out. Several batteries were taken over by the batteries. There was much aerial activity during the week.	see

WAR DIARY or INTELLIGENCE SUMMARY

Army Form C. 2118.

81

Place	Date 1916	Hour	Summary of Events and Information	Remarks and references to Appendices
Field	Dec 17th		No 4384 Br FARQUHARSON, J.A. Bat Cay. was killed. No 1612 Gr. SMITH, E.M. A Battery and No 4396 W.H. BOWEN, D.A. Battery, No 4654 Gr. EMSLIE, J.A. Battery were wounded in action. No 1376 Gr. STEWART, W.A. Battery, No 4120 Sgt. CUTHILL, R.A. Battery were wounded. No 7012 L. MORRIES, W. Bge. A Battery was accidentally injured from shell splinter.	See
	11th to 21st		A great deal of trouble was experienced for the night was very trying. No op- was able to do any firing. Several battle stations were shifted by working parties. No op- were selected for the Batteries, and the billeting of the men was also selected and the billeting of them was commenced; reinforcing parties were much depleted by general work on many days. The observation was much interfered with.	See
	21st to 28th		A fresh lot of guns for firing as at night was allotted. The usual am firing took place and further the Inspection Officers were many working parties were dispatched. Damage Battle stations were found. Ventral huts were very muddy, weather improved, very difficult and enemy's artillery were Shifted. The enemy were far inactive long the new position and the OPs were strengthened and made habitable. Rations were normal as ammunition found above.	See
	28th		12 round 5 shrapnel 65 lyd. guns. Capt. S.O. SHEPHERD, A.D.C. rejoined the Bde. and reported to D/Battery. Shelling was normal. Observation was impossible during periods and when it got misty towards dusk.	See
	31st			See
2/1/17				

J.O. Shepherd, Capt. R.F.A.
Comdy. 256th Bde. R.F.A.

-2-

barrage shooting is shooting "from the Map" and not "from registers" it is most important that allowance be made for the angle of sight which will effect both the range and fuze.

The only data for this is the contours of the Map.
It is possible to observe at a time when but little shooting is going on, some useful facts as to height of burst might be got even by observation during the two bombardment days, X and Y.

7. 255th Brigade R.F.A. will detail one 18 pounder Battery to take in "area calls" from aeroplane, and deal with "targets of opportunity".

O.C. Brigade will arrange his battery zones so that this may be done without leaving gaps in the barrage.

When not so employed this battery will thicken the barrage fire on its Brigade front.

8. As soon as YELLOW line is reached, the 179 and 184th Brigades R.F.A. of 39th Divisional Artillery attached to 51st Division will come under the orders of 63rd Division and will be available from that time on for barrage or other work on 63rd Division front. At the same time the 161st and 168th Brigades of 32nd Divisional Artillery attached to 51st Division will come under the orders of 2nd Division and will be available from that time on for barrage or other work on 2nd Division front.

9. As soon as the attack begins to move forward from YELLOW line 51st Divisional Artillery will stop firing.

10. The Z day and the zero hour will be notified later. 5.45 a.m.

11. Watches will be synchronised at 6 p.m., on Y day and at 12.30 a.m., on Z day.

12. Divisional Headquarters will be established at FORCEVILLE from 8 p.m., Y day.

ACKNOWLEDGE.

Issued at 9 a.m.

MAJOR R.A.,
BRIGADE MAJOR.
51st Divisional Artillery.

```
Copy No.1 to 161st Brigade R.F.A.
     2 to 168th Brigade R.F.A.
     3 to 179th Brigade R.F.A.
     4 to 184th Brigade R.F.A.
     5 to 255th Brigade R.F.A.
     6 to 256th Brigade R.F.A.
     7 to 260th Brigade R.F.A.
     8 to 51st D.A.C.
     9 to D.T.M.O.
    10 to 51st Division "G"
    11 to R.A., V Corps
    12 to V Corps Heavy Artillery
    13 to 2nd Divisional Artillery
    14 to 63rd Divisional Artillery
    15 to 39th Divisional Artillery
    16 to 32nd Divisional Artillery
 17 & 18      Diary
    19        Office.
```

SECRET.   COPY No. 21

51st DIVISIONAL ARTILLERY.

OPERATION ORDER No. 59.

10th November, 1916.

1. The attack of V Corps on Z day will not go beyond YELLOW Line except on right of 63rd Division, where an advance will be made from YELLOW Line to include the village of BEAUCOURT.

    The II Corps attack will go as far as HANSA LINE.

    The XIII Corps attack will go as far as WALTER Trench on left of V Corps attack.

2. From now on, up to and including Z day, there will be a bombardment every morning from 5-30 a.m. to 6-0 a.m. as follows:-

    5-30 a.m. - Heavy Artillery open fire at a slow rate and increase gradually till 5-45 a.m.

    5-45 a.m. to 6-0 a.m. - Heavy Artillery fire at an intense rate - Field Artillery join in.

    Targets for 18-pdrs. - Communication Trenches and approaches as far back as YELLOW Line.

    Targets for 4.5" Howitzers - Communication Trenches and trench junctions.

    Targets will be varied from day to day, in Brigade zones, so that every trench and approach gets its share.

    Ammunition allotted for this - 1 round per gun per minute. 18-pounders will fire 1/3rd shrapnel and 2/3rds H.E.

    Up to Z day there will be a pause in firing every morning from 6-0 a.m. to 7-0 a.m. On Z day the pause will be from 6-0 a.m. to zero hour.

3. There will be a 48 hours bombardment commencing at 7-0 a.m. on X day.
    During this period Field Artillery will fire on the enemy's wire where necessary, up to and including the YELLOW Line.
    In addition to this bombardment, wire cutting will go on all day on X and Y days where necessary.

    Cancelled by BM.546.

4. The Command of Batteries of 39th and 32nd Divisional Artillery now in action on 51st Division front will pass to C.R.A's. 63rd and 2nd Divisions, as previously ordered.

5.   Ammunition

51st Div: Arty. Operation Order No. 59 (continued).

5.   Ammunition will be expended as required, except that all units must have at least the following dumps in addition to full echelons on the morning of Z day:-

    18-pounders ....400 rounds per gun.
    4.5" Howitzers.......350 "   "   "

In addition Batteries must also have 50 rounds per gun and howitzer to be fired during Y/Z night.

The order that all ammunition is to go up to the guns in G.S. wagons is now cancelled, it may be taken up in either Ammunition Wagons or G.S. Wagons as most convenient.

6.   Acknowledge.

MAJOR, R. A.
BRIGADE MAJOR, 51st (HIGHLAND) DIV. ARTILLERY.

Issued at 4-45 p.m.

Copies 1-5 to 161st Brigade, R.F.A.
    6-10   168th   "   "
    11-15   179th   "   "
    16-20   184th   "   "
    21-25   255th   "   "
    26-30   256th   "   "
    31-34   260th   "   "
    35-38   51st Division "G".
    39   R.A. V Corps.
    40   V Corps Heavy Arty.
    41   2nd Div. Arty.
    42   63rd Div. Arty.
    43-47 retained.

SECRET 51st D.A. No. BM.304/37.

255 Bde R.F.A

1. Table A issued with Operation Order No.58, is cancelled. An Amended Table A is issued herewith.

2. In order that the Infantry can enter the trenches West and South West of Y RAVINE at O plus 5 minutes. O.C., No.2 Group will arrange that the barrage on front trench between Q.11c.45.45 and Q.10d.6.8 will be from O to O plus 5 minutes only. It will then lift to its own part of line B and the barrage on that portion of line B will be from O plus 5 minutes to O plus 11 minutes.
From line B onwards lifts will be uniform all along the line

3. The Battery detailed to enfilade Y Ravine will fire on it until O plus 6 minutes but O.C., No.4 Group will arrange that it lifts sufficiently at the Western end at O plus 5 minutes to admit of the Infantry going in at Q.10d.6.8.

Major R.A.
Brigade Major,
11th Novr.1916. 51st Divisional Artillery.

Distribution of Amended Table 'A'

161st Brigade R.F.A.   5 copies
168th Brigade R.F.A.   5 copies
179th Brigade R.F.A.   6 copies (one for Liaison Officer)
184th Brigade R.F.A.   5 copies
255th Brigade R.F.A.   7 copies (- do -   )
256th Brigade R.F.A.   7 copies (- do -   )
260th Brigade R.F.A.   6 copies (- do -   )
51st Division "G"   4 copies
R.A., V Corps   1 copy
2nd Divisional Artillery 1 copy
63rd Divisional Artillery 1 copy

S E C R E T.
* * * * * *

Latest

TABLE A.

51st DIVISIONAL ARTILLERY.
Amended Barrage Table for 18-pdrs.
REFERENCE Maps shewing Brigade Zones issued with Operation Order No. 58 and amendments to it issued with 51st D.A.No. BM/304/28.

TIME.	TASK.	Rounds per gun per minute.	REMARKS.
0	Barrage opens 75% of 18-prs on line A. 25%, 50 yards short.	4.	
0 plus 1 minute.	The 25% 18-prs. lift on to line A.	4.	
0 plus 6 minutes.	Barrage lifts from line A to line B.	4.	
0 plus 11 minutes.	-:- -:- B -:- C.	4.	
0 plus 16 -:-	-:- -:- C -:- D.	2.	
0 plus 21 -:-	-:- -:- D -:- E.	2.	
0 plus 26 -:-	-:- -:- E -:- F.	2.	No. 4 Group gradually lifts on to and off the GREEN line as shown in tracing issued with 51st D.A. No. BM/304/28.
0 plus 31 -:-	-:- -:- F -:- G.	2.	
0 plus 36 -:-	-:- -:- G to GREEN LINE.	4.	
0 plus 41 -:-	-:- from GREEN LINE to line H.	2.	
0 plus 41 to 0 plus 44 mins.	Barrage on line H.	2.	
0 plus 44 mins to 1 hr. 1 min.	Barrage on line H.	1½.	
0 plus 1 hr. 1 min. to 1 hr. 6 mins.	Pause in firing.		
0 plus 1 hr. 6 mins. to 1 hr. 21 mins.	Barrage on line H.	1½.	
0 plus 1 hr. 21 mins. to 1 hr. 26 mins.	Pause in firing.		
0 plus 1 hr. 26 mins. to 1 hr. 36 mins.	Barrage on line H.	1½.	
0 plus 1 hr. 36 mins. to 1 hr. 41 mins.	Pause in firing.		
0 plus 1 hr. 41 mins. to 1 hr. 51 mins.	Barrage on line H.	1.	
0 plus 1 hr. 51 mins. to 1 hr. 56 mins.	Pause in firing.		
0 plus 1 hr. 56 mins. to 1 hr. 58 mins.	Barrage on line H.	4.	
0 plus 1 hr. 58 minutes.	Barrage lifts from line H to line I.	3.	
0 plus 2 hrs. 03 minutes.	-:- -:- I -:- J.	3.	
0 plus 2 hrs. 08 minutes.	-:- -:- J -:- K.	3.	
0 plus 2 hrs. 13 minutes.	-:- -:- K -:- L.	2.	
0 plus 2 hrs. 18 minutes.	-:- -:- L -:- M.	2.	
0 plus 2 hrs. 23 minutes.	-:- -:- M -:- N.	2.	
0 plus 2 hrs. 28 minutes.	-:- -:- N -:- O.	2.	
0 plus 2 hrs. 33 minutes.	-:- -:- O -:- P.	4.	
0 plus 2 hrs. 38 minutes.	-:- -:- P -:- Q.	3.	
0 plus 2 hrs. 47 minutes.		3.	

Table A – Continued

TIME.	TASK.	Rounds per gun per min.	REMARKS
O plus 2 hrs. 41 minutes	Barrage lifts from line Q to YELLOW LINE	4	
O plus 2 hrs. 46 minutes	Barrage lifts to 150 yards beyond YELLOW LINE	2	
O plus 2 hrs. 46 minutes to O plus 2 hrs. 49 minutes	Barrage 150 yards beyond YELLOW LINE	2	
O plus 2 hrs. 49 minutes to O plus 2 hrs. 56 minutes	– do –	$\frac{1}{2}$	255th Brigade R.F.A. only which will cover what will be the whole of the Division front from Q.6c.9.3 to Q.6 central in accordance with instructions contained in 51st D.A. No. BM.304/27
O plus 2 hrs. 56 minutes to O plus 3 hrs. 01 minute	Pause in firing	–	
O plus 3 hrs. 01 minute to O plus 3 hrs. 11 minutes	Barrage 150 yards beyond YELLOW LINE	$\frac{1}{2}$	
O plus 3 hrs. 11 minutes to O plus 3 hrs. 16 minutes	Pause in firing	–	
O plus 3 hrs. 16 minutes to O plus 3 hrs. 26 minutes	Barrage 150 yards beyond YELLOW LINE	$\frac{1}{2}$	
O plus 3 hrs. 26 minutes to O plus 3 hrs. 31 minutes	Pause in firing	–	
O plus 3 hrs. 31 minutes to O plus 3 hrs. 41 minutes	Barrage 150 yards beyond YELLOW LINE	$\frac{1}{2}$	
O plus 3 hrs. 41 minutes to O plus 3 hrs. 46 minutes	Pause in firing	–	
O plus 3 hrs. 46 minutes to O plus 3 hrs. 48 minutes	Barrage 150 yards beyond YELLOW LINE	4	

From 3 hrs. 48 minutes onwards act according to situation

The 4.5" Howitzer Barrage will keep 100 yards beyond the 18-pounder Barrage.

S E C R E T.
* * * * * *

51st D.A. No. BM304/38.

SPECIAL TASK FOR ONE 18-pdr. BATTERY OF NO. 1 GROUP.
Cancelling the table issued with 51st D.A. No. BM./304/32.

TIME.	TASK.	ROUNDS PER GUN PER MINUTE.	REMARKS.
0 to 0 plus 6 mins.	4 guns enfilade trenches from Q.5.c.2.6. to Q.5.c.2.6.	4.	
0 plus 6 mins. to 0 plus 27 mins.	1 section enfilade road from Q.5.c.90.15. to Q.5.d.4.8.	2.	
0 plus 27 mins. to 0 plus 36 mins.	1 section enfilade trench from Q.5.d.25.35. to Q.5.d.75.65.	2.	
0 plus 36 mins. to 0 plus 1 hr. 58 mins.	1 section enfilade trench from Q.5.d.42.48. to Q.5.d.75.65.	1/2	Pauses in firing. from 0 plus 1 hr.1 min. to 1 hr. 6 mins. from 0 plus 1 hr. 21 mins. to 1 hr.26 mins. from 0 plus 1 hr. 36 mins. to 1 hr.41 mins. from 0 plus 1 hr. 51 mins. to 1 hr. 56 mins.
0 plus 6 mins. to 0 plus 40 mins.	1 section enfilade trench from Q.11.b.2.5. to Q.5.d.9.1.	2.	
0 plus 40 mins. to 0 plus 1 hr. 58 mins.	1 section enfilade trench from Q.11.b.4.7. to Q.5.d.9.1.	1/2	Pauses same as above.

From 0 plus 1 hr. 58 minutes onwards this Battery will conform to the tasks of the remainder of its Brigade.

11th November 1916.

Copies to No. 1 Group.
2 Group.
3 Group.
4 Group.
51st Div: "G".
R.A. V Corps.
V Corps Heavy Art'y.
2nd. Div: Art'y.
63rd Div: Art'y.

Major, R.A.
Brigade Major,
51st Divisional Artillery.

SECRET.

Copy No. 25

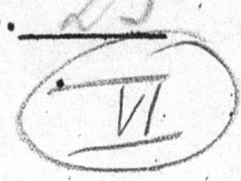

51st DIVISIONAL ARTILLERY.
OPERATION ORDER No. 60.

14th November, 1916.

Reference BEAUMONT HAMEL Map, 1/5,000.

1. The 51st Division will continue its advance to-day.

   1st Objective - MUNICH TRENCH.
   2nd Objective - FRANKFORT TRENCH.

2. The zones for the Artillery Brigades will be the same as allotted to them in Operation Order No. 58, except that the 168th Brigade's southern limit will be a line running through Q.6c.10/05, Q.6c.80/05 and Q.6c.90/05.
   The 1st barrage line will be on the north and south line running from Q.6a.0/0 to Q.12a.00/55.
   The 18-pdr. barrage will open on this line at 5-50 a.m. lifting 100 yards at 6-5 a.m. and again at 6-8 a.m. and on to the trench running from Q.6c.80/05 to Q.6a.55/00 at 6-12 a.m., remaining on this trench until 6-20 a.m. when it will lift to trench running from Q.6c.90/05 to Q.6b.0/0.
   The 168th Brigade R.F.A. will arrange the zones of at least two batteries so that they fire on the trenches from Q.6c.80/05 to Q.6c.6/3 and from Q.6c.90/05 to Q.6c.9/3.
   The barrage will remain on trench from Q.6c.90/05 to Q.6b.0/0 for one hour when it will lift to a line 150 yards beyond it.
   Rate of fire for above:-
      From 5-50 a.m. to 6-20 a.m. - 2 rounds per gun per minute.
      From 6-20 a.m. until ordered to cease fire - ½ a round per gun per minute.
   O.C. 256th Brigade, R.F.A. will detail one 18-pdr. Battery to enfilade the trenches from Q.5d.8/7 to Q.6c.0/7 and Q.5d.9/1 to Q.6c.0/1 from 5-50 a.m. to 6-0 a.m. This battery will then join in the barrage with the remainder of its Brigade.
   4.5" Howitzer Batteries will open fire at 5-50 a.m. and fire as follows:-
      D/256 - along LEAVE AVENUE from Q.6c.0/7 to Q.6c.5/3 keeping 100 yards in front of 18-pdr. barrage and lifting to FRANKFORT TRENCH at 6-8 a.m.
      D/260 - from Q.6c.0/1 to Q.6c.4/0 keeping 100 yards in front of 18-pdr. barrage and lifting to FRANKFORT TRENCH at 6-5 a.m.
   Remaining 4.5" Howitzer Batteries will open fire on trench from Q.6c.80/05 to Q.6a.55/00 at 5-50 a.m. and lift on to trench from Q.6c.90/05 to Q.6b.0/0 at 6-10 a.m.
   Rate of Fire for Howitzers - ½ round per gun per minute.

3. All Liason Officers will remain as they are at present.

4. <u>Acknowledge by wire.</u>

MAJOR, R.A.
Issued at 2-0 a.m.   BRIGADE MAJOR, 51st DIVISIONAL ARTY.

Copies 1-5 to 161st Bde R.F.A.   Copies 38. to 51st Div. G.
       6-10 " 168th   "   "   39. to R.A. V Corps.
      11-15 " 179th   "   "   40. to V Corps H.A.
      16-20 " 184th   "   "   41. to 2nd Div. Arty.
      21-26 " 255th   "   "   42   to 63rd Div. Arty.
      27-32 " 256th   "   "   43-45 retained.
      33-37 " 260th   "   "

"A" Form.
MESSAGES AND SIGNALS.

Army Form C.2121 (in pads of 100).

TO: No 2. Group.

Sender's Number: BM 563
Day of Month: 14

AAA

Line for S.O.S. barrage tonight will be 150 yds beyond Yellow line. Zones for each Bde. are as detailed in O.O. 58. Each Group will fire occasional bursts on this line & will also search the more distant approaches especially the roads & tracks in R1 & R2. This fire will extend over all the hours of darkness especially towards dawn. Ammn to be expended on night firing 400 Rds 18 pdr per Bde & 50 Rds per How= Bty.

51 D A
6.30 p.m

"A" Form.
MESSAGES AND SIGNALS.

Army Form C.2121 (in pads of 100).

TO No 2 GROUP

Sender's Number.	Day of Month.	In reply to Number.
*BM 564	15th	

AAA

Attack on Frankfort Trench will be continued to-day aaa. Our infantry now in new trench 100 yards west of Munich trench aaa Germans hold Munich trench aaa at 9 AM 256 Bde will open fire on Munich trench from Q6c5.8 to Q6A55.00 and 255 and 260 Bdes will open fire 50 yards beyond Munich trench aaa at 9.6 AM all Btys will lift back 50 yards aaa at 9.10 AM 256th Bde will lift back 50 yards and 255 and 260 Bdes will lift back on to Frankfort trench aaa at 9.15 AM 256 will lift back on to Frankfort trench aaa

"A" Form.
MESSAGES AND SIGNALS.

Army Form C.2121 (in pads of 100).

at 9.20 AM All guns will lift to 150 yards beyond Frankfort trench aaa All Howitzers of 3 Bde will fire on Frankfort trench from 9 AM to 9.10 AM and on BEAUMONT SERRE ROAD from 9.10 to 9.25 AM when they will stop firing aaa Zones for 255 and 260 Bdes as follows aaa 255 Bde Southern Boundary LEAVE AVENUE inclusive aaa Northern Boundary line running through Q6C67.7 and Q6D6.9 aaa 260 Bde Northern Boundary Q6A6.0 to Q6B0.0 and along GLORY LANE aaa Our new trench west of Munich trench will be marked with biscuits

"A" Form.
MESSAGES AND SIGNALS.

Army Form C.2121 (in pads of 100).

AAA

tns aaa Rate of fire for 18 PRS 4 rds per gun per minute up to 9.23 AM then gradually slacken off to ½ rds per gun per minute aaa 4.5 Howitzer 1 rd per gun per minute throughout aaa ~~Acknowledge~~

For your information

From: 51. O A

Time: 6 AM

51st D.A.No. BM/504/41.

Headquarters,
    No. 1 Group.
        2 Group.
        3 Group.
        4 Group.
    51st Div: "G" (for information).

Line for S.O.S. barrage to-night will be notified later.

Zones for 255th, 256th and 260th Brigade's will be as allotted in my BM/504 of to-day. These Brigade's will fire occasional bursts on the S.O.S. line, and will be responsible for barraging for a S.O.S. Call.

Ammunition to be expended as necessary.

Night firing by the remaining Brigades will be carried out throughout the night on the more distant roads and approaches.

Ammunition to be expended for this 400 rounds per Brigade.

Major, R.A.
Brigade Major,
15/11/15.   51st Divisional Artillery.

"A" Form.
MESSAGES AND SIGNALS.
Army Form C.2121 (in pads of 100).

TO — Trunk —

Sender's Number.	Day of Month.	In reply to Number.	
BM 565	15th		A A A

Re my BM 304/41 of today
Line for SOS barrage tonight
will be as follows:—
256 Bde on Frankfort Trench &
NOT East of it.

255 & 260 Bdes 50 yds east of
Frankfort Trench.

Sapp.
4.10 pm

"A" Form.
MESSAGES AND SIGNALS.

Army Form C.2121
(in pads of 100).
No. of Message ....

Prefix .... Code .... m.	Words	Charge	This message is on a/o of :	Recd. at .... m.
Office of Origin and Service Instructions.				Date ....
....	Sent		.... Service.	From ....
....	At .... m.			By ....
	To		(Signature of "Franking Officer.")	
	By			

TO — Trunk

Sender's Number.	Day of Month.	In reply to Number.	
* BM566	16		AAA

Night firing tonight same as last night but there must be no firing within 100 yds of LEAVE AVENUE between Q6C9.3 & Q6D2.4. Ammn for 255th Bde. 250 & 260 Btys as required. For 161 & 163 600 Rds 18pdr per Bde & 50 Rds 4·5 per By.

51. D.A.
8-20 pm

From
Place
Time

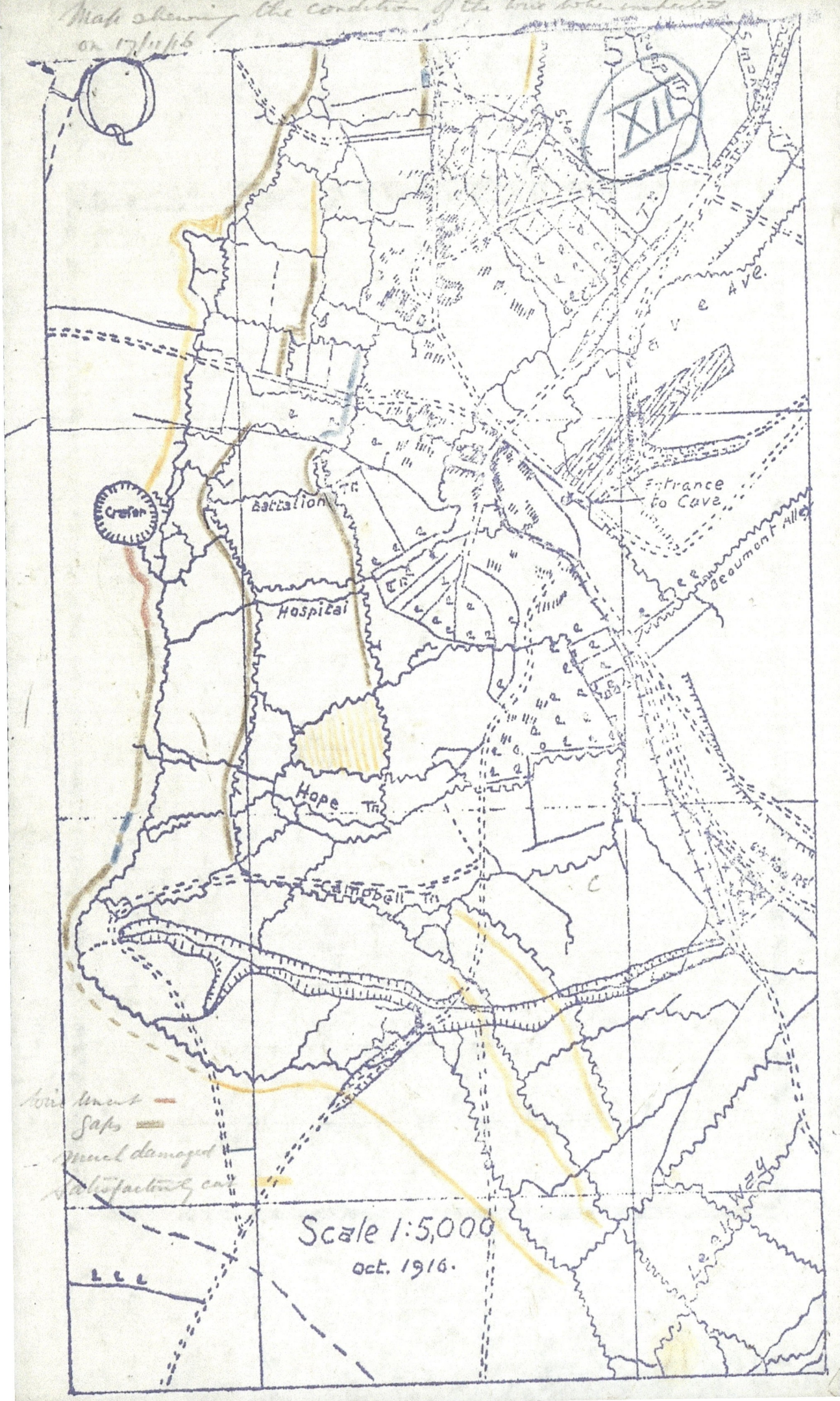

29 Ersatz Regt. 223 Div.   Our approximate Front Line and
121 R.I.R.) 26 Res. Div.   Enemy Forces opposing
99 R.I.R.)   17th Nov, 1916.
23 I.R., 12 Div.
173 I.R. 223 Div.
169 I.R.) 52 Div.
66 I.R.)

Scattered Remnants
   only.
III/22
144 I.R. 223 Div.
55 R.I.R. 2 Gds. Res. Div.
62 I.R., 12 Div.

XIII

Part of Sheet 57D.
Scale 1/20,000.

V. Corps Intelligence
   Oct. 1916.

No. 1 Gun   Add 30" M.R.   CORRECTOR ⓍⅣ   132 (85)
                                              148 (80)

TIME	ALTERATION		FUZE	RATE OF FIRE	LINE	A.S.	RANGE	TARGET
6. AM			9.5	4½	2.30 R	-15"	3300	A
6.6	15" ML A.S. -20	Add 125	10	4	2.15 R	-20	3425	B
6.11		" 225	10.7	4	"	"	3650	C
6.16	15" ML AS -25	" 100	11.1	2	2° R	-25	3750	D
6.21	AS -30	" 100	11.4	2	"	-30	3850	E
6.26		" 50	11.6	2	"	"	3900	F
6.31	15" ML	" 125	12	2	1.30 R	"	4025	G
6.36		" 25	12	2		"	4050	GREEN
6.41	AS -20	" 175	12.6	2		-20	4225	H
6.44							"	"
6.44 to 7.56	Pauses 7.4 & 7.6 7.21 & 7.26 7.36 & 7.41 7.51 & 7.56			½ ½			"	"
7.56 & 7.58			11.1 12.6	4			"	"
7.58	15" ML AS -15	Add 100	11.4	2	1.15 R	-15	4325	I
8.3	AS -10	" 125	11.8	2		-10	4450	J
8.8	15" ML AS Zero	" 75	12.1	2	1° R	Zero	4525	K
8.13		" 100	12.4	2	"	"	4625	L
8.18		" 100	12.7	2	"	"	4725	M
8.23	15" ML AS +5"	" 100	13.1	2	45' R	+5	4825	N
8.28		" 75	13.3	2	"	"	4900	O
8.33		" 50	13.5	4	"	"	4950	P
8.38	15" ML	" 75	13.8	2	30' R	"	5025	Q
8.41		" 100	14.2	4			5125	YELLOW
8.46 & 8.49				2				BEYOND
8.49 to 9.46	Pauses 8.56 & 9.1 9.11 & 9.16 9.26 & 9.31 9.41 & 9.46			½				" "
9.46 & 9.48				4				"

CONFIDENTIAL
No 21(m)
HIGHLAND DIVISION

Vol 21

War Diary
of
256th Brigade, R.F.A.
from 1st Jan 1917 to 31st Jan 1917

WAR DIARY
of
INTELLIGENCE SUMMARY.

(Erase heading not required.)

Army Form C. 2118.

CONFIDENTIAL
No 2710
HIGHLAND DIVISION

Place	Date	Hour	Summary of Events and Information	Remarks and references to Appendices
Field	1917 January 1.		There was the usual daily firing and in addition to this a few extra bursts of fire were fired as minimum "hates" sps to	see
	2nd		Orders were received to prepare to hand over in the night of the 5/6th.	see see
		7.9 pm	A few gas shells were sent over by the enemy.	
	3rd		C.O. B/2/e and C/2/c Batteries of relieving division were shown round the position my new [?] Batteries were assigned as C/2 [?] to A Battery, A, C, & B Batteries myself had 1 to A Battery. Thus my batty B battery. to be taken over by 2 guns of C but 1 to A battery and 1 to some one [?] batteries were to be guns.	see
	4th		no further [?] M.D. & green [?] Oil batteries to be relieved and B battery gathers [?] here guns did some indirect actions [?]	see
		4.30pm	and proceeded to [?] level [?] There was only little shelling on our part.	
	5th	12.30pm 5.30pm	Brigade and Battery commanders proceeded to take over the relief was completed by H.Q. Group of A.F.A. the 16th, 9th and 41st Batteries in battery A.C.D. Batteries of effecting Batteries [?] began [?]	see

Army Form C. 2118.

WAR DIARY
or
INTELLIGENCE SUMMARY.
(Erase heading not required.)

Instructions regarding War Diaries and Intelligence Summaries are contained in F. S. Regs., Part II. and the Staff Manual respectively. Title pages will be prepared in manuscript.

Place	Date	Hour	Summary of Events and Information	Remarks and references to Appendices
Field	Jan. 1917		The Brigade marched to AUTHIEULE and three Billeting Knight Eye	
	6th		" " " OUTREBOIS	Eg.
	7th		" " " MAIZICOURT	Eg.
	8th		" " " PORT-LE-GRAND	
	9th		" " " PORT-LE-GRAND, 152 Final destinations and	
			settled army there. PORT-LE-GRAND is on the right bank of the	
			SOMME about 8 kilometres North of ABBEVILLE. 57 (H) Dir.	
			LIEUT E.C.TACK was attached as A.D.C. to the C.R.A. Horse had been very	Eg.
			Billets men inspired. Horse standings commenced fifty yards of the march	
			In addition to daily games at ill, the 3rd of the march was paid between batteries, and	
			against the units in the Division	
		12.31H	Lectures were given by BRIG-gen L.D.OLDFIELD, D.S.O, C.R.A.,	
			by the A.D.V.S., by the A.D.V.S., and by MAJ. H. FRASER, A/216.	
			[signature]	
	1/2/17		Recd Lt. R.F.A.	
			Cmdg 316 L Bde R.F.A.	

Vol 22

WAR DIARY

OF

256th BRIGADE R.F.A.

From 1st February 1917 to 28th February 1917.

WAR DIARY
or
INTELLIGENCE SUMMARY.

Army Form C. 2118.

84

Place	Date	Hour	Summary of Events and Information	Remarks and references to Appendices
Field	1917 February 1st		Brigade remained in training at PORT-LE-GRAND.	See
	2nd			See
	3rd		Orders were received to proceed to FONTAINE-SUR-MAYE. Brigade stayed there for night 3/6 & 7/6.	See
	4/5		Bgde proceeded to FILLIEVRES and stayed there the night	See
	6/2		Brigade " " CROISETTE " "	See
	7/2		Brigade " " BAJUS and stayed there until	See
	8/2			See
	9/2		the 18th when orders were received to proceed into action. Division formed 17 Corps 3rd Army. Brigade proceeded into action in their positions alongside road running from A.26.c.7.2. to A.26.a.5.3. with Bde HQrs at A.26.a.25.5.6.; all Trench Map ROCLINCOURT 51B NW. Till 23rd positions were day and camouflages and telephone wires laid as observation was impossible two days 24th Feb relief D battery calibrated two howitzers A, B, + C battery calibrated their guns and D battery checked guns calibration. Owing to bad light, calibration was impossible. Batteries continued calibration. Battery attempted to cut wire but owing to bad night it was found to be impossible.	See See See See See See See See
	24th			
	25th			
	26th			
	27th			
	28th			

2/3/17

Mulvany Lieut-Col R.A
Comdg. 256 Bde R.F.A.

Vol 23

War Diary
of
236th Bde R.F.A.

From 1st March 1917 to 31st March 1917.

WAR DIARY
INTELLIGENCE SUMMARY

Army Form C. 2118.
85

Place	Date	Hour	Summary of Events and Information	Remarks and references to Appendices
Field	March 1917 1st		The Brigade remained in the positions previously occupied by it.	app
	5th	6.10 am	Wire cutting on the left battalion front was carried out from A.23.d.50 to A.30.a.2.35. Lt. Bn. Sutton (Hughes) raided enemy's trenches. The raid was very successful. 1 officer, 20 other ranks and 1 machine-gun being captured. Identifications were obtained and many of the enemy killed.	app
	4 pm		Lieut. Sec. L.M. DYSON took on a force of one gun or 6 4th Army Field Artillery	
	14th		During the first week of this month the battery positions were improved and work was begun on 13 dugouts and 3 primary OPs.	app
			During the week the enemy infantry in his trenches increased slightly though no attempt was made to return. He [said] he would cut [—] in battery positions. The work on OPs was continued and also on battery positions. In addition to this Eng. Factory had to prepare a reinforcing position. Apart from this, the ST. SIXTE was practised to this brigade to dig position for another brigade.	app
	17th	6.15 am	The 8th Bn Argyll & Sutherland slightly raided the enemy trenches on the same front that the 6th Bn [Argyll] raided. They raid was also very successful, inflicting 10 [??] on the enemy killed, 10 prisoners [??] [????] casualties were very high but only slight wounds.	app
	21st		During this week many working parties were supplied by our Bde. Work (putting [?]) was carried out on the ammunition supply, nearly 2000 rungs of ammunition completed. [????] for the gun line almost completed. The free back OPs were completed and [???] [??] continued on the OPs, dugouts and [????] dugouts and two others. The Brigade being dug by the S.A.O. parties were made ready to take the guns forward and the Brigade was brought up to these new positions. Ammunition was brought up to these new positions.	

WAR DIARY
or
INTELLIGENCE SUMMARY.

(Erase heading not required.)

Army Form C. 2118.
86

Place	Date	Hour	Summary of Events and Information	Remarks and references to Appendices
Field	23rd		The brisk system of rifles for the attack was started.	app
	24th		Hostile aeroplane flew over battery position and brigade HQrs at a height of about 300 feet.	app
	25th		No reconnaissance of hostile planes coming over C battery was shelled from 9 am till 11 am with 5.9 How. C battery commander came to brigade HQ to perform under this heavy fire	app
	26th		1 A/256 y. Field artillery brigade came into temporary position by by batteries	app
	27th		1 Army Field Artillery Bde came into temporary position by by batteries	
	28th		Recs B. gun succeeded to register. Ammunition of batteries brought up to 200 rounds per gun. Wire was cut and fair intended raid to left of RE of bde front. A great many rounds fired by Hun of 4/5's to bring our system was better. 635698 St. J. LAING C33598 Sgt. FORBES 90 Bdr TAYLOR C battery were wounded NO 183 — 61 TAYLOR C battery were wounded	90C
	29th			
	30th			
	31st	8:30pm	A raid was carried out by 6 Black Watch No prisoners were taken but identification was obtained. The raid was fairly successful. 2/Lieut L.B. BRIERCLIFFE B battery was killed while observing at forward O.P. 635 639 K HUGHES B battery was wounded At 6:15 am of 1st Brigades in this group began register and were ready to shoot in barrage lines.	
	2/4/17			

Lieut Col RA.
Cmdg 256 Bde R F A

51st

Vol 24

WAR DIARY
of
256th Brigade R.F.A.
From 1st April 1917 to 30th April 1917

WAR DIARY
INTELLIGENCE SUMMARY

Army Form C. 2118.

Place	Date	Hour	Summary of Events and Information	Remarks and references to Appendices
Field	1917 April			
	2nd		The Brigade remained in action in the positions previously occupied by it. The preparations for offensive operations were continued, and all necessary barrage tables and other programmes were prepared that Z day would be 8th April. Orders were issued that Z day would be 8th April. Nominal roll of officers in Bde at beginning of month is in Appendix E. (attached) — we received Operation order 28 contained in Appendix B (attached) from which Preliminary Bombardments (Appendix C attached) and Barrage Tables for Z day (Appendix D attached), were made up and sent out to Batteries.	Gog
			The first day } Preliminary bombardments "W" day	Gog
			"W" day }	
	4th		"X" day } with tables in appendix C.	Gog
	5th		"Q" day }	
	6th		"Y" day }	Gog
	7th		On the night of 4/5th One section of 113 battery moved to a forward position at A.28.b.28 on the night of 7/8th one section of A+ one section of C battery moved to forward positions respectively at A.28.c.45.45 and A.28.b.45	Gog

Army Form C. 2118.

88

WAR DIARY
INTELLIGENCE SUMMARY.
(Erase heading not required.)

Place	Date	Hour	Summary of Events and Information	Remarks and references to Appendices
Zulu	1917 April		Original junctions of battalions are given in Appendix B. The other Battle was 1st Canadian Divn. 51st (Highland) Divn on 34th Divn own. Canadians on right, 57th in centre, and 34th on right. The Division attacked with 2 Inf Bdes in the line each with 2 battalions, the 152nd Inf Bde on left, and the 153rd Inf Bde on right. The attack was planned for a limited objective called the BROWN LINE, that with 2 intermediate lines called the BLACK LINE and the BLUE LINE. The Divisional artillery was supplemented by 4 Army field artillery Bdes the 34th, 64th, 84th, and 315th Army field artillery Bdes and was divided into 2 groups as follows:- No 1 group. Commded by Lieut-Col. M. M. Duncan V.D., C.M.G. 235th Bde R.F.A., 34th A.F.A. Bde, and 64th A.F.A. Bde. on right of divisional zone No 2 group Commded by Lieut-Col. L. M. Dyson R.F.A. 256th Bde R.F.A. 84th A.F.A. Bde and 315th A.F.A. Bde. on left Divisional Zone with 256th on left, 84th in centre and 315th on right. The Zones were as shown in Appendix A which also shows the lifts in the barrages and the times of lifting.	

Army Form C. 2118.

WAR DIARY
or
INTELLIGENCE SUMMARY

(Erase heading not required.)

Place	Date	Hour	Summary of Events and Information	Remarks and references to Appendices
Field	9/4/17		From the night 1/2 Lieut. Col. L.M. DYSON proceeded to the Hd.Qrs. 174th Infantry Brigade as liaison Officer for the Group. The back O.P. was manned by CAPT. S.O. SHEPHERD. B/ Battery, assisted by 2/Lieut. B.W. JOHNSTON. A battery. The forward O.P. was manned by CAPT. E.C. WELSH D/ Battery. 2/Lieut. S.F. SMITH was liaison Officer with left Battalion. 2/Lieut. E.V. ASTON was liaison Officer with right Battalion. The Rifle Zone was covered on the right by A Battery on right and B Battery on left and C Battery covering the whole zone.	E99
		5.30 a.m.	Attack began.	
		8.55 a.m.	Up till this time the barrage had been normal, and up to time, and the BLUE LINE was captured. Prisoners coming in were very much demoralised.	
		9.15 a.m.	It was thought that enemy was counter-attacking. The rate of fire on the protective barrage was increased.	
		9.38 a.m.	Programme was resumed. The attack was very successful then objective the centre did not quite reach the BROWN LINE, but the flanks gaining their objective. At night-fall the situation was somewhat obscure, and it was reported that the infantry were holding TOMMY TRENCH which they thought was the BROWN LINE. About 1200 prisoners were taken by the Division.	
		12.26 p.m.	The guns of the forward sections started firing	

WAR DIARY

INTELLIGENCE SUMMARY

Army Form C. 2118.
90.

Place	Date	Hour	Summary of Events and Information	Remarks and references to Appendices
Field	April 1917 9th	2 pm	Batteries started moving guns up to forward positions; this was confined to forward sections in the afternoon. The Bde did not move from the Wagon Lines in the G, 2 & G 18th D battery moved to forward position alongside A battery at dawn. 10th. Reconnaissance was made from actual situation. Throughout it was seen that the infantry was not quite BROWN LINE. The whole day was spent in clearing up the situation.	See. See.
	10th			
	11th	9 am	A bombardment of the BROWN LINE which was not captured was begun by the Heavy and Siege batteries; to enable this to have effect the infantry were withdrawn & returned to BROWN LINE and started forward again and reached	See
		6.30 pm	Situation remained the same.	
	12th		The 170th Bde of the 31st Div relieved the 256th Bde who withdrew to their Wagon Lines.	See
	13th		Major FRASER, CAPT. S.O. SHEPHERD & Lieut. J. McFARLANE MC. D Battery, reconnoitred positions for the brigade in action. Ref. map afterwards F (3, B. N.W.); and orders were received that the Bde would move into action on the 14th; and some news that these orders had however the following morning the orders to move into action were cancelled and Bde was more into position A battery in the command of the 4th Div. Arty.	See
	14th		A battery moved into action at H 9 C 18 Lieut-Col. L.M. DYSON; LIEUT. G.C. COULL and the other three battery remaining	See

Army Form C. 2118.

9/1

WAR DIARY
INTELLIGENCE SUMMARY.
(Erase heading not required.)

Place	Date 1917	Hour	Summary of Events and Information	Remarks and references to Appendices
Field	April 14th (cont.) 15th		went forward and reconnoitred positions for the three remaining Bde Hd.Qrs. moved in return, and the Hee Batteries B, C, and D, at positions H14 a 90 45, H 8 d 88, H9 c 26 and H14 b 34 respectively. The following casualties occurred:— Killed No 636917 Gr. MITCHELL, A., A battery " No 663024 Gr. PARTRIDGE, T., D battery Wounded No 635322 Cpl. RILEY, D. A battery No 663,046 2/Lt. HERD, R. D battery, arms and forearms (20/4/17) No 10937 Gr. HOWELLS, E., D battery No 663028 Gr. HUGHES, J. D battery	G.G G.G. G.G
	16th		The Bde Hd.Qrs. moved to the railway cutting at H7 d 93. The batteries continued entrenching and reporting. Casualties wounded 635536 Gr. GOW, G., A battery.	G.G
	17th–18th		The Bde came under the command of the 62nd Div. artillery. The No 635120 Gr. STARK, F., C battery who was wounded. The moved carrying and firing and one was carried in. Killed 636 418 Gr. EDGAR, J., C battery Wounded 635038 Bdr. THOMSON, J.S., C battery	G.G
	19th		The Bde came under the command of the C.R.A. 51st (High) Div. Killed 663025 Gr. MITCHELL, W., D battery Wounded 119064 Gr. MORSE, A., D.	G.G
	20th		The several gas and conveniently shelling the day was very hull and conveniently all shelling was done from the mg. At night the batteries were fairly heavily shelled with gas shells, intermixed with 4.2" hows H.E.	G.G

Army Form C. 2118.

92

WAR DIARY
INTELLIGENCE SUMMARY.
(Erase heading not required.)

Place	Date 1917	Hour	Summary of Events and Information	Remarks and references to Appendices
Field	April 21st		Our batteries continued sniping and several working parties were dispersed. Orders were received that the division would attack on the morning of the 23rd. During the night the batteries were very heavily shelled with H.E. and the shells intermixed with 4.2" gun and howitzer H.E. and the following casualties occured :-	See app.
	21/22		Wounded No 635159 Sgt. SLIDDERS. W. C Battery	
			" No 635075 Gr. BROWN, Q., "	
			" No 635114 Gr. PAUL, D., "	
			" No 636103 Gr. CHARLES, R., "	
			" No 635110 Gr. BURNETT, G., "	
			" No 635006 Gr. PATTERSON, T., "	
			" No 635044 Gr. REID, J., "	
			" No 635702 Sgt. FORBES, J., B Battery. Since died (24/4/17).	
			" No 650423 Gr. GRANT, C., "	
			" No 635337 Gr. MAXWELL, H., "	
			" No 635403 Dr. DONALDSON, E., "	
			" (Gassed) No 636379 Br. DEXTON, C., HQ Po.	
			" " No 636423 Gr. BLYTHMAN, T., C Battery	
			" " No 635214 Gr. McADAM, A., "	
			" " No 1016 Gr. SMITH, W.K., "	
			" " No 635328 Gr. NUGENT, J., A Battery	
			" " No 127722 Br. SHELDON, F., "	See

Army Form C. 2118.

93

WAR DIARY
INTELLIGENCE SUMMARY.
(Erase heading not required.)

Place	Date	Hour	Summary of Events and Information	Remarks and references to Appendices
Field	1917 April 22		Ammunition was brought up, and all arrangements made for the attack on the 23rd. A few working parties were dispersed, and my wire which had been put out by the Chinese was carefully cut by our pts.	
		8 pm.	Lieut-Col. L.M. DYSON went to HdQrs 153rd Inf Bde to liason there for the group.	
			MAJOR. A.F.S. NAPIER A was in charge of the BnW.O.P. noted by	
			2/Lieut. P.W. JOHNSTON A battery.	
			Lieut. F.V. ASTON " " F.D.O.	
			LIEUT. R.R. ALEXANDER was liason officer right battalion	
			2/Lieut W. HANWORTH was liason officer with left battalion	
			2/Lieut J.M. COUPER was liason Officer	
			The left Group of the 51st D.V. Artillery under the command of Lieut-Col. L.M. DYSON consisted of the 256th Bde R.F.A. the 14th H. Artillery Bde, and the 50th Army Field Artillery Bde, covering the 153rd Inf. Bde. The infantry line and 1st objective are shown in attached map Appendix G, and also the lanes and barrage lines, with 1st objective viz the BLACK LINE, the 2nd the BLUE LINE and the 3rd objective the BROWN LINE.	
			The Barrage lines and objectives are shown on map Appendix O. (attached)	
	23rd	4.45 am.	Barrage opened out at 4.50. the infantry assaulted At first the attack was successful, both the CHEMICAL WORKS and ROEUX being taken; no infantry trumps and no opp. advancing as far as it is likely on the map. (Appendix D G.). The infantry attacked very heavily and was successfully driven off an obsvered attack ultimately we were driven back to a line which	ECG

Army Form C. 2118.

94

WAR DIARY
INTELLIGENCE SUMMARY.
(Erase heading not required.)

Place	Date	Hour	Summary of Events and Information	Remarks and references to Appendices
Field	1917 April 23 (cont).		included the CHEMICAL WORKS and FORT ST ROEUX. The fighting was fairly intensely fierce all through. About 1380 prisoners were taken by the Division. Casualties Killed :- 2/Lieut J. McFARLANE M.C. D Battery No. 636703 Gr. STOREY, A. A Battery No. 107211 Gr. WREN, G. C Battery Wounded :- 635208 Sgt. CUNNINGHAM, M. C Battery; 635208 Br. HARRIS, J., C Batt.; 645944 Br. ORMISTON, G., A Batt.; 635249 Dr. LOWRIE, T., C Batt.; 12.8650 a/Br. HARDMAN, G., A Batt.; 167057 a/Br. HORSBURGH, F., A Batt.; 776353 Gr. OWEN, W., A Batt.; 636389 Gr. BARRON, A., A Battery; 13273 Gr. SULLIVAN, T., C Batt.; 84114 Gr. HOWES, W., C Battery.	G.C.C.
	23/4/17		During the night the enemy again counter-attacked and we were driven out of ROEUX and the CHEMICAL WORKS, and the line held was then as shown on map.	R.C.Y.
	24th		The day was spent in clearing the situation, which was still a little obscure. Another counter-attack was driven off by the artillery fire. No 635739 Gr. MACKIE, D., B Batt. was wounded. Infantry of Division were relieved by that of 34th Div.	R.C.Y.
			Several working parties were prepared by our fire, in addition	G.Y.
	25th 26th 27th		2/Lieut F.B. PATTERSON B Batt. was carried out. 663610 Gr. PHINN, D, D batt., wounded 635, 418 Sgt. MILLAR, C. A batt. wounded on the 28th. Plans reviewed for an attack.	
		8 pm	The Officers as follows went to heavy artilleries in addition: MAJ. H. FRASER as a Liaison Officer to Batt & 102 H.A.G. CAPT. S.D. SHEPHERD to Batt O.P. 2/Lieut J.M. ANDREW to Bde O.P. as F.O.O.	

Army Form C. 2118.

95.

WAR DIARY
or
INTELLIGENCE SUMMARY.
(Erase heading not required.)

Place	Date	Hour	Summary of Events and Information	Remarks and references to Appendices
Field	1917 April 27th (cont'd)	?	2/Lieut J. NIVEN to left Battalion as Liaison Officer. 2/Lieut D.L. McMASTER to Rifle Battalion as Liaison Officer.	CCF
	28th	4.25 am	Barrage opened and at 4.20 am infantry assaulted. Barrage line and objective and lanes as shown in appendix G. Barrage line was uneventful. MOUNT PLEASANT WOOD was lost by the infantry and retaken in the afternoon about 3.— Very few prisoners were taken. HdQrs. 323241 Gr. NUNN, W.J., wounded, at duty. 636461 Gr. GORSTORPHINE, J.C. battery, wounded. Harassing fire kept up all day.	Seg
	29th – 30th		O.C. Rifle and Batt Cmdrs reconnoitred forward positions East of FEUCHY with a view to moving the batteries. The bay was very quiet. We shop shell caused the following casualties:— Killed 635128 Gr. STRACHAN, G. C battery. 636049 Gr. STEVENS, A. C battery; 636093 Gr. ROBERTSON, J. C battery; 636147 Gr. CLARK, W. C battery; 636149 Gr. EAGLE, W., C battery. During the month the following names were sent up for honours in connection with the operations 9/4/17 to 16/4/17: April:- Capt. C.C. WELSH, R.F.A. 2Lt. EVASTON, R.F.A. (T.F.) N? Serjt. CALLAGHAN 2/235 R.F.A. G. N? NIVEY D/285 R.F.A. Infantry & 34th Divisions always at Lieut: and Brest Penneuendre Hd Dw Gnr.	
	2/5/17		As only one copy of the afternoon, they have been sent to Home Records with the duplicate copy. Among 256th Bde R.F.A.	

Lieut-Col R.F.A.
Among 256 Bde R.F.A.

WAR DIARY
of
256th Brigade R.F.A.
From 1st May to 31st May 1917

Vol 25

Army Form C. 2118.

96

WAR DIARY
INTELLIGENCE SUMMARY
(Erase heading not required.)

Place	Date 1917	Hour	Summary of Events and Information	Remarks and references to Appendices
Gill	May 1.		The Bde remained in the positions occupied by it last night.	ELF
	2.	4am	A barrage was put down on the enemy's trenches to simulate an attack, and was replied to & relieved by the enemy. Works were successfully bombarded by no. ELF	ELF
	3.	3.45 am	Attack by the 4th Div. Infantry, 9 & SW on left, our 17th Div. on right, did not progress at all. The situation at night still was obscure.	EY
	4.	8pm	At this hour an attack was again made on the CHEMICAL WORKS and on ROEUX and again at 11 pm an attack was made. Both attacks were successful and the troops gained their objectives but owing to heavy machine gun fire, and shell enough, the attacking force was obliged to retire, and finally this Bn held on to the 32 to the original line. CAPT. S. O SHEPHERD B/ Batt. was wounded at duty.	ELF
	5.		Harassing fire was carried out by day and night.	ELF
	6.	6am	An attempt was made by the infantry to capture the buildings in I 13 just north of the railway. This was unsuccessful owing to machine gun fire.	ELF

Army Form C. 2118.

97

WAR DIARY
or
INTELLIGENCE SUMMARY
(Erase heading not required.)

Place	Date	Hour	Summary of Events and Information	Remarks and references to Appendices
Field	7th May		Enemy was very much quieter during this period. Harassing fire was kept up by us by day and night. Reputedly were mag of our rifle attacks on the CHEMICAL WORKS and on ROEUX CEMETRY	App 7
	8th			App
	9th			
	10th			
	11th			App 5
	12th	7.30pm	The CHEMICAL WORKS and ROEUX were attacked successfully and remained in our hands.	
		6.30am	A further attack was made on CORONA TRENCH N.W. to railway. The attack was unsuccessful but South of the railway, the trench was taken and held. During the day no attempt was made by the enemy to retake the ground lost. During the night Brig of 51st Division relieved the inf. of the 34th Division.	App
	13 R		During the day the enemy artillery were very active on our newly won ground.	App
		11.30pm	2/Lieut J. NIVEN B/Lieut was killed at the battery position 7th B. THOMSON, J. T.M.B. was wounded. ROEUX was taken unopposed by our infantry.	

A5834 Wt. W4973/M687 750,000 8/16 D. D. & L. Ltd. Forms/C.2118/13.

WAR DIARY
INTELLIGENCE SUMMARY.
(Erase heading not required.)

Army Form C. 2118.

98

Place	Date 1917	Hour	Summary of Events and Information	Remarks and references to Appendices
Field	May 14th		During this day the enemy's artillery was very active in or about the trenches N. of the CHEMICAL WORKS.	A.S.
	15th		During the day the enemy fire was quite and during the night practically died down firing.	S.S.
	16.	3.30am	Enemy opened a very heavy barrage in our trench lattice positions, and roads and approaches; and launched an attack against the CHEMICAL WORKS and ROEUX. Very fierce fighting took place. The enemy gained much behind the CHEMICAL WORKS from the NORTH and some of the enemy even got so far as CALABAR Trench.	
		8.30am	A strong counter-attack was launched by us and all ground was taken again. The enemy suffered very severely indeed. 2/Lieut J. FAIRLIE B/batt who was taken prisoner escaped and helped to capture some prisoners.
Battalion killed.
636031 Pte. WILSON, J. D/batt killed.
636390 Pte. CRUICKSHANKS, J. A/batt killed.
The following officers were wounded at duty 2/Lieut. D. NICOLL B/batt. and 2/Lieut W.B. MUTTER C/batt.
The following N.C.O's and men were wounded:- 635709 Cpl. COLEMAN, T. B/batt; 635.887 L. McLENNAN, J. B/batt; 636211 Bdr. STOUT, J.M., D/batt; 454.00 Sgt. CALLAGHAN, C. D/batt; 4/10843 Br. GUY, F. D/batt; 77687 Br. CARTER, D. A/batt; 165307 Br. GREENWOOD, H., T.M.B attached B/ue; 635280 Br. THANE, J. D/batt. (Since died of wounds)	G.S.

Army Form C. 2118.

99.

WAR DIARY
INTELLIGENCE SUMMARY.
(Erase heading not required.)

Place	Date 1917	Hour	Summary of Events and Information	Remarks and references to Appendices
Field	May 17		Very heavy harassing fire was kept up by us by day and night in approaches and trenches. The enemy replied very quiet and only shelled the CHEMICAL WORKS with a few shells.	aep
	18	12.15 am 1.30 am	Enemy was shelled by us at these times.	aep
	19	3.45 am 4.45 am	The enemy opened very heavy barrage on our trenches & replied vigorously but no attack developed.	aep
		3 a.m.	Hostile artillery who again very active in the CHEMICAL WORKS and in ROEUX and during the early morning there was Explosive B was required. Aerial activity on the part of the enemy. The enemy opened a very heavy barrage on the GAVRELLE-ROEUX Rd, and kept it up for an hour.	aep
	20		Our own artillery was very active in the early morning. The hostile aerial activity was very much greater than normal. The enemy again shelled the CHEMICAL WORKS between 4 and 6 p.m.	aep
	21		13th. AUCHTERLONIE w; A.Lieut was wounded. The enemy was quiet except for occasional bursts of fire on the CHEMICAL WORKS and on ROEUX.	aep
	2/14/22		D/ battery moved from its position to a new position at H 22 c 86 Ref. map France 57¹³ N.W. 1/20.000.	

A 5834 Wt. W 4973/M 687 750,000 8/16 D. D. & L. Ltd. Forms/C.2118/13.

Army Form C. 2118.

WAR DIARY
or
INTELLIGENCE SUMMARY.
(Erase heading not required.)

Place	Date	Hour	Summary of Events and Information	Remarks and references to Appendices
Field	May 21st(Mon)		During the morning B. battery moved two guns to new position at H.22.b.6.1. During the day except for the shelling of CHEMICAL WORKS, H.22.b.30.7 by GREEN W.D. H.M. trench mortars B.H.Q. was informed.	See
	22nd		Registered B/D Battery heavily shelled just outside of Brigade Hqtrs R.F.A. will 20%d & 25%p Blue R.F.A. were formed up to Bgs positions) & battery. The remainder of B/13 battery moves to H.22.c.45.05 and proceeded to dig in.	See
	23rd		B. Battery entrenched its position at H.22.c.45.05 and proceeded to dig in. Our artillery continued its harassing fire by day and by night.	See
	24th		The enemy artillery was fairly active all day, and quiet at night. A battery moved into action in a new position at H.22.d.50.65 and proceeded to register. Hostile artillery was very active. Enemy aerial activity was normal.	See
	25th		During the day the enemy artillery was very active especially in the neighbourhood of the Divisional Zone.	See
	26th		Enemy's artillery was again very active principally in our rear system of trenches. On Flanks there very active during the day.	See
	27th		Hostile aircraft were very active in the early morning. The hostile artillery was less active; at number of new in the neighbourhood of Lehny mills were noticed. No 6630%g Gr. COWAN, G. D/Batt was wounded.	See

A5831 Wt W4973/M687 750,000 8/16 D.D. & L. Ltd. Forms/C.2118/13.

Place	Date	Hour	Summary of Events and Information	Remarks and references to Appendices
Field	May 1917 28th		The enemy's artillery was again less active than usual. Our aeroplanes were very busy after. Seven [?] in reconnoitering the enemy was carried out during the day. The shelling of 'a Chinese' attack by night this scheme was carried out. Shelling fire was kept up by the artillery on approaches and roads with a view to any movement seen. Chinese burp guns carried out.	S.S.
	29th			S.S.
	30th		At 3.15 am another "Chinese" attack was carried out. The enemy replied very feebly. Began during the afternoon a 'Chinese' attack was carried out. Hostile artillery was much quieter than the previous day except for [short] bursts of fire. Hostile aircraft inactive.	S.S.
	31st		Harassing fire kept up during the day and night. 3.30 am we bombarded the enemy's trenches. The enemy's reply was feeble. Enemy aircraft were inactive.	S.S.

2/6/17

R.G.R.
Major R.T.R.
Cmdy. 256 & 13 de R.T.R.

WAR DIARY

Vol 26

From June 1, 1917 to June 30 1917

256th Bde R.F.A.

WAR DIARY

INTELLIGENCE SUMMARY.

(Erase heading not required.)

Army Form C. 2118.

102

Place	Date	Hour	Summary of Events and Information	Remarks and references to Appendices
Field	June 6/17 1		The Bde remained in the positions occupied by it last month. The C.R.A. 9th Div. took over command from C.R.A. 57th Div.	ecs
	2		A "Chinese attack" was carried out successfully.	eg
	3		Hostile artillery was very active to-day.	eg
	4			ecs
	5	8 p.m.	Barrage opened by artillery prior to an attack by the infantry. Ref. Appendix A original line and objective shown. The objective was taken. Several pickets of Germans in isolated shell holes held out for a time but were ultimately driven off by our infantry. During the night the enemy kept up a fairly heavy fire on the CHEMICAL WORKS and vicinity. 49 prisoners were taken.	ecs
	6/6/17		During the night the S.O.S signal was sent up five times at 7.50 p.m.; 8.10 p.m.; 10/10 p.m.; 11.30 p.m.; 12.32 a.m. and 3.50 a.m. The enemy did not attack but his firing during the night was heavier than usual.	ecs

WAR DIARY
or
INTELLIGENCE SUMMARY

Army Form C. 2118.

103

Place	Date	Hour	Summary of Events and Information	Remarks and references to Appendices
Judd	June 1915 7		Our artillery was very active during the day, and at 9.45 p.m. enemy's trenches were heavily bombarded in response to an S.O.S. sent by the infantry.	909
	8th		At 8.30 a.m., 11.45 a.m. & 12.55 a.m. practice barrages were fired by the artillery with good effect. Enemy artillery was considerably quieter. V/Lieut-Col. L.M. DYSON, MAJ. N.K.O SHEPHERD, and MAJ. H. FRASER were awarded the D.S.O. 2nd Lieut. D.L. McMASTER D/battery was awarded the M.C. for gallantry during recent operations. Activity normal.	890
	9th 10th 12th		D/Battery had 5 casualties: 663060 A/Br. McMATH, J., killed; 438 Gr. THOMAS, J.; 636467 Gr. BARTRAM, C.; 200,052 Gr. McMEEKING, R. 636372 Gr. RUSSELL, N.T., wounded. From 9th creeping barrage was carried on as per Appendix B.	900

Army Form C. 2118.

104

WAR DIARY
or
INTELLIGENCE SUMMARY.
(Erase heading not required.)

Place	Date	Hour	Summary of Events and Information	Remarks and references to Appendices
Field	1917 June 15th		2/Lieut. J.M. FAIRLIE B Battery was granted the M.C. for gallantry displays on 16th May 1917.	
	15/16th		Enemy relief suspected. Batteries fired during night on approaches and Trenches and D Battery fired lethal shell at suspected mtgs.	See
	16/4/17		The Bde withdrew from the line and went into rest billets at Lutrincourt South of ACQ.	
	23		2/Lieut A.V. ASTON formerly C battery was awarded M.C. for gallantry during operations 9th April. Bde remained in rest at ACQ until the end of the month, during which time Guns and Stores were overhauled.	See
	8/7/17		[signature] Lt Col R.F.A. Comdg 77th Bde R.F.A.	

No diaries for period between June and December 1917

CONFIDENTIAL
No 91(A)
HIGHLAND DIVISION.

96 32

War Diary
of
256th Bde R.F.A.
from 1st to 31st Dec. 1917

WAR DIARY
or
INTELLIGENCE SUMMARY.

Army Form C. 2118.

Place	Date	Hour	Summary of Events and Information	Remarks and references to Appendices
	1-12-17		Dull morning & low visibility owing to thick mist. No change of importance has taken place in the situation. Harassing fire barrage was carried out between 6 & 7 A.M. An attack was attempted by the enemy W of LA FOLIE WOOD early this afternoon which was however completely broken up by our Artillery & M.G. fire. Other local counter attacks W of BOURLON WOOD were made, but they were all repulsed. Heavy losses being inflicted on the enemy. Hostile artillery activity showed considerable decrease.	R.T.C.
	2-12-17		Situation unchanged. Enemy artillery less active. Harassing fire kept up. "D" Battery was withdrawn to position in L.19.b. 226315 Gr. Clark W.S. (D/By) wounded 2/Lt. W.A. Wilkinson (D/By) killed. Good visibility. Night firing kept up. Enemy aircraft active, and several engagements took place in which 2 enemy machines were brought down. S.O.S. calls were answered at 4-30 P.M. & 8 P.M. In consequence of recent operations & in accordance with flaw our Batteries were all withdrawn between 6 & 10 P.M. to position W of RUBECOURT in K.30.c. Lines & men were laid out covering a line just W of MARCOING to assist the 6th Division if need be. This zone was well within our lines & fire would only be opened if the tactical situation demanded it. 635497 Dvr. Pringle F. (D/By) Killed. 635498 Dvr. Hill A. (A/By) Wounded	R.T.C. R.T.C.
	3-12-17			

WAR DIARY
or
INTELLIGENCE SUMMARY.
(Erase heading not required.)

Army Form C. 2118.

No. 138.

Instructions regarding War Diaries and Intelligence Summaries are contained in F. S. Regs., Part II. and the Staff Manual respectively. Title pages will be prepared in manuscript.

Place	Date	Hour	Summary of Events and Information	Remarks and references to Appendices
	4-12-17		Cloudy & heavy ground mist throughout the day. Quiet day. Hostile artillery less active. Hqrs moved back to their Hqrs in K 35 b 99 W of RUBECOURT. Battery positions dug and camouflaged. Battery wagon lines moved this afternoon to new wagon lines in the vicinity of METZ. Unusual movement reported behind the enemy's line. Harrassing fire scheme carried out on selected targets between 8 P.M. and 12 midnight. Ammunition sent up from forward positions.	A.T.C.
	5.12.17		In accordance with plans the troops of the V th & III Corps were withdrawn during the night to pre arranged positions. The operation was successfully carried out without interference from the enemy's artillery. Our new positions are now being consolidated. This afternoon Enemy assembled for attack WEST of ANNEUX, but his attack was completely broken up. L/256th assisted firing on the village of ANNEUX. Small parties of the enemy seen in the open & successfully engaged by our 18 Pdrs. especially around BOURLON WOOD. Our vacated positions were shelled at intervals during the morning. Usual harrassing fire carried out throughout the night.	A.T.C.

WAR DIARY
or
INTELLIGENCE SUMMARY

Army Form C. 2118.

No. 139.

Place	Date	Hour	Summary of Events and Information	Remarks and references to Appendices
	5-12-17		635960 Gr. Arthur, C. (C. Bty) wounded 179210 Gr. Russell, E. (A. Bty) " 680924 Dr. Hickson (A. Bty) " Fair weather.	16 T.C.
	6-12-17		Quiet morning. Our new infantry positions were further consolidated. About 1.30 P.M. the enemy attempted to be manning the trenches S.W. of CANTAING. About 2 P.M. he began shelling our new positions heavily. Later on at 3.20 P.M. he was reported advancing in large numbers on FLESQUIERES. He massed at the Brown Roads at L 8 & 28 & attacked at about 4 P.M. After heavy fighting the enemy was driven back & retired. It is believed that he suffered extremely heavy losses from the intensity of our Artillery and M.G. fire. Our batteries fired on the barrage. Hostile aircraft was very active. Battery wagon lines moved from METZ back to new wagon lines near HAVRINCOURT WOOD in Q 15 b. 256th Bde became attached to 6th Divisional Arty for tactical purposes from 6 P.M. to-day; the Bde came under the Left Group commanded by W. G. 2/4 Bde R.F.A. supporting the 18th Infantry Bde 6th Division. Special zones allotted E. of FLESQUIERES from Southern boundary of V Corps to L 20 central. 635758 Bar Vait. W. (B. Bty) wounded 9369 Sgt. Hardman, G. (C Bty) "	N.T.C.

WAR DIARY
INTELLIGENCE SUMMARY
(Erase heading not required.)

Army Form C. 2118.

No. 140.

Place	Date	Hour	Summary of Events and Information	Remarks and references to Appendices
	7-12-17		Our new positions were further consolidated last night. Enemy artillery showed very little activity & majority of shelling is done by H.V.Guns. At 6-30 P.M. the outpost line of the 59th Division was attacked, also a strong point at the BEETROOT FACTORY. The attack was driven off all batteries fired in a 5 minute concentration scheme at 3-5 P.M., 3-30 P.M. & 3-55 P.M. Harassing fire carried out on enemy's roads & approaches.	
	8-12-17		Concentration Scheme carried out this morning at 6 A.M., 6.5 A.M., & 6.20 A.M. Enemy artillery quiet. No change of any importance has taken place during the last 24 hours. The night was quiet except for intermittent shelling. The consolidation of our new positions was continued. The enemy barraged our trenches around FLESQUIERES & the village itself was heavily shelled from 5 P.M. to 7 P.M. No infantry action followed. Many small enemy working parties seen in the open & successfully engaged by our 18 Pdr. Parties A/256 moved back to new position in K.35.c.	16 J.C.

WAR DIARY
or
INTELLIGENCE SUMMARY.
(Erase heading not required.)

Army Form C. 2118.

Place	Date	Hour	Summary of Events and Information	Remarks and references to Appendices
	8-12-17		57840 Bdr Blunt, D. (H.Q) Killed	
			207863 Dr Bagwell (D) Killed	
			185123 Dr Bowman, A. (A) Wounded	
			212165 Dr Russell, G.H. (A) Wounded	
			855043 Sgt Buckett, P. (D) Wounded	
	9-12-17		Dull wet morning	
			No change in the situation	
			Our wagon lines were shelled during the night by H.V. Guns.	
			Harassing fire Concentration Scheme carried out (See appendices)	
			Hostile Artillery quiet. B Battery was shelled between 11 A.M. & 12 noon.	
			D/256 moved to new position this morning in K.29.b.	
			B & 6/256 moved to new positions in the afternoon in K.29.a.	
			635907 Bgr Collins, T. (B) Wounded	
			635929 Cpl Sampson, W. (B) "	
			635398 Gnr Chisholm, J. (B) "	
			636399 Gnr Watt, G. (B) "	
			635667 Sgt Purvis, G. (B) Killed	
	10-12-17		Good visibility. No change in the situation. Night firing was carried out as usual.	
			One section of each of the batteries was relieved corresponding sections of 296th Bde. R.F.A., 59th D.A. covering 57th Division in the line	
			(See appendices)	

WAR DIARY
or
INTELLIGENCE SUMMARY.
(Erase heading not required.)

Army Form C. 2118.

Place	Date	Hour	Summary of Events and Information	Remarks and references to Appendices
	11-12-17		Usual night firing carried out. Second Section relieved by T. relieved corresponding sections of 59th D.A.	16.J.C.

	12-12-17		Relief completed. New Battery positions as follows :-
			 A/256 J.9.6.21.21
			 B/256 J.2.6.62.18
			 D/256 J.14.a.18.91
			 H'qrs I.12.6.90.10
			 C/256 remained at Wagon Lines.
			 Dual Arty covering the Divisional front consisted of two Groups.
			 Lt. Col Byron took command of the Left Group which consisted of :-
			      256th Bde. R.F.A.
			      310th Bde. R.F.A.
			 The Right Group under Lt. Col. Fleming. 255th Bde consisted of :-
			      255th Bde. R.F.A.
			      5th R.H.A.
				16.J.C.

WAR DIARY
or
INTELLIGENCE SUMMARY.
(Erase heading not required.)

Army Form C. 2118.

Place	Date	Hour	Summary of Events and Information	Remarks and references to Appendices
	13.12.17		A Hostile attack was expected this morning on the BULLECOURT FRONT. At 6 A.M. the 2nd & 57th Inst Art'ys in co-operation with Heavy Artillery II Corps carried out a bombardment of the Enemy's trenches which lasted until 7.30 A.M. No attack was made. Situation normal.	6.I.C.
	14/77/6 17/77		During this period vigorous harassing fire was carried out by night	6/6 egg
	18th		Dull day. Arty very active. Observation was repeated. The Right Group and	
	23rd		The artillery in Rt division was repeated the Right Group and [?] was carrying out the [?] harassing fire. 255th & 57th (Army) and 310th Rotgades, and also the 256th Bde - Bde. During the past week's firing to many weather observation was held. But impossible, and harrowing fire was carried out by day and night on selected stocked roads, railways and trench junctions.	egg egg
	27th		3.10 a/m Re R.F.A. was relieved by 2 F. Bde R.F.A.	
	28th		Light very good. Many parties of the enemy were taken successfully by the 18 pdr batteries.	

Army Form C. 2118.

144

WAR DIARY
or
INTELLIGENCE SUMMARY.
(Erase heading not required.)

Place	Date	Hour	Summary of Events and Information	Remarks and references to Appendices
Field	1917 Sept 28 (cont'd)		An enemy 'plane was brought down by an A-A battery. Harassing fire was carried out as before, and continued on the Battery positions & O.P's.	See

A. Russell. Major R.F.A.
Cmdg 281 Bde R.F.A.

2/1/18

Vol 33

Confidential

War Diary

of

256th Bde., R.F.A.

From 1st to 31st January. 1918.

WAR DIARY or INTELLIGENCE SUMMARY

Army Form C. 2118.
256 Bde. R.F.A.
145

Place	Date	Hour	Summary of Events and Information	Remarks and references to Appendices
Field	1918 Jany 1/8		The Brigade remained in positions occupied by it last month. No event of any importance took place. That usual harassing fire was carried out by Bde. on many communication trenches, tracks, approaches and back areas. Sniping was carried out by day when visibility was good. Over the wholy visibility was poor during the period under review. Casualties 2/1/18 212284 Gnr. Whitehead, G. (B) wounded 3/1/18 655698 Dvr. Taylor, B. (B) wounded	
	9th/14th		The only event of any importance which took place during the week under review, was the S.O.S. between 8 P.M. and 9 P.M. on the 11th, on the right of the Divisional Zone to which our Batteries replied. During the week the usual sniping and harassing fire was carried out. Casualties 10/1/18 194321 Gnr. Thompson, G. (6) wounded & 636427 L/Bomdr. McGann, D. (6) at duty.	to T.C.
	14th/21st		Nothing unusual occurred during the week. During the past three weeks hostile artillery was fairly quiet, and enemy aerial activity was also inactive. This Battery positions were completed, OP's constructed, and our trenches generally consolidated by our Infantry.	to T.C.
	21st		One section of A.C. & D. Batteries were relieved by one section of 21st Bty, 42nd Bty, and 87th Bty respectively of 2nd Bde. 6th Divl. Artillery	to T.C.

WAR DIARY
or
INTELLIGENCE SUMMARY.

Army Form C. 2118.

146

Place	Date	Hour	Summary of Events and Information	Remarks and references to Appendices
Field	21st		Relieved sections withdrew to their wagon lines at FREMICOURT. (see appendices) Casualties 27009 a/Bomb. Ford. W. J (A) Wounded.	W.T.C.
"	22nd		Remaining sections of A.C. & D Batteries were relieved by corresponding sections of relieving battery. Command of 2nd Brigade R.F.A and troops passed to 1st Brigade Commander, 2nd Brigade R.F.A. Headquarters and relieved sections proceeded to wagon lines. B/256 remained in action and came under the orders of Brigade Commander 2nd Brigade R.F.A. Casualties } 164792 Gnr. Watkins. J. J. (B) Wounded.	W.T.C.
"	22nd/31st		During this period batteries were re-equipped and began a general scheme of training at the wagon lines. Tactical fullness the Brigade remained in reserve and stood ready to go into action at short notice. Enemy aeroplanes were active each night during the week bombing back area. As a result of this bombing the following casualties occurred on 29/1/18. 635026 S.S. Robb. J. (C) } Wounded 676208 Gnr. Haydd. S (D) 338222 Gnr. Thornton A (B) } Wounded & 636459 Dvr. Dunn. D (B) at duty	W.T.C.

A.T. Travers. Major. R.F.A.
Commdg. 256th Brigade. R.F.A.

16134

Confidential

War Diary
of
256 Brigade R.F.A. (T.F.)

From 1st February 1918 - To 28th February 1918.

(Volume   )

WAR DIARY
INTELLIGENCE SUMMARY
(Erase heading not required.)

Army Form C. 2118.

147

Place	Date	Hour	Summary of Events and Information	Remarks and references to Appendices
Field	1918 Feby 11/12	1	During the period under review the Batteries (except B/255 which remained in action under 6th Div. Arty) continued their General Scheme of Training at their wagon lines at FREMICOURT. All the guns & Howrs. of A.C. & D Batteries were calibrated at FRICOURT Firing Range on 6th 9th & 10th insts. respectively.	W.J.
	12th		Various guns & Howrs. were handed over to 25th Div. Arty. in exchange for old guns in the line.	W.J.
	13th	4 pm	One section (heavy) of A.C. & D Batteries relieved in action corresponding sections of 21st Battery & 42nd Battery & 87th Battery (2nd Brigade) 6th Div. Arty. – guns being taken over in pits (see appendices)	W.J.
	14th	11 am	C.R.A. 51st Divl. Arty. assumed command of the Fd. Artillery covering the 51st Division which had relieved the 6th Division in the line on the night 12th/13th & 13th/14th.	W.J.
		4 pm	Remaining sections of A.C. & D Batteries relieved remaining sections of 2nd Brigade – guns being taken over in situ (see appendices). Bde. Hdqrs. closed at FREMICOURT at 3pm & reopened at I.12.b.81 at 3pm when command of Bde. Group passed to O.C. 257 Bde.	W.J. W.J. W.J.

Army Form C. 2118.

WAR DIARY
or
INTELLIGENCE SUMMARY.
(Erase heading not required.)

148

Place	Date	Hour	Summary of Events and Information	Remarks and references to Appendices
Field	1918 Feby. 14th		The disposition of the Field Artillery covering the 37th Division was as follows:—	
			Right Group — 255th Brigade R.F.A.	
			293rd Army F.A. Brigade	
			Left Group — 238 Brigade R.F.A.	
			Battery positions as follows:—	
			A/238 4 guns I.12.d.90.25	
			2 guns J.9.b.26.18	
			B/238 4 guns I.18.a.64.70	
			2 guns J.2.a.62	
			C/238 4 guns I.18.b.63.93	
			2 guns J.7.b.95.92	
			D/238 4 How. I.12.c.93.65	
			2 How. J.9.c.45.52	JWS
			The 6th Division relieved the 25th Division in the line on our left on 13th & 14th inst.	
			The 17th Division went in the line on our Right — the IV Corps consisting of the 51st Division, 6th Division in the line & the 25th Division at rest.	JWS
	15th–22nd		During the week the usual Registration were carried out. Sniping by day when visibility good, was also vigorously done — many enemy parties seen in the open being successfully engaged by the Batteries.	JWS

Army Form C. 2118.

149

WAR DIARY
INTELLIGENCE SUMMARY.
(Erase heading not required.)

Place	Date	Hour	Summary of Events and Information	Remarks and references to Appendices
Field	Feby 15/22		Hostile Batteries were generally quiet during the week. Enemy aeroplanes were most active & 3 or 4 were brought down by our machine & a.a. fire. The Battery positions were improved whilst Rienynpeng & Reserve positions were begun to be made by all Batteries. Casualties :- 2nd Lt 4/30824 Driver Smith T. "D"Bty wounded.	nil
	22/28"		The only event of any importance which occurred during the week was a completed Enemy Relief on the night of the 25th. A special Harassing fire scheme in conjunction with our Heavy Arty, was carried out on the Enemy's Trenches, Communication Trenches & Approaches (see appendices) work was continued on all the Battery positions including the Rienynpeng & Reserve positions. Casualties nil. Ammunition expended from 14th to 28th inst. 2015 rds. 18 pdr. 494 " 4.5 How.	nil

1/3/18.

[signature] Lieut Col.
Comdg. 252 Brigade R.F.A.

51st Divisional Artillery

WAR DIARY

256th BRIGADE

ROYAL FIELD ARTILLERY

MARCH 1918

256 Brigade RFA (TF)   WA 35   51 Div

War Diary
of
256 Brigade RFA (TF)
From 1st March 1918 To 31st March 1918

(Volume   )

WAR DIARY or INTELLIGENCE SUMMARY

Army Form C. 2118.
150.

Place	Date	Hour	Summary of Events and Information	Remarks and references to Appendices
Field	March 1st 1918		Visibility poor during morning but good later. Much enemy movement seen during the day & successfully engaged by our 18 pdrs. Hostile artillery quiet.	Nil.
	2nd		During last night the front of the 51st Div. was reorganised & divided into three Permanent 1. Brigade Sectors as follows:—	
			Right Sector (SEMICOURT Sector) held by the 154 Infantry Bde. & permanently the Right group (293rd Army F.A. Brigade).	
			2. Centre Sector (BOURSIES Sector) held by 152 Infantry Bde. & covered by the Centre group (255 Brigade R.F.A.)	
			3. Left Sector (LOUVERVAL Sector) held by 153 Infantry Bde. & covered by Left group (258 Brigade R.F.A.). Left Group Commander Lt. Col. L.M. Dyson D.S.O. (see Appendices).	Nil.
			S.O.S. lines were distributed accordingly. (see Appendices).	
			Visibility good from 10 am onwards. Many enemy working parties were seen during the day & dispersed.	
			The usual night harassing fire scheme were carried out. Enemy Artillery has remained practically inactive.	
	3rd to 6th		During this period much firing was done on Enemy movement & casualties inflicted. Harassing fire was kept up during the nights on Enemy approaches, tracks &c.	Nil.
	7th	1 am to 2 am & 8.10 am & 9.10 am	Between 1 am & 2 am and again between 8.10 am & 9.10 am a special bombardment of PRONVILLE was carried out in conjunction with heavy artillery. (see Appendices)	Nil.

Army Form C. 2118.

157.

WAR DIARY
or
INTELLIGENCE SUMMARY.
(Erase heading not required.)

Instructions regarding War Diaries and Intelligence Summaries are contained in F. S. Regs., Part II. and the Staff Manual respectively. Title pages will be prepared in manuscript.

Place	Date	Hour	Summary of Events and Information	Remarks and references to Appendices
Field	1918 March 7		In addition vigorous harassing fire throughout the night by forward 18pdrs with the exception of intermittent shelling of the CAMBRAI ROAD & acc. N.W. of DOIGNIES, the enemy artillery was practically inactive.	2ng.
	8.		During the night our forward guns had co-operated with Heavy Arty. in bombardment of PRONVILLE & QUEANT. The usual harassing fire was kept up in rear. The enemy during the day remained inactive — an open plane in which an general slump the day — no enemy movement was seen — no evidence of our aeroplanes was obtainable — our aeroplanes were active above our hostile lines which tried to come near our lines. Hostile artillery activity — most of the shelling being in the LOUVERVAL vicinity. The Reinforcing Reserve positions dug by the Brigade (Nº 69-72 W. of BEAUMETZ) (Nº 5B-56 N. of BEUGNY) were inspected today by B.E.R.A. IV Corps. who thus arrg by 255 Bde. R.F.A. The result of the Comparison was as follows:— 1st prize A/256 — BEAUMETZ positions. 2nd prize C/256 equal with B/255 — BEUGNY positions 1st brge. R Battery positions S. of LEBUCQUIERE.	2ng.
	9.		Work was commenced on another set. R Battery positions. During the night our forward guns shone harassed PRONVILLE roads shacks in the vicinity. Enemy artillery any are rigidly concealed was all movement Stationary. Parties in area. Today hostile artillery has been abnormally quiet.	2ng.

Army Form C. 2118.

WAR DIARY
INTELLIGENCE SUMMARY.
(Erase heading not required.)

152

Place	Date	Hour	Summary of Events and Information	Remarks and references to Appendices
Lille	1918 March 10th		A bombardment of MOEUVRES was carried out in conjunction with the Heavies 1.5 am / 1.35 am 4 am / 4.20 am 6.30 am – 6.50 am The Vicinity of the AGACHE was subjected to a descending sweeping harassing fire scheme during the night heavy morning. Nothing unusual has been reported – the general situation remains quiet. Hostile artillery has been very slight.	
	11th		There was much aerial activity today several combats – one hostile machine was seen to shut down heard & 2 others falling out of control. Special concentrated shoots on enemy Battle Helps Coy. Helps Railway & Trench Junctions were carried out. Today many hostile batteries were seen engaged. Hostile artillery practically inactive except for slight shelling by field guns of the KONVERVAL area.	M.I.
	12th		Up till 4.30 am the usual harassing fire took place. Special shoots were arranged from that hour onwards in view of information received of a hostile enemy attack. The Scheme was however cancelled. No abnormal hostile artillery activity has been reported today. Mural fires were seen in INCHY and QUÉANT a renewed fortan during? by our Heavies	M.I.
	13th		Today the usual indirectual movement was observed in enemy lines taken on by our forward guns. Harassing fire carried out slightly as usual. Several aerial combats took place today. Two planes were seen burne down in flames. Hostile Artillery inactive.	M.I.

WAR DIARY
INTELLIGENCE SUMMARY
(Erase heading not required.)

Army Form C. 2118.

153

Place	Date	Hour	Summary of Events and Information	Remarks and references to Appendices
Field	1918 March 14		Visibility all day very bad making observation practically impossible. No enemy fire on enemy front system was observed tonight. At 6.50 p.m. Transport was reported by Aeroplane call moving along road in D11.6 northwards. Our forward 18pdrs replied with good results. An O.K. was received.	W.S.
	15		Visibility today was good. Considerable movement was found engaged during cavalier horse carriages. An enemy transport in D.16.6 was fired on by our 18pdrs. Dispersal and about one about 100 explosions burst. Two explosions were seen in the vicinity of QUÉANT. Hostile artillery less pronounced very quiet. Hostile aircraft displayed no activity.	W.S.
	16	3 a.m.	Visibility bombarding the morning improving later. The went movement new taken in many enemy ammunition dumps were seen to be bursting during the day. The principal ones being E. of PRONVILLE & about D.22.a. The grass N.of AGACHE Road from about D.10.0.0 for some hundreds of yards to EAST was set on fire by our 18pdrs. Large numbers of the enemy were seen to rush about making efforts to put the fire out. A large number of small explosions occurred in the burning grass. An 18pdr at 5.30 p.m. kept up heavy rending sweeping fire on the area N. Enemy artillery was more active. BEAUMETZ area was shelled with 8". Hostile aircraft was much more active than usual. At 7 a.m. two of our Scouts engaged two E.A. One E.A. was seen to break up and into flames the other E.A. spiral down out of control.	W.S.

Army Form C. 2118.

154

WAR DIARY
or
INTELLIGENCE SUMMARY
(Erase heading not required.)

Place	Date	Hour	Summary of Events and Information	Remarks and references to Appendices
Field	1918 March 17/20		During this period in accordance to the usual harassing fire scheme by night special concentrated shoots in conjunction with Heavy Arty were carried out in non-suspected enemy positions. Service in Aeroplane Photographs. These shoots were carried out by day & by night. Many bivouacs camps were again lit up by our & Heavy Arty. & Enemy Arty & Enemy large explosions were particularly observed about QUEANT, INCHY, PRONVILLE. During the period from 1st to 20th ordt. ammunition guns fired 10725 Rounds 18 Pdrs. & 3515 Rounds 4.5 Hows.	N.T.R
	20.		Unusual movement on the divisional front on our left was reported during the afternoon by our Division. Liaison point to an attack known warning special harassing fire schemes arranged carried out in addition to harassing fire concentrated shoots. Batteries neared to keep away enemy.	N.T.R
	21.	5am	Heavy Enemy Barrage put down which consisted mainly of Gas shells in good proportion of 5.9". The enemy was simultaneous in our front. & Front RAMICOURT & BEAUTMETZ - MORCHIES Line & on the RIDGES in the BEAUTMETZ - MORCHIES Road. & the main Battery positions & the same time a destructive fire was opened in the area further back reaching the destruction of all our lines communications with the rear.	

Army Form C. 2118.

WAR DIARY
or
INTELLIGENCE SUMMARY.
(Erase heading not required.)

Instructions regarding War Diaries and Intelligence Summaries are contained in F. S. Regs., Part II. and the Staff Manual respectively. Title pages will be prepared in manuscript.

1535

Place	Date	Hour	Summary of Events and Information	Remarks and references to Appendices
Field	1918 March 21		The barrage was intense on the 6th Divisions area on our left also in the Valley between 6th & 51st Divisions until nearly 8 am when it slackened slightly.	
		5.15am	The S.O.S. was sent up from our front line about 5.15am when reported to advanced Infantry Bde from SOLE POST that no attack appeared impending, this was stopped. Counts Preparation "B"	
		5.38	S.O.S. Defence Preparation "A") — I.M° ordered 5.38 a.m. (see Appendices 51st I.D. Defence defence Prep: A) — T.M° was ordered to stop firing rates by Supportine 153rd Infantry Bde just increased & Counts Preparation "A" moved	
		6.22	At 6.22 am enemy shelling on Supportine 153rd Infantry Bde just increased & Counts Preparation "A" moved	
		7am	"Gosling" O.P. reported that shelling was practically all enfused to front of Division on left	
		7.52am	that the front of 152 Infantry Bde was being shelled apparently to support line but this happened just further to the right.	
		8.12am	at 8.12 a.m. supplied intimation to Right Group 6" D.A. that their front was quiet.	
		8.19am	Returned to Counts Preparation "B"	
		9.25am	Gosling O.P. reported situation unchanged friendship very low — a thick ground mist	
		9.53am	Gosling reported seeing a few men moving on top of ground between front trystine lines unable to distinguish whether they were ours or this quiet.	
		9.55	O.P. reported there to be Germans 153rd Infantry Bde informed BDE.S.G. at S.O.S. rate between 100 yards clear of PRIMROSE (A/256 Anti Tank Gun) Candle (C/255 Anti Tank Gun) and Gosling O.P.	
		10 am	Gosling reported that Germans had just pressed 2 tanks down Chuppto their support places reached on also that Infantry in CHEAPSIDE round O.P.	gW.J.

WAR DIARY or INTELLIGENCE SUMMARY

Army Form C. 2118.
152

Place	Date	Hour	Summary of Events and Information	Remarks and references to Appendices
Suid	1918 March 21	10.3	GOSLING O.P. reported that the enemy had ceased their communications with Ritton ceased though the line still showed a descent from the tree mounds. No enemy were in view of the Battery position. Battery Commanders engaged their own fronts by direct observation though visibility remained poor until advance. As regards the work done by Lts Tank forward going there is little information available. 2/Lt. Mackie C Bty. who was at GOSLING took charge of Cowslip with the detachment but the gun was knocked out by a direct hit into the ammunition returning by another route. The detachment under Sgt. P.S. were buried inside the Battery. They lost one 2/Lt. Burke collecting the detachment of PRIMROSE (A/258 Lata Tank Gun) running them back. This was after it had been out looking at this Gun Pit in Burrow stream't have been knocked out of the "PRIMROSE" detachment and then returned to his Battery. He was wounded then evacuated.	
			As to SNOWDROP (B/258 Tank Tank Gun) when the enemy began attack we more (D Bty) who was Liaison Officer with Batt Headquarters collected the detachment & went to the gun. It was dark & the enemy was quite near that be told the detachment to stand by under cover, The gun was hit & wheel damaged The Stn N.C.O. in charge decided the gun was unfit before in emergence to withdraw his detachment. Until afterwards Lieut Gun Cooper (B/1Bty) arrived from B/258 from Gun Pit r/p/Lt Morse & with the gun into action a fresh of 2nd Corps was hit by a M.G. bullet was taken to Batt. Hagn. Dressing Station closely on returning to the gun a 2/Lt Morse found it had been hit & knocked out.	
			As regards the forward Guns French Battery. A/258 was under the charge of 2/Lt. a B.W.Owen. He made many attempts to get to this gun but coming in the severity of the enemy barrage	gud

Army Form C. 2118.

WAR DIARY
INTELLIGENCE SUMMARY
(Erase heading not required.)

Instructions regarding War Diaries and Intelligence Summaries are contained in F. S. Regs., Part II. and the Staff Manual respectively. Title pages will be prepared in manuscript.

157

Place	Date	Hour	Summary of Events and Information	Remarks and references to Appendices
Field	1918 March 21		Especially the amount of gas in the Valley between 6° & 132°. But was only able to read it & get it into action by shortly after 7am. This gun maintained uninterrupted with the Battery in spite of many hits on the line till late in the day. At 10 am the Gun was pulled out of action of the Lnt. Strongpoint were large parties of the enemy were seen coming down the Valley & were engaged at ranges from 800 yards to 400 yards — many casualties being inflicted. By this time the enemy was in possession of "C" Battery forward (rear man) position rather to S.E. & somewhere they brought a Heavy Rifle & M.G. fire to bear on the gun team which opened fire about 400 yards away. Yet H.Q. was prepared to two batteries the gun increasingly & at Co. Section took the Lewis Gun & remainder of his detachment forward to the Sunken Road to keep fire on the enemy on his left. He kept on firing until 2 drums were left & then withdrew to the BEAUMETZ – MORCHIES line receiving & there rejoined his Battery. Forward Gun of B/256. Lieut. J. M. Cooper 17/H.R. H.C. Isham were in charge. They made several attempts to get through the barrage & to the gun but were unsuccessful as the gun intervene only side & was shortly after 7am. Shortly afterwards the gun was knocked out & the ammunition catching fire so Lieut Cooper went to join B/257 Anti Tank Gun (Knowsley) into action & Lt. Isham took charge of the Lewis Gun keeping it in action knocking successive withdrawal with it undertone of making the BEAUMETZ – MORCHIES line the town from where he wrote to the Infantry & the detachment rejoined this Battery. Forward Gun of C/256. This Gun fired a considerable number of rounds until knocked out half buried about 12 noon. The detachment then withdrew after removing the gun & thereafter sights were regained the enemy Battery position	

J.W.J.

WAR DIARY
or
INTELLIGENCE SUMMARY

Army Form C. 2118.

158

Place	Date	Hour	Summary of Events and Information	Remarks and references to Appendices
Lieu	1918 March 21		Forward Howitzers of D/256. There was much change of F.H. ammunition & all its ammunition was expended. Two Lewis Mountain places in the area the gun mounts. The detachment then retreated (carrying the gun sights) about 11 am and escaped from the front left front.	
			BOOLING OP was manned by 2/Lt W.H. Cowen (B/256) & 2/Lt. T. Street (C/Bty)	
		10:47	Dispatch was sent to the neighbourhood to have all teams & gun-limbers ready to march to a position if necessary in the neighbourhood of I 16 c.	
			Nine S.O.S. lines went out to the Batteries at various times during the day. The Batteries continued firing throughout the day. Target being engaged by direct observation.	
			127 Siege Battery (6" How.) atmosphere along with us in action on the B-M Road have given Target images to Annes where the enemy were reported to be massing.	
			The Left Group was reinforced by 2 Batteries of the 112" Bde. R.F.A. (25th Division) (Position 62 v 63 m I 23 c) batteries not actually in action until about 7 pm on a line - I 8 c 27 - I 2 c 47	
			S.O.S lines were given and - for the night - on a line - I 8 c 27 - I 2 c 47	
			Casualties:- Officers 2nd Lieut. R.M. Cooper B/256 Wounded missing	
			2/Lt R. Cronkie C/256 missing	
			2/Lt G. Street "	
			2/Lt W.H. Cowen D/256 "	
			2/Lt T.A. Brown wounded D/256	
			Capt. Harcourt D/256 wounded gas.	
			Other Ranks: 69787 S/Sgt. E.R. Jones (C) Killed 18766 Bdr. S. Green (D) Killed	
			125557 Gunner G. McFarland (D) Killed	

948

(A7992) Wt. W12859/M1293. 750,000. 1/17. D. D. & L., Ltd. Forms/C.2118/11

Army Form C. 2118.

159.

WAR DIARY
INTELLIGENCE SUMMARY
(Erase heading not required.)

Instructions regarding War Diaries and Intelligence Summaries are contained in F.S. Regs., Part II. and the Staff Manual respectively. Title pages will be prepared in manuscript.

Place	Date	Hour	Summary of Events and Information	Remarks and references to Appendices
Field	1918 March 21		Casualties Cont'd. Wounded (Negro) missing 1120 Gr. Sadrus J(A) 190882 Gunnr Bell F(A) 425963 Dffr. Whitfield W (Negro) missing 1120 Gr. Sadrus J(A) 190882 Gunnr Bell F(A) 238835 Gr. Whitehead A(A) 24836 Shotroot C(A) 59528 Dr. Field A(A) 109109 Gr. Robertson M(C) 636138 Gr. Bunce C(C) 636454 Gr. Bruce C(C) 636430 Gr. Lithaloe M(C) 636706 Gr. Watson T(C) 635074 Gr. Lymington (C) 147882 Gr. Read M(C) 204107 Gr. Wilson A.R.(C) 162705 Gr. Hale W(C) 635249 Dr. Lowrie T(C) 233289 Gr. Gunner W(C) 640138 Bdr. Baillie F(D) 645624 Bdr. Turnbull T.B.(D) 229885 Gr. W. Marsh(D) missing Wounded 316302 Spr Scott S W (H.Q.) 635661 Gunr Cochrane J (H.Q.) 55979 Dvr W[armatt] 4(H.Q.) 635765 Gunr Wylie H(A) 636394 L/Bdr Gilmour J(A) 63469 G. Higgins E(A) 755324 Cpl. Knox F(A) 635398 Dr. Wyuck G(A) 12358 Dr. Bryant A(A) 26759 Dr. Cobbold T(A) 635637 G. Cumming A(A) 155964 Gr. Willy W(A) 635410 Dr. Panton D(A) 635199 Dr. Stewart W(A) 636049 Dr. Anderson J(A) 636074 Dr. Reed A(A) 115456 Dr. Galway H(A) 636013 Dr. McGann J(B) 635854 Bomb. Morris H(B) 635733 G. Smith A(B) 635191 Dr. Leslie J(B) at duty 91400 G. Parker A(B) at duty 635877 Gr. Clark W(B) at duty 635503 Cpl. Muir W.F.(C) 636422 L/Br. Rattray S(C) 662 Br. Matthews W(C) 166181 Gr. Douglas R(C) 935134 Gr. Sullivan T(C) 169942 Dr. Martin J(C) at duty 3293 G. Rayner E G(C) at duty 149099 G. Mead G(C) at duty 31822 Cpl. Simms H.R.(C) 280056 Gr. Greenwood J(C) 36210 Gr. Stout E(D)	GWJ.
	22	12am	Batteries were ordered to withdraw by sections from advanced positions to N.E. 33.54.55 v 58 NE of Beugny (at Maj A.G. appendix). This move was completed together with the salvage of all ammunition (except 300 rds of 4.5 How Gas Shells in a few limbr shells). Very 5 am. Brigade began without attack and fired	

(A70991). Wt. W12859/M1293. 75,000. 1/17. D. D. & L., Ltd. Forms/C.2118/14.

Army Form C. 2118.

160

WAR DIARY
INTELLIGENCE SUMMARY
(Erase heading not required.)

Place	Date	Hour	Summary of Events and Information	Remarks and references to Appendices
Field	1918 March 20th	12a.m.	Bde. with Hdqrs. 153rd Infantry Bde. to Sunken Road (MORCHIES — BEUGNY).	
		6.30 a.m.	Bde. Hdqrs. received orders to go to Divisional H.Qrs. at FREMICOURT & shortly afterwards the two remaining Batteries of 112. Bde. came under orders of Left Group. Batteries observing the enemy continued his attack. During the first half of the day Batteries observing from the left ground about I.17.c engaged the enemy just E. of the BEAUMETZ — MORCHIES line with good visible effect. During the afternoon the Brigade guns fired concentrations E. & N. of MORCHIES. As the tendency of the enemy to outflank us on this side became more pronounced, very many excellent targets were offered. Infantry the enemy attack between MORCHIES & MARICOURT Wood later in the afternoon came under very heavy fire from this Brigade & never developed beyond this line. Tanks were not employed in the afternoon & counter-attack & did excellent work. B/256 fired a number even when they counter attacked. Very large numbers of the enemy were then seen to leave the above line in confusion & retire northwards & were caught by the concentrated fire of the Brigade. An enemy Battery coming into action N.E. of MARICOURT Wood (no doubt against our Tanks) was neutralised by B/256 & 4 Teams shot down & never got round off till just after dark (about 3 to 4 hrs later) & then only fired with 2 guns altogether for 4 hours the 18pdrs. using open sights fired continuously at the enemy both advancing or retiring. During this period the 4.5 How. of the Brigade in a semi covered position close by, but from which the B.C. by standing on a timber could get direct observation at his target, fired also continuously using	9.8.V

Army Form C. 2118.

WAR DIARY
INTELLIGENCE SUMMARY
(Erase heading not required.)

Place	Date	Hour	Summary of Events and Information	Remarks and references to Appendices
Field	1918 March 22		106 targets. The enemy could quite plainly be seen to suffer very severely from this fire. As the average range was but little over 2000 yards visibility was excellent. The opportunity for judging the effect of the fire was most favourable. No other Batteries fired in this Zone during the day although well within the area allotted to the Division on our left. Towards dusk as our infantry had vacated the BEAUMETZ MORCHIES Line by being turned from the north our S.O.S. Barrage was called for that even on a line W. of it reaching backwards towards the BEAUMETZ - MORCHIES Road, other than this was definitely known to be vacated our S.O.S. Line for the night was put down just E. of CHAUFFEURS WOOD and searching fire by types from that line Eastwards. At 7.30 pm Batteries were ordered to withdraw to positions in the neighbourhood of MILL CROSS, in I 26 d. This was carried out by sections, the larger proportion of Ammunition being saved. Of the Ammunition expenditure for the 21st & 22nd with fairly accurate figures are available. This expenditure does not include that of forward Anti-Tank guns is as follows:—	161.

Battery	No of Guns	No Rds.	No of Rds. per Gun		Battery	No of Guns	No Rds.	No of Rds. per Gun
21st A	5	4800	960	22nd	A	5	5100	1020
B	4	3600	900		B	4	7000	1750
C	5	4000	800		C	5	6000	1200
D	4	3700	925		D	4	2500	625

WAR DIARY
INTELLIGENCE SUMMARY

Army Form C. 2118.
162

Place	Date	Hour	Summary of Events and Information	Remarks and references to Appendices
Field	1918 March 22nd	9 p.m.	On coming into action in new position at MILL CROSS, the Brigade laid out lines of fire to cover Sunken Road from J.7.a.0.0. – I.12.a.97. 112 Bde. R.F.A. were also ordered to withdraw to new positions in I.26.c. & their H.Qrs. were also established beside our Bde. H.Qrs. in FREMICOURT.	N.I
		10.30 p.m.	S.O.S. lines for the night were ordered as follows:- 256 Bde. R.F.A. – I.12.c.47 – I.12.a.45 112 Bde. " – I.7.c.00 – I.12.c.47 Casualties on 22nd 136407 Gr. Woodward J. (B) 39178 Dr. Bullock W. (B) 16988 Gr. Nebraham H. (B) 63809 Gr. Mcdicken D (B) 635144 Bdr. Craig J. P. (C) 635381 Gr. Seabrook F (C) 122632 Gr. Shepheran P (C) 170646 Gr. Coates T (C) Wounded.	N.I
	23	7.15 a.m.	New left group S.O.S. lines were ordered as follows:- on a line from J.13 central through I.12 central to I.6.c.00. The dividing point between 256 Bde & 112 Bde being I.12.d.55.	
		10.40 a.m.	New S.O.S. lines were ordered as follows:- 256 Bde. I.12.c.00 – I.12.a.00. 112 Bde. R.F.A. " I.8.a.00 – I.12.a.00. " I.11.b.03 – 112 Bde R.F.A.	
		11.30 a.m.	Group H.Qrs. moved to more back to BANCOURT to H.Qr. of 57th & 58th Infantry Bdes. (19th Division) support them with 255, 256, 112, 104, 235 & 293 Brigades R.F.A. & 29th Heavy Bde. R.G.A. – The whole group to be under the command of Lt.Col. L.M. Ogan. D.S.O. 256 Bde. R.F.A.	
		12 noon 2 p.m.	Group H.Qrs. were established with H.Qrs 56 & 58th Infantry Bdes. at A.34.d.38 & 3 p.m. our Brigades moved back to BANCOURT area – 256 Bde. taking up position in O.1.G. Communication with these Brigades was established by some dismounted orderlies. Group Commander acted as C.R.A. of forward area & however he instructions to artillery was arranged as	N.I

Army Form C. 2118.

163

WAR DIARY
INTELLIGENCE SUMMARY.
(Erase heading not required.)

Instructions regarding War Diaries and Intelligence Summaries are contained in F.S. Regs., Part II. and the Staff Manual respectively. Title pages will be prepared in manuscript.

Place	Date	Hour	Summary of Events and Information	Remarks and references to Appendices
Field	1918 March 23		Follow:—	
			Right group. No.1 Subgroup (Lt.Col. A. Mayne D.S.O) consisting of 104 & 293 Army F.A. Bdes. covering the 56" Infantry Brigade S. of the CAMBRAI Road.	
			No.2 Subgroup (Lt.Col. Larun D.S.O) consisting of 253 & 112 Brigades R.F.A. covering the Paris Brigade S. of CAMBRAI Road.	
			Left Group. (Lt.Col. J. Fleming D.S.O.) 255 & 235 Brigades R.F.A. covering the 58" Infantry Brigade N. of the CAMBRAI Road.	
			Zones were allotted as follows:- (see Map A Appendices)	
			Right Group I 29 c 05 – I 28 d 45 30 – I 22 d 00 along Railway to I 21 d 37 – I 21 b 05	
			Left Group I 21 b 05 – I 15 c 80 – I 15 c 32 – I 15 a 10.	
			The night remained quiet.	
			Casualties Killed 635013 Dr. O'Brien P.(A)	
			Wounded 705460 Dr. Murphy H.(A) 635054 Dr. Edward S.(A)(at duty) 6493 Bdr. Ferris J.(H) 633581 Gr. Bain J.(B) 231330 4/Bdr. Meade P.(B) 760740 Dr. Hemmann J.(C)	nil.
	24"	5.15 am	Groups, Subgroups, & Heavy artillery bombarded on S.O.S. Lines resuming forward by 100 yards to a depth of 500 yards.	
		6.15 am	The programme was again repeated except that the 6" Hows. of Heavy Bde. searched through BEUGNY eastwards from N.E. of 2nd line between I 15 v 21 and I 16 v 22 .	
			During the day our F.O.O's sent in various reports of enemy movements & concentrations between LEBUCQUIERE & BEUGNY. There were all dealt with by concentrations of fire from all Brigades — the Right Group & 29 & Heavy Bde. Enemy casualties inflicted are heavily considered in the Sunken Roads in I 24 c and I 23 b & d was particularly dealt with & very heavy casualties	nil.

WAR DIARY
or
INTELLIGENCE SUMMARY

Army Form C. 2118.

164

Place	Date	Hour	Summary of Events and Information	Remarks and references to Appendices
Field	1918 March 24		Much valuable information was given in by an F.O.O. of 112 Bde at DELSAUX FARM Hy. 2/Lt. Isherwood B/256 from a house on the S.E. outskirts of BEUGNY who brought it back quickly in advance on threatened points. In one case the assistance of 2 Army Brigades was obtained through 51st D.A. A searching barrage from them through the uneven ground in I.17.d & I.18.c prevented a threatened attack developing from this direction.	M.J
		12 noon	As our infantry of the Green Line became much weakened, only a matter of time before our Troops withdrew to the BAPAUME Line for rearrangement. The 29th Heavy Bde was ordered to withdraw at 12 noon.	M.J
		1 p.m.	At 1 pm Field Brigades were also ordered to withdraw. Itching left to Group Art. Groups Commdrs to carry out the withdrawal in their covering force on their own together. Guns were out of action at once. Batteries accordingly withdrew to LE TRILLOY were in action there by 6 p.m. The meantime groups Hdqrs. transferred from 38 & 39" Infantry Bdes. to 152 & 153 Infantry Bdes. (57th Div.) Hdqrs. at the BRICKFIELDS S.W. of BAPAUME.	M.J
		7 p.m. 9.30 p.m.	A further withdrawal was then ordered the Brigades marching to ACHIET LE PETIT covered by 256 & 293 Brigades R.F.A. These ceased firing rearwards at 9.20 p.m. Brigades remained bivouc control of 51st D.A.	M.J
			Casualties in 24th of Lt. H. Strachan attached A/256 from D.A.C. wounded Wounded 635468 Gr. Coleman B. (C) 129333 Gr. Thomas P. (C) 950915 9/Bdr. Edwards A.E. (C)	M.J

Place	**Date**	**Hour**	**Summary of Events and Information**	**Remarks and references to Appendices**

Army Form C. 2118. 165

WAR DIARY or INTELLIGENCE SUMMARY

Place	Date	Hour	Summary of Events and Information	Remarks
Field	1918 March 25	10 am	The following artillery arrangements were made to cover the Infantry holding a line on the E. side of LOUPART WOOD. 255, 293, 104 & 112 Bdes. R.F.A. came into action in the area L.27, 28, 23 & 24. 29" R.F.H. & 71 Bde R.G.A. came into action in the neighbourhood of PENDANT COPSE & L.31 reporting there. They were to rendezvous about 2 mile S.W. of SERRE in about N.29.c. just clear of the road. In order to cover any stirring through with the line EAST of GREVILLERS, 258 Bde. & 235 Bde. were ordered to counter action in S.21. & to be in action by 6 am.	R.J.
		3 am	Orders were accordingly issued. The group consisting of 258 & 235 Bdes. under Lt. Col. L.M. Dyson D.S.O. The enemy were reported to be in BAPAUME & further advance by him to the West was to be looked for. 19 Scot. Infantry were holding a line running N. & S. from H.22.00 (southward) to N.26.00. 258 Bde. to take up positions of observation at S.21.a. to cover the northern half. For H.20.00 – H.32.00 yds. withdrew to PUISIEUX (via Bucquoy) where the Infantry began to come back. 235 Bde. R.F.A. to take up position about S.21.d. to cover the southern half of the Zone. & to withdraw to PUISIEUX (via Bucquoy) when situation demanded it.	
			As the position of the line was very doubtful each Bde. sent forward 2 Officers mounted patrol to maintain touch with the Infantry	
		9 am to 10 am	Owing to advance of hostile control of back of the occupation of the MIRAUMONT Road in MIRAUMONT where Balloons having arrived about 11 km. Moonlight rendered the brought clear of the Village till 9 am. The Brigades opened fire at 10 am.	R.J.
		11 am	At 11 am parties of 51st Scot. Infantry (whomever holding LOUPART WOOD) were seen retiring from it. Stragglers afterwards intercepted reported enemy advancing in force there.	
		11.30 am	About 11.30 am Infantry of 19 & Division & 61 & Division were seen retiring N. of GREVILLERS. This	R.J.

Army Form C. 2118.

WAR DIARY
INTELLIGENCE SUMMARY
(Erase heading not required.)

Place	Date	Hour	Summary of Events and Information	Remarks and references to Appendices
Field	1918 March 25th	11.30am	This retirement was carried out in the direction of BIHUCOURT. 235 Bde. was then ordered to withdraw & carry out portion at 12.15pm. Embracing rearguard to Col. Fleming. Liaison officers with 152, 153 & 154 Infantry Bdes. of IRLES of this retirement.	W.J.
		1pm	256 Bde. was ordered at 1pm via BEHIET-LE-PETIT, BUCQUOY, PUISIEUX to a position of assembly in K24 d. to take up position at SERRE whole doing so were ordered to	
		3pm	Brigades were ordered	
		6.30pm	continue the withdrawal to COLINCAMPS. On arrival at the latter place about 10.30pm they received further orders to move to FONQUEVILLERS where they arrived about 12 midnight.	
		12m	Casualties for 25th Nil	
	26th	2am	The position was as follows: The 51st Division was concentrated at SAILLY-au-BOIS with outposts covering the COLINCAMPS and HEBUTERNE Roads. The artillery covering the 51st Bri. being 255, 256 & 293 Brigades R.F.A. The 19th Division was similarly concentrated at HEBUTERNE with outposts on high ground to the south of the City, covering the 19th Bri., being 104, 235 & 112 Brigades R.F.A. The City covered 51st Divi. was ordered to come into action near the FONQUE VILLERS – SOUASTRE Road – the position to the south by the road leading to near SAILLY-au-BOIS, many positions towards SOUASTRE. 256 Bde. D30 a. rt. 255. D23 c. rt. 293 E25 a. rt.	W.J.
		8.30am	Orders were received to take up positions WEST of HEBUTERNE. 256 Bde. was complete by this G.K. in gun from 255 Bde. were moving into action S.W. of HEBUTERNE when it came	

WAR DIARY
INTELLIGENCE SUMMARY

Army Form C. 2118.

Place	Date	Hour	Summary of Events and Information	Remarks and references to Appendices
Field	1918 March 26		under enemy M.G. fire from HEBUTERNE at a range of about 800 yards. The Brigade halted about 2 miles west of Battery East & 3 Battalion West of the FONQUEVILLERS – COLINCAMPS Road, facing enemy reported advancing on HEBUTERNE from the S.E. The Leading Battery A/256 was subsequently withdrawn a further 400 yards S.W. Remainder of Brigade in rear to cover the nightflank from an attack from direction of COLINCAMPS. Enemy from various reports estimated at a strength of about 2 Battalions was concentrated for an attack S.E. of Colincamps. The attack never developed properly on the M.S. on HEBUTERNE has eventually charged by one of our tanks.	
		4 p.m.	About 4 p.m. 258 & 293 Bdes moved back to a position for observation near SOUASTRE in D24.d to cover the SAILLY-AU-BOIS – COLINCAMPS line & the HEBUTERNE Ridge — approximately from K14.c.00 – K14.central. Fire was not to be opened until turns definitely ascertained that our infantry had withdrawn to the HEBUTERNE Ridge.	
		6.30 p.m.	Brigade were in action covering that line. Boisallie. Major H. Farel wounded. (A)	
		11 p.m.	9th Bde H.Q. Bead Boissallied (at early) Bde Hdqrs established at D23.6.59.	
	27th	–	The Brigade remained in action at SOUASTRE (D24.d) without firing. Officers hounded patrols were sent forward as usual to maintain touch with the Infantry.	
		6 p.m.	Orders were received for the Bde. to go into action tomorrow night 28th in position in the vicinity of FIENVILLERS. These orders were however subsequently cancelled	
	28th	1 p.m.	The Brigade marched today to 51st Divisional Concentration Area N.W. of DOULLENS – reserve to take over billets last on certain operations	

Army Form C. 2118.

WAR DIARY
or
INTELLIGENCE SUMMARY.

(Erase heading not required.)

168

Place	Date	Hour	Summary of Events and Information	Remarks and references to Appendices
Field	1918 March 28		The Bde was billeted in LE SOUICH marched from SOUASTRE via AUTHIE, SARTON - DOULLENS - NEUVILLETTE arriving LE SOUICH 8.45pm	Nil.
	29	12 noon	The march was continued today, the Bde marching to FILLIEVRES via BOUQUEMAISON - CANTELEUX - VACQUERIE, LE BOUCQ, arriving FILLIEVRES 6.30pm	Nil.
	30		The Bde remained at FILLIEVRES	
	31	12 noon	The march was continued to St. POL area via Bois LINZEUX - CROISETTE - RAMECOURT arriving St. POL 4.30pm	Nil.

6/4/18.

[signature]
Lieut Col
Comdg. 258 Brigade R.F.A.

51st Divisional Artillery

WAR DIARY

256th BRIGADE

ROYAL FIELD ARTILLERY

APRIL 1 9 1 8

14　51

Confidential

Vol 36

War Diary
of
256 Brigade R.F.A. (T.F.)
from 1st April 1918 to 30th April 1918

(Volume I)

Army Form C. 2118.
169

WAR DIARY
INTELLIGENCE SUMMARY
(Erase heading not required.)

Instructions regarding War Diaries and Intelligence Summaries are contained in F. S. Regs., Part II. and the Staff Manual respectively. Title pages will be prepared in manuscript.

Place	Date	Hour	Summary of Events and Information	Remarks and references to Appendices
Field	1918 April 1	6.30 am	The Brigade continued the march from St. Pol to BARLIN via OSTRAVILLE - MONCHY - BRETON - LA COMTE - HOUDAIN - arriving St. Pol 12.30 pm.	nil.
	2nd 3rd		Brigade remained at BARLIN. 51st Div. Arty were concentrated in this area under I Corps. They were noted to be in readiness to move into action at 3 hours notice to support 46th Div.	nil.
		12.30 pm 2d	H.Q. again proceeded to 46th D.A. Hdqrs at FONQUEREUIL W of BETHUNE to obtain particulars of Corps & Divisional duties &c.	nil.
		11 am 8th	Orders were received to move to AMETTES area.	nil.
	4th	6.30 am	Brigade marched from BARLIN to AMES via HOUDAIN - DIVION CAMBLAIN - CHATELAIN - CAUCHY-a-la-TOUR - arriving AMES 12 noon.	nil.
	5th – 8th		Brigade remained at AMES. 51st Div. Arty were concentrated in this area in reserve and Army Artillery. During this period reconnaissance of the reserve Battery Positions for defence of 46th Div. Sector was carried out. The positions reconnoitred were all on the LIEVIN area. (see Appendices)	nil.
			The usual training was carried out & also practice on the Rifle Range. The 18ther Battery M.G. were calibrated at the Calibration Range WESTREHEM N.W. of AMETTES.	M.L.
	9th	6 am	Intimation was received that 152 Infantry Bde had been ordered at 5 am to proceed to the Battle front covering the left division of the XI Corps.	
		10 am	Orders were received to be prepared to move to SONNENEM. N.W. of BETHUNE (see 16th appendices)	
		11 am	The Local Adjutant were ordered to proceed to HINGES N of BETHUNE where XI Corps Hdqrs	nil.

Army Form C. 2118.

170

WAR DIARY
INTELLIGENCE SUMMARY.
(Erase heading not required.)

Instructions regarding War Diaries and Intelligence Summaries are contained in F. S. Regs., Part II. and the Staff Manual respectively. Title pages will be prepared in manuscript.

Place	Date	Hour	Summary of Events and Information	Remarks and references to Appendices
Field	1918 April 9	11:30am 1:50pm	Brigade received orders to proceed to GONNEHEM. Colonel reiterated reports to 11th Corps H.Qrs. at HINGES. Information received was confirmation of that heard previously namely that the enemy had broken through an entire Portuguese front but that an a two small parties of the latter were still holding out — in isolated localities. 152nd Infantry Brigade had taken up a position on the LOCOUTURE - LE DRUMEZ - NOUVEAU MONDE Line & 258 Bde was ordered to take up position from in to action covering the left of that line.	N.J.
		2:30pm	Position was exceedingly precarious as indicated by 4/m v guides, post back to GONNEHEM to bring the Batteries forward to position. During the afternoon severe fighting was taking place & arrangements were made whereby the 153 Infantry Bde were to take up a defensive line of the Canal DE LA LAWE with outposts across the Canal — the 152 Infantry Bde falling back to this line also.	N.J.
		7pm	The Brigade came into action H.Q CORNET MAKO - MARMUSE Rd, as follows: A/256 Q 30 a 97 B/256 Q 24 c 7510 - Q24 c 54 C/256 D/256 Q 30 a 95 H.Qrs. were established in conjunction with H.Qrs. 255 Bde RFA at Q 30 a 20 Lt Col Styer D.S.O. M. Col. Glenning D.S.O. (255 Bde) acted as Liaison Officers with the Brigadier Condg. 152nd British Infantry Bde. Headquarters 152nd Infantry Bde. H.Qrs. was established at R26 a 74 (subsequently moving to R256 22) The command of 256 Bde devolved on Major R.R. will whilst reorganised	N.J.

Army Form C. 2118.

WAR DIARY
INTELLIGENCE SUMMARY
(Erase heading not required.)

Instructions regarding War Diaries and Intelligence Summaries are contained in F. S. Regs., Part II. and the Staff Manual respectively. Title pages will be prepared in manuscript.

17/1

Place	Date	Hour	Summary of Events and Information	Remarks and references to Appendices
Field	1918 April 9	7.0 p.m.	Line was formed at 7.10 p.m. on a line from R24 6 9999 – R24 6 9900 – R35 6 95 – reaching all Ronci Village in rear of as above. Mounted officers' Patrol, pioneer officers were sent forward to get into touch with the Infantry friends out the situation.	
		9.23 p.m.	New S.O.S. lines were laid and up as follows: 236 Bde from R23 a 06 – R29 6 47 – R29 central – R29 c 50 rendezvous of fire reaching back the line was by day –	Ju.J.
		10.30 p.m.	Wagon Lines for Firing Battery 7." had Wagons were established in neighbourhood of R27 b. 153" Infantry Bde had arrived by this time & new S.O.S. lines were laid out at 10.30 p.m. to cover it as follows: From R16 c 86 – R16 c 73 – R23 a 06 – R23 a 06 – R23 c 00 – R23 c 00 – R29 c 47 – R29 c 50.	
			There was very heavy throughout the night Visibility was bad owing to mist throughout the day. Casualties: 2/Lt F. Elliott "A" Bty wounded at duty. 1234065 Gr. Beard E. (c) wounded	Ju.S.
	10		Enemy in action. A/258 - 5 B/258 6 C/258 6 D/258 4 New S.O.S. lines were received as follows: R16 c 86 – R16 c 73 – R23 a 06 – R23 c 00 – R29 c 47 – R29 c 50. Severe fighting took place all the morning especially in the neighbourhood of the locks on R96 & R16 c where much movement had previously been reported by Patrol officers. These locks changed hands several times & remained intimately in the hands of the Enemy. Bridge here had been reported as destroyed but it is doubtful if this was the case. Brigade fired on reported locations of the enemy weapons	Ju.S.

Army Form C. 2118.

172

WAR DIARY
INTELLIGENCE SUMMARY.
(Erase heading not required.)

Instructions regarding War Diaries and Intelligence Summaries are contained in F. S. Regs., Part II. and the Staff Manual respectively. Title pages will be prepared in manuscript.

Place	Date	Hour	Summary of Events and Information	Remarks and references to Appendices
Field	1918 April 10	10.30am	New S.O.S. lines were again ranged on the following line :- R9c58 following line of River southwards to R16a02 to R16c07 - R16c83 - R23a06 - R22a25 - R28c26. The defence of the S.O.S. line in R22b6ol was necessitated by the very determined stand made in FOSSE POST by early of King Edwards Horse who had the many attacks inflicted heavy casualties. They were reinforced by a company of the 3rd Seaforths. It was intended to relieve these by a company of the 7th Blackwatch but the Post was captured in the evening before this could be effected. A large dump of Ammunition was reported here & after the withdrawal of our troops a concentrated shoot was carried out on the place by 6" How: of 116 S.B. & 8/255. After dark the enemy was seen hurrying in this direction but no further information could be obtained of it was the one fired on.	Nil
		5pm	2/Lt. R.Scott C/256 (since killed) whereas Liaison Officer with 7th Blackwatch, saw enemy digging in near head of River R3c24 moved from R2d70 - R2d75. He immediately asked the Battery for a gun to mount up for a close enfiry shoot. The gun from C/256 arrived at 5.30pm at a position picked by him Officer who had made all arrangements, previously for opening fire & fired 94 rds with excellent results, causing casualties. The work was most appreciated by the Infantry. The gun was withdrawn at 8.35pm.	96I
		7pm	Between 7pm & 8pm intense enemy Heavy Rifle & m.g. fire occurred in the area R9d & R10c at the regual. 1 Infantry fire was opened on S.O.S. lines.	
		9.15pm	At 9.15pm Bde. Liaison Officer reported that LESTREM POST at R9c20 had fallen & that the Enemy were advancing along the road towards R14.6.0.9. A Barrage was placed & immediately put down on the Roads leading from LESTREM POST eastwards & the wood between FORK Roads in R9c96 & the tracks in R9c.	Nil

(57093). Wt. W1285g/M1293. 750,000. 1/17. D.D. & L., Ltd. Forms/C.2118/14.

WAR DIARY
INTELLIGENCE SUMMARY

Army Form C. 2118.
173

Place	Date	Hour	Summary of Events and Information	Remarks and references to Appendices
Field	1918 April 10	9.27 p.m	At 9.27 p.m. an enemy attack on LESTREM POST having been ordered, a barrage was put down on line R9c67 – R9d20 with 2. 18 pdr Batteries O.P. near R29 b09 that there was heavy M.G. & Rifle fire about Railway in R21 d & Patrols were sent out to gain touch with the situation.	M.S.
	10.	10 p.m	About midnight O.P. reported that at present Infantry in its immediate front had been withdrawn to a line immediately E. of O.P. (which was also Battalion Hdqrs.) & parallel to the Railway. During the time continuous fire was being kept up. Two platoons of 8th Royal Scots were detrained to X Roads R20c82 & ½ Coy. to R20 a 52 & 1 Coy. to EPINETTE.	M.S.
			Casualties during 10th. 636359 Wheeler Beckingham H. (A) Wounded 645 459 S.S.Cpl. Ford F (D) Wounded 6788 Sr. Smith W (D) Wounded at duty	M.S.
	11.	1 am.	About 1 am. a P reported enemy were advancing W. in strength, probably afterwards that he was attacking the O.P. where Battalion Hdqrs were. During this time a continuous rate of fire was kept up an enemy Barrage lines as ordered by Brigade during offices.	M.S.
		2.30 am	O.P. reported that the Enemy had got Bn Hdqrs held in North & South & that Lt Scott had ordered the Infantry E. of it to fall back on the Cross Roads R20c82. Information received at same time that 152 & 154 Inf. Bdes appeared to be holding their own further to the South. A Barrage was accordingly put down on line R21a05 – R21c03 & the cover between that and the Canal was cleared.	M.S.

Army Form C. 2118.

174

WAR DIARY
INTELLIGENCE SUMMARY.
(Erase heading not required.)

Place	Date	Hour	Summary of Events and Information	Remarks and references to Appendices
Field	1918 April 11		The O.P. Officer just left the O.P. as it was being surrounded. Telephonic communication with his signallers along the O.P. wire, tapping in & sending information constantly during the withdrawal.	
			By 4.15 am the enemy had pressed further forward very rapidly & had got through the line held by us in R20 a 7 t & R26 a & our troops were falling back towards PARADIS between the road leading to Battery Position in Q.30 a.	N.S.
			Firing a S.O.S. rate was hopeless as his ammunition carriage by pack horses & Officer owing to the situation it was decided to withdraw the Batteries one at a time as the Enemy were within 700 yards of the Position & were machine gunning the Batteries. The Batteries were ordered to withdraw accordingly to positions which had been previously reconnoitred.	
		6.45am	The withdrawal was B/256 & 1 Section D/256 followed by C/255 & the remaining section of D/256 & lastly A/256. A quick rate of fire was maintained by our guns & Batteries fell back withdrawing with all our own & prior sights & the enemy's progress was slow A/256 especially keeping up a very heavy fire after the other Batteries had withdrawn.	N.S.
			New positions were taken up as follows:- A/256 Q.27 a 77 B/256 Q.26 d 48 C/256 Q.27 c 65 30 D/256 Q.26 b 22	
			Bar. Hoggs (together with three of 255 Bde) came in action again by 7:50 am their place being the whole Brigade was in action again by 7:50 am their place being nearly full of ammunition. Fire was directed along the approaches to PARADIS from the East. Our Infantry had fallen back on troops holding PARADIS from the Church to	N.S.

WAR DIARY
INTELLIGENCE SUMMARY

Army Form C. 2118.

172

Place	Date	Hour	Summary of Events and Information	Remarks and references to Appendices
Field	1918 April 11		to BOUZATEUX FARM with a front at EPINETTE, met at about Q14d98 Vanithen at R25a59, at the same time 2 Battns of the 61st Div which came under orders of 153 Infantry Bde were ordered to dig in on a line from Q29 central in front of VACANT - Q11671 - Q6a59 - Q6a59 - 6th Warwicks n. S. of 4th D.C.L.I in N. About 9.30 am our Infantry and men withdrawing from PARADIS & PETITE BOIS Herm. The Bde Hqrs of both 152 & 153 Infantry Bdes were at Q23d02 withdrew to Q27a56 & 57. By 10.30 am enemy had apparently established himself in N of PARADIS and 1 Company of 8th Royal Scots still held out from the Church to Q30d68 where it was in touch with 5th Seaforths at this time H. Col. Dyson D.S.O. was ordered to take temporary command of 153 Infantry Bde in place of Brigadier General Beckwith (sick) Capt. L. Coull D/256 was sent up to do Liaison Officer with the Brigade. Two officers from B + C Batteries (2/Lt H. Ruben & 2/Lt D. McGregor) & 2 other from the 12th Australian Army F.A. Bde who had just come up, were ordered to go with the Infantry to reorganise them & lead them. An O.P. was established at Q23 c 28 observing the day General fire was very successfully carried out on enemy movement near PARADIS. Y. enemy approached by the infantry. The fire was kept up all day but at 2.35 pm B/256 was ordered to withdraw to Q76 d 48. Two aeroplane calls were responded to during the afternoon to by A/256 on enemy Batteries. In the evening Batteries were withdrawn to positions as follows:—	

WAR DIARY
INTELLIGENCE SUMMARY

Army Form C. 2118.

17b

Place	Date	Hour	Summary of Events and Information	Remarks and references to Appendices
Field	1918 April 11		A/256) & line Q19c67 - Q19c59. These positions were all reconnoitred B/256) carlier in the day. C/256 Q19c6545 } ROBECQ D/256 Q19c1525. These moves were all accomplished between 6.30pm & 8pm. excepting B/256 which was postponed the return of 255 Bde for tactical purposes in case of enemy Depot. to this position at 10pm after having fired about 700 rds. Harassing B/256 withdrew to the return of the other Batteries. During the withdrawal of B/256 fire covering the return of 255 Bde in its place. Wires laid in the following A/256 came under the return of 255 Bde in its place. Wires laid in the following SOS line if required R25c33 - R25c6085.	Yes L.
		8pm	New Hdqtrs. Bn. Hdqrs. were established at Q19.6.07.(Eastern end of ROBECQ) Harassing fire from new Positions on Roads, Tracks & Approaches to Village of PARADIS in vicinity with typhoon. about 60 rds. per Battery per hour being expended. The O.P. at Q23c28 was manned by 2 Officers ie Liaison Officer was sent to Battn. Hdqrs. of 64 Warwicks at Q22d87. SOS lines for the night were put down as follows:- PARADIS Road - Q18a28 - Q24d67 - R19c48. Casualties 1 & 36 W482 Lt. Winnard "B"Bty. wounded.	Yes L.

Army Form C. 2118.

WAR DIARY
INTELLIGENCE SUMMARY
(Erase heading not required.)

Place	Date	Hour	Summary of Events and Information	Remarks and references to Appendices
Field	1918 April 12	1.45 a.m.	Orders were received for a special 10 minute shoot in conjunction with the Heavy Artillery to take place at 5 am on line Q24c56 to Q24a2570 — 4.5 How. 300 plus. The whole shoot quickly rose from the aforementioned shoot was carried out.	
		5.15 a.m.	O.P. reported that the enemy were advancing in the neighbourhood of the O.P. (Q23c 37) that our Infantry were withdrawing to the VACANT LINE. Fire was opened on SOS lines & SOS rate of fire.	
		5.35 a.m.	About this time a burst of Rifle & M.G. fire was heard on RIEZ–du–VINAGE at very close range. This was not however known from until after the Bat. was ordered to retire.	No 1
			No further communication could be got with the O.P. — 153 Infantry Bat. or 258 Bat. About 6 a.m. Enemy M.G. & Rifle fire was directed on Battery Position. It was then known that the Enemy had broken through our advancing our ROBECQ8S during this time a heavy fire was being kept up from SOS lines. total open SOS (who was then in command of 153 Infantry Bat.) along with his Staff had been almost surrounded in RIEZ-du-VINAGE & had to retire. Any manner of the Batteries for the situation.	
			The Bat. was ordered to retire immediately N.W. rates as was. Machine Gun fire at range 300 to 400 yards range. The Cd Battery B/258 to retire keeping one Section in action by 6.35 a.m. kept up a heavy fire on the Roads leading to RIEZ-du-VINAGE & CORNET MALO & surrounding area. Thereafter a preparatory casualties to horses, but the Bat. got away covered by detachments many Rear Rifle system bursts.	No 2
		10.30 a.m.	Ou Liaison from 18pdr Battery was ordered to concentrate certain knolls on the main ROBECQ — St VENANT Road alongside the Ammunition dump at P16c 89. These Sections were in action by 6.35 a.m. & kept up a heavy fire on the Roads leading to RIEZ-du-VINAGE.	No 3
		8 a.m.	The remaining Sections of B/258 came into action on the St VENANT — BUSNES Road as follows. A/258 P15a 14 B/258 P16 b9515. C/258 Pg d 14 D/258 P14 d 46. Fire was opened	No 4

WAR DIARY
or
INTELLIGENCE SUMMARY
(Erase heading not required.)

Army Form C. 2118.
178

Place	Date	Hour	Summary of Events and Information	Remarks and references to Appendices
Field	1918 April 12		RIEZ au VINAGE & LE CORNET MALO & approaches thereto. In the meantime 153 Infantry Bde HdQrs (there being no other officers) assisted by Officers of 2/6 Bn. r 12" Australian Army F.A. Bde. collected all stragglers & formed a line in Q.19 of facing SE. A further line was formed on the ROBECQ – LES AMUSOIRES Road. The forward sections previously in action with the ammunition dumps in their neighbourhood had been set on fire (by mules). They then rejoined the main Battery Positions. As the main line of defence was to be the ROBECQ – LES AMUSOIRES Road. Positions further back across the LA BASSEE CANAL were reconnoitred. Machine mounted & kept look-out forward as usual to get into touch with our Infantry & find out the situation – the Batteries keeping up a slow rate of fire. Positions across the Canal were selected & the Batteries withdrew – one Battery at a time only, moving to the next moving & when the previous one was in action. These moves were all accomplished between 11:30 am & 1:30 pm – the positions taken up being as follows:- A/256 P.19.b.95.40 B/256 P.19.b.40.35 C/256 P.20.a.02.25 D/256 P.19.b.25.90 These Positions were all in LA PIERRIERE. Bde. HdQrs. were established at P.19.a.85. & communication immediately established by wire with 153 Infantry Bde. HdQrs. also now at P.20.c.99. Runners from each Battery & HdQrs. Reported the Bridges across the Canal in P.13 & P.20. The mounted officers Lewis Gun were posted to cover the Bridges across the Canal. Patrols continual in the morning had brought in valuable information as to location of the enemy & general situation. Fire was kept up at a slow rate for any positions.	
		7/pm	The Arty covering the 61st & 51st Divisions was now general throughout as follows:-	

(A7591) Wt. W12590/M1293. 750,000. 1/17. D.D. & L., Ltd. Forms/C.2118/4.

Army Form C. 2118.

179

WAR DIARY
INTELLIGENCE SUMMARY
(Erase heading not required.)

Place	Date	Hour	Summary of Events and Information	Remarks and references to Appendices
Field	1918 April 12		(a) 51st Divisional Arty. (H.Q. Br. SNES). 255 Bde. R.F.A. 12 Australian Bde. R.F.A. (b) 61st Divisional Arty. (H.Q. MOLINGHEM) 336 Bde R.F.A. 177 } Bden. R.F.A. 16"S.A. 180 }	Liaison arrangements with the Infantry were also formed.
			The Heavy Arty. covering both fronts was:— 28" } 10" } Bden. R.G.A. act. to be grouped 49" } in the neighbourhood of GUARBECQUE	N.J.
			Harassing fire for the night was ordered to be put down on Area Q.10 central & Q.25 a.79 & Q.25'b.23 & Q.20 c.1 d.05 = 100 R.H.D. rds. per Gun, those with an increase expenditure from 4.30 to 5.30 a.m.	
			At 10 p.m. the Guns of A/256, which had been bogged on the retreat on the evening 9/10 April, were shelled. All ammunition left behind was also salved.	
			Casualties on 12th: Capt. G.C. Conell O/256 Wounded. 2/Lt. A.R. Rennie C/256 Wounded. 2/Lt. R. Scott C/256 Killed. Officers 2/Lt. Winton-Carlane D/258 Wounded. 2/Lt. Warwick Dickinson R.H. Wounded.	
			Other Ranks: B/256 635649 a/Bdr Oliphant A.D. 690370 Gr. Dickinson R.H. Wounded. C/256. Killed 835576 Gr. Morecroft H. 220940 Gr. Clark C.J. 740675 Gr. Rennie. Wounded 142857 Coll. Quigley 57948 S. Hughan 68609 Y. Mathie 169982 Y. Riddle 11576 3 Gr. Greenwood T. 635355 Gr. Br. Ford M.S. 635384 Gr. Pritchard S. 635047 Gr. Rotherham. 237094 Gr. Palfrey H.	N.J.
			Helgo. 636383 S. Cagie Wounded at duty.	
			The Ammunition expended by Batteries up to this time in rounds From 7 Jan. 9.16 (When Bde. moved into action) to 6.30 a.m. 12th (when Batteries withdrew to CARNET NHD Position). 69-20 rds 18 pdr: P 13"20 rds. S.How.	N.J.

From

WAR DIARY or INTELLIGENCE SUMMARY

Army Form C. 2118.
180

Place	Date	Hour	Summary of Events and Information	Remarks and references to Appendices
Field	1918 April 12	From 6.30 am 11th to 6 am 12th	12th when Battns withdrew to ROBECQ – ST VENANT Rd. 8970 rels 18 Febr 1850 rels 4.5" How.	
	13th		Nothing unusual happened during the night. Patrols were pushed forward & they reported that all was unchanged. Fresh mounted Patrols were pushed forward from O.P. was established on the Canal Bank at Q31a92. Havergaye crept out & showed no Infantry on back area.	
		11 am.	4 Col. 1 Trooper D.S.O. rejoined Bde from 153 Infantry Bde.	
		2.30 pm	251 Bde Hqrs moved to new Hdqrs at P19c74 Havergaye fire & was stopped at 1 pm.	
		4 pm.	The commanders of the two brigades made by our mounted Patrols are reported as follows:— From Q1 central to Q8a00 – Q14c36 down to & including J BAQUEROLLES Farm – Q20a – Q19 central – Q19c87 – Q19c00 thence to Canal Bank & along the Canal to about Pt. LEVIS where the men line East.	N.J.
		7.30 pm.	Orders were received today as ordering most to O/C 4th Infi under & in the case of an S.O.S. an immediate front. This was because certain Infantry Garrisons were to take place N J Canal towards RIEZ du VINAGE.	N.J.
		11 pm.	Orders were received as to alteration in the disposition of the Artillery covering the 51st & 61st Divl fronts. They are as follows:— 255 Bde R.F.A. to cover 51st Div front 61st Div 253 Bde R.F.A. " " 184 Infantry Bde. 61st " 12 lands' Q 182 " Canal " 182 – Do – Do – 197 Bde. R.F.A. " Canal " 183 – Do – Do – since the The Following boundaries between Divisions & Bdes. Northern boundary of 57 Div front – a line through P24 al 63 parallel to LA BASSEE Canal (exclusive) Southern " 184 Infantry Bde: Northern Boundary – Q14.C central back to LES AMUSOIRES (A9 6-29) 182 – Do – " – The Railway " – Q1, 2 & 3 183 – Do – Northern " – The Railway " 188 – Do – Northern " – The St VENANT – MERVILLE Canal S.O.S. lines were arranged accordingly.	N.J.

Army Form C. 2118.

WAR DIARY
INTELLIGENCE SUMMARY
(Erase heading not required.)

Place	Date	Hour	Summary of Events and Information	Remarks and references to Appendices
Field	1918 April 13		The Brigade O.P. on the Canal Bank was manned by a Signals mounted look-out party, while Battn patrols on their flanks kept before any change in the situation. The night was fairly quiet. Casualties 95272 Pte Osborn C. H/10988 Pte Cliff W. 635763 Pte Corrigan W. 4/3553 L/Bdr Joss W. 48379 Pte Carter L. 206687 Pte Hawkins C. (at duty) all 1/258 Wounded 73874 Pte Smedley S. (B) wounded	181
	14		It was concluded during the night that the enemy would renew their attacks in the morning. No attack took place but the morning was generally quiet. During the night Farm at Q14 a 52 was taken by our M.G. captured at/c Farm at Q20 a 51. During the day minor Infantry operations took place about Q20 where 18th Infantry Bde pushed their line from Q20 a 65 along Roads to Q30 c 95 60 taking about the southwestern outskirts of Riez du Vinage. This line was known gown it is the glorious.	W.I.
		6 p.m.	The 4th Division made night attacked covered by an Artillery Barrage. The position was was taken by the Zouaves Q20 x Q21. & Riez were occupied to reassure the new Battery Position on N. & S. Ldmns Q20 x Q21. & Riez were occupied to reassure the new Battery Position north of the Canal about P34 — Viridity the front the day was hot. The night was generally quiet but positions were improved & consolidated. Casualties Ptes. 406264 Sgt. S. Bass. H.Qrs. (attached from 51st Bn. Signals) Killed	2nd J.
	15th		Our heavy Artillery kept up a vigorous harassing fire throughout the night. The position of our front this morning was as follows: Q. central Q8a52 — Q14c56— round Barleaux Farm inclusive to Q19c63 — Q19c98 - Q25c80 - Q25b74 — Q26a63 round Riez au Vinage inclusive to Q26d80 thence to Canal with Patrols the Bois au Pacaut about Q33 central.	
		6.30 a.m. 12 noon	New Battery Position whereas was established :— P23 West of Robecq r N. of the Canal A/258 - Q28a 36 C/258 Q22c 34 Battle was at as Positions as follows :— B/258 - Q22c 62 Q22c 67.	3rd J.

WAR DIARY
INTELLIGENCE SUMMARY

Army Form C. 2118.

192

Place	Date	Hour	Summary of Events and Information	Remarks and references to Appendices
Sieur	1918 April 15	3 p.m.	Lewis gun fire was kept up covering the N & S. grid line between squares Q20 & Q21. Bde. HQrs. moved to new HQrs. under Batteries at Q21 d 2.4	
		5.30 p.m.	Orders were received to the effect that 184 Infantry Bde were to attack at 7.30 p.m. recapture the Road from Q20 a.58 to Q20 d.05. The 4th Division were likewise establishing a line approximately as follows: From W10 6.8.7 to Q28 d.93 thence along Road to Q27 a.36 thence approximately the 4th Divn. would co-operate with the 184 Bde attack at 7.30 p.m. by getting into touch with them at Q20 d.05 afterwards pushing out from Riez-au-Vinage together. Howrs. at Q26 6.95. (See appendices) The artillery covering the attack consisted as follows: 3 – 18 pdr Batteries 1 – 4.5 How. Battery 2 – 60 pdr Batteries 1 – 2 Batteries of 6" Hows. as available. accompanying 184 Bde attack. The attack of the 4th Division on the right was successful. They captured Riez-au-Vinage & established themselves on the Road along the Road through Le Cornet Malo as far as the Rain running through Q20 a. & t.c. The attack by the 184 Bde also proved successful & they established themselves on the Road from Bacquerolles Farm to Q20 d.06 & thereout as far as the Rain running through Q20 a & t.c. Just prior to the attack it was reported that the enemy were massing for a attack near — Q14 c 7 Q15 a. They were engaged by Rfle. Rio & M.G. fire & were caught in an enbarkment which started at 7.30 pm. Heavy casualties were inflicted on them. The artillery fire supporting 184 Bde attack was kept up until 8.30 p.m. for instructions to Bde Liaison officer. Before 9 p.m. "counter attacks" were attempted & taken up & regained by us. Ultimately our men were forced to withdraw to their original line. 107 bris were fired down covering the 184 Bde front as follows: — From Q14 b (central) to Q20 b (south) to Q21 c 00. 255 Bde. R.F.A were responsible for covering during the night approaching hararing fire was kept up on all roads approaches to Bde. sector. Casualties for 15th 7 3 1 9 St Royalt O Bdy wounded	

Army Form C. 2118. 183

WAR DIARY
INTELLIGENCE SUMMARY
(Erase heading not required.)

Place	Date	Hour	Summary of Events and Information	Remarks and references to Appendices
Field	1918 April 16	6·0 a.m.	Owing to this morning remained much the same as it was y/day. The 4th Division however had withdrawn slightly their line from about Q26 a.53 near RIEZ-du-VINAGE inclusive to Q27 c.00 where it runs to the Canal. Harassing fire was kept up during the day. Visibility was bad. Enemy artillery & aircraft were active.	Sgd
		4·0–4·30 p.m.	B/216 moved to new position at P28 c 79.	
		5·30 p.m.	Enemy artillery bombarded area Q28 a a/b where enemy Batteries were reported active over 15 pdr & 4·5 How's anticipated	
		6 p.m.	S.O.S. lines for the night enemy 184 Bde removed the same	
			Casualties Nil.	
	17"		Throughout the night continuous harassing fire was kept up. Enemy's artillery was particularly quiet during the night. Visibility this morning was good though out but the day. Batteries neglected their lines of calibration. Special shoots on Newin, in which Enemy machine Guns were suspected, were taken by standard ranging. Fire was observed. S.O.S. lines covering 184 Bde were readjusted as follows:– From Q21 c 00 along Road to Q29 c 99 to Q30 b 35 and with 18 Q 14 d 35 with 4·5 How's on special targets. 255/336 was performed on same zone.	Sgd
		3/–	Bde H.Qrs moved to new H.Qrs. at P26 6·80. The 61st Divfront was divided into 3 sectors as follows:– "A" Sector held by 184 Infantry Bde covered by 255 & 257 Bdes R.F.A. "B" Sector held by 182 – D° – covered by 180 & 12th Australian Bdes R.F.A. "C" Sector held by 183 – D° – covered by 177 Bde. R.F.A. A addition to the above Field arty. the 28" Bde R.F.A. was tactically under the orders of R.A. 57 Div, its additional Heavy Arty. could be turned on through G.O.C. RA XI Corps. Harassing fire from chink smoothis was kept up	See Appendices & tracing

Army Form C. 2118.

WAR DIARY
INTELLIGENCE SUMMARY
(Erase heading not required.)

184

Instructions regarding War Diaries and Intelligence Summaries are contained in F. S. Regs., Part II. and the Staff Manual respectively. Title pages will be prepared in manuscript.

Place	Date	Hour	Summary of Events and Information	Remarks and references to Appendices
Field	1918 April 17th	6.30 pm	A special Barrage was put down supporting a dusk attack by 8th Battalion to retake a fort near BACQUEROLLES FARM. The Barrage was repeated at 10 pm and 11 pm. The fort was finally taken & established. Casualties - 17th Nil	M.J.
	18th	3 am 3.15 am	Enemy put down a heavy Barrage & general fire around attack area. #Battery Positions were replied to with artillery of ours and changed to S.O.S. after about 5 minutes of rapid fire. A number of prisoners were captured who stated that an attack was intended but was completely broken up by our artillery fire on 4th Division front. The enemy made attempts to effect a crossing over the Canal at BOIS de PACAUT. They were however driven off & suffered heavy casualties. A number of prisoners were also taken. During the day our Batteries were kept active engaging small parties of the enemy in D.20.b. Vd.	
		8.30 pm & 11 pm	A special barrage was put down by Bde. at 8.30 pm & again at 11 pm covering a small attack by 184 Bde. to capture BACQUEROLLES Farm. The attack was successful. The usual night firing was maintained.	
			Casualties on 18th: Capt. R.C. Mayhew D/251 Wounded at duty, Lieut. J.H. Gay attacked H.Bty from D.A.C. Wounded. 2/Lt. J.H. Pilleer (B) 249356 494 Bulley J (H.Q.) attacked sick on signed Wounded at duty. 636704 Sgt. Christie A (A) 633361 Bdr. Lillie C (A) 638584 D. Trueman A (A) 635345 S. Robson (A) Wounded 2659 Pdr. Macrae W (B) 1032384 Pr. Nicholson J (B) 776 836 P. Orrville H (D) 13800 P. Green C (D) Wounded.	Maj. J.
	19th		Having fired our barrage during the night covering infantry touching the over, Enemy artillery inactive. D/258 fired special Harrasschede for frames Co. who were with good effect. Casualties 19th Nil	M.J.
	20th	2.30 am	At 2.30 am, this morning the enemy attacked near RIEZ-au-VINAGE likely by a Bn. surprise was against but the attack was held up by the front line & the enemy driven back into PACAUT WOOD. A number of prisoners were taken. The remainder were quiet.	M.J.

(A7092). Wt. W12859/M1293. 750,000. 1/17. D. D. & L., Ltd. Forms/C2118/14.

Army Form C. 2118.

185

WAR DIARY
INTELLIGENCE SUMMARY.
(Erase heading not required.)

Instructions regarding War Diaries and Intelligence Summaries are contained in F. S. Regs., Part II. and the Staff Manual respectively. Title pages will be prepared in manuscript.

Place	Date	Hour	Summary of Events and Information	Remarks and references to Appendices
Field	1918 April 20th		ROUX and E. of RIEZ au VINAGE were improved during the day. Several prisoners captured. Special photo on Buildings which were peacefully carried out in squares Q21C & Q20b. Enemy artillery inactive but shelling back area. Our aeroplanes were active during the day. Pilots reporting. An S.O.S. was responded to at 7.30 pm. Casualties Nil.	No. 1.
	21st		The situation remains unchanged. Vigorous night firing maintained by our Batteries. Visibility today again good. Many enemy balloons up. 4 Hostile cancelled special bombard -ment of Harass in Q21C & Q20b. S.O.S. calls at 7.30 pm & 10.20 pm responded to. No attacks developed. Casualties 2. Nil	No. 2.
	22nd		Special Harassing fire shoot by 18 pdrs commenced between 3.30 am & 5.30 am on areas Q20 & rd. etc throughout the night on Roads, Light Railway & Q20 & rd. etc throughout. At 4 am enemy overnight advanced their positions on the at 5.30 am. 4th Division reported they had improved their positions on the southern edge of PACAUT WOOD. Batteries replied to an S.O.S. call at 5.30 am - firing until 6 am. 10 minute Concentrate shoots were carried out by D/256 at 11.20 am - 2.15 pm - 4.30 pm & 6.15 pm in Harass in Q20b & Q21C. - 2.18 pdr Batteries reached the area with Shrapnel during enhancement of the bombardments. - Enemy arty fairly quiet all day. The enemy's over the Canal were shelled at intervals throughout the day. Casualties 22. Nil	No. 3.
	23rd	4.30 am	Harassing fire was actively kept up during the night nearly morning at 4.30 am. The 184 Infantry Bde (61st Div) in conjunction with 4th Div on Right carried out attack with the object of making good the following line. Inastine & Roads Q27 a 26 52 - Q20d 6895 - Farm Q14c 58. The	No. 4.

Army Form C. 2118.

WAR DIARY
INTELLIGENCE SUMMARY
(Erase heading not required.)

18B

Place	Date	Hour	Summary of Events and Information	Remarks and references to Appendices
Field	1918 April 23		The Artillery supporting the attack of the 184 Infantry Bde. was as follows:— 255, 256 & 12" Australian Bdes. & 28" Bde. R.F.A. assisted by 57" Aust. T.M. Bty. & a proportion of XI Corps Heavy Arty.— (see Appendices). Major Buffin 255 Bde. was liaison officer with 184 Bde. H.Qrs. Battalion. 2/Lt. S.C. Galpin D/256 was liaison officer with attacking Battalion. The attack was successful with our objectives near gained. Considerable casualties were inflicted on the enemy. 120 prisoners were captured by us & 5 machine guns. The attack took the enemy completely by surprise. They had just come into the line during the night. Our Barrage led and were utterly demoralising. Efforts searching opponents statements. Harassing searching fire was kept up during the day. Visibility poor. Enemy Artillery much more active. Forward area — Canal Bank Crossings. Casualties 119 O.R. 3 O.R. Penny, E. C/256 wounded.	Rev.J.
	24.		During the night officer 1 8hr. Rolling Barrage was carried out at 9.10pm & 10.30pm. 3.30am & 4.30am who opened concentration shoots 4.45hr. at 11pm. 1am 3am 4am. After persistent heavy shelling & enemy artillery preparation throughout the night. The enemy made a determined attack at 5.0am on our entire line in Q20b. With the object of retaking the ground which recaptured yesterday. The attack was made by great Battalion. The enemy were completely repulsed & failed to gain a footing on our front. The attack was taken up by our artillery Barrage. Mr.G.s, Rifle fire & very heavy casualties were inflicted. about 80 prisoners were captured including 5 officers & 9 N.C.O's. Throughout the day the 187 ptr. were rested except for occasional bursts of fire. Enemy Artillery quieter during the day. Visibility poor. Casualties. 6 O.R. 3 25. 1/Bar J. Coplin (A) wounded.	Rev.J.
	25.		Morning fine was maintained including cloud Rolling Barrage. That the enemy's unsuccessful attack of yesterday morning, & has remained quiet. No further efforts have been made to retake his line. During the day we caused interest about on Snipers Post, M.Gs & L.Gs posts. Observer at 9.30pm the previous nights bombardment was repeated in anticipation of a repeated operation as neutral refused there line was advanced (?) about 30 yards a S.O.S. Battn replied to an S.O.S. Visibility low all day. Casualties: Nil	Rev.J.

Army Form C. 2118.

WAR DIARY
INTELLIGENCE SUMMARY
(Erase heading not required.)

184

Instructions regarding War Diaries and Intelligence Summaries are contained in F. S. Regs., Part II. and the Staff Manual respectively. Title pages will be prepared in manuscript.

Place	Date	Hour	Summary of Events and Information	Remarks and references to Appendices
Field	1918 April			
	26		Harassing fire throughout the night was vigorously maintained : situation this morning unchanged. Visibility this all day. Hostile artillery quiet. The Battery Positions were shelled for a short period between 12 noon & 7 pm. Casualties. 635758 4/Bar. T.a.S.W. wounded	Nil
	27		Situation remains unchanged. Harassing & general shooting Hants & covered out. Hostile artillery more active shelling forward Back Areas. Visibility low, the morning improving later. Casualties. Nil.	Nil
	28		A special Harassing fire rolling Barrage in conjunction with 258 Bde. was carried out. Enemy artillery was active shelling both forward Back Areas including Battery Positions. The men between R.B.E.C9 & the Canal & stations, the Canal & BUSNES receiving special attention. Aircraft activities. Casualties. Nil.	Nil
	29		Harassing fire maintained. Visibility very low making observation difficult. Hostile artillery again very active & Battery Positions & surrounding Area was heavily shelled in the early morning & again during the afternoon & evening. This was of a persistent nature no particular attention being paid to any one place. R.B.E.C9 was shelled all calibre up to 15 cm Casualties. 635885 S. Mackenzie P (B) 104708 S. Robbie A(C) 71932 Gr. Wallace S (D) 663207 Lt. Mounds (D) W.J. all wounded	W.J.
	30		Harassing fire & usual was carried out & Burst of fire maintained during the day, & back Area. Enemy Artillery again very active shelling Bde. W.J. R.B.E.C.9 & Battery Positions area between Canal & BUSNES. Blue Cross Gas Shell was fired on area around Battery Positions during the night. Aircraft in action. Visibility low. Casualties. Capt. S.A.D. MacDowell (C) Wounded Lieut. C.A. Cater (C) Gassed. 2/Lt. T. McGiollan Gassed. 1447344 Gr. Pritchard (C) Wounded 310767 Gr. Rooker Dvr (C) killed block 930887 Gr. Catten L.A. Gassed	W.J.

(A7092). Wt. W12339/M1363. 750,000. 1/17. D. D. & L., Ltd. Forms/C2118/14.

Army Form C. 2118. 188

WAR DIARY
or
INTELLIGENCE SUMMARY.
(Erase heading not required.)

Place	Date	Hour	Summary of Events and Information	Remarks and references to Appendices
Field	1918 April 30		Ammunition expended from 9th April to 30th April.	
			from 9th April to 12th April . 8970 rds. 18 pdr. 1850 rds. 4.5 How.	
			" 13th " to 30th " 28,610 " 7329 " 300 Gas Shell	
			Totals for month 37,580 9179 300 Gas Shell	

2/5/18.

T.W. Johnston Captain
for Lieut. Col. Comdg. 237 Brigade R.F.A.
(T.F.)

Confidential

War Diary

256 Brigade R.F.A. (T.F.)

From 1st May 1918 to 31st May 1918

(Volume -I-)

WAR DIARY
INTELLIGENCE SUMMARY

Army Form C. 2118.
189

Place	Date	Hour	Summary of Events and Information	Remarks and references to Appendices
Field	1918 May 1st		Harassing fire scheme carried out between 3.30am & 4 am. Situation otherwise quiet during the night. Hostile artillery again very active mainly in the area W of ROBECQ & the area between the Canal & BUSNES including Battery positions. The area P27 & P28 was gas shelled during the night. Visibility was bad throughout the day preventing aeroplane working. Casualties: 635327 Bdr. E Jones 98673 G. Bate H.9638098 G. Taylor W "A" Battery killed. 14993 G. alic F.C. 687369 G. Hudson R.635892 L/Bdr. Pollard A/A/Bty wounded 635498 G. Gunn A/A/Bty wounded at duty.	W.J.
	2nd		Hostile Batteries were very active during the night mainly shelling CARVIN ROBECQ & back areas. Visibility during the day was very bad making observation very difficult. Harassing fire during the day & night was maintained. Casualties: 147503 H/Bdr. Mulryment F.D 134y wounded.	
		10/-	At 10 pm. an Offr. escorted by 60/pdr 6" How. & trench Mortars opened enemy Bombardment of the enemy's defences. Fronts left rectile rectification - 182 & 183 Infantry Bde formed Barrage & 18 pdrs along Patrols, which moved up all [illegible] & under cover of everything the enemy's positions with a view to gaining identifications. Personnel of 256 Bde. cooperated in the Creeping Barrage. The operation was entirely successful resulting 3 prisoners in addition a number of the enemy were killed in NoMs Land. - Hostile retaliation was slight.	W.J.
	3rd		Enemy artillery much quieter during the night. Harassing fire was carried out. 1/256 fired 200 rds gas shell into PARADIS during the night from forward positions. Visibility today good. Aircraft were active. Hostile Battery in action at Q.24.c.67. was engaged by C/256. Enemy arty/ balloons decreased activity Casualties Nil.	W.J.

Army Form C. 2118.

WAR DIARY
INTELLIGENCE SUMMARY.
(Erase heading not required.)

190

Place	Date	Hour	Summary of Events and Information	Remarks and references to Appendices
Field	1918 May 4		The "night" was quiet. We find the usual night harassing fire. Our Heavies were more active. Enemy Artillery showed intermittent activity against SE WARANT & surrounding Area. At about 5 Stunds our Battery positions were shelled by 105 m.m. at 11 p.m. the Bridge – 29C was heavily shelled. Aircraft showed little activity. Casualties Nil.	2us.f.
	5th		Harassing fire maintained as usual. Heavy Artillery carried out short Gun Bombardment between 4 am & 6 am on area Q3d, Q4b, & Q9b. 236 Bde co-operated by harassing Roads & Cross Roads in Q9a, b, y, c. No marked retaliation followed. Gas Bombardment on a small scale carried out by the Brigade on Q9c, Q4b & Q5a-b. Enemy artillery showed increased activity today. Area NE of BUSNES was shelled between 11.30 am & 12 noon & again between 1-2 pm. Aeroplanes inactive but there was a marked increase in the number of Observation Balloons.	2us.f.
	6th		Usual harassing fire on Roads, Tracks &c during the night. At 12 noon rifle fire from Enemy Posts. A Shoot was carried out. Ireland Q16 d 3.9. 4 Shots & Concentrations. Concentrated on Enemy forward Gun Locations. Unluckily pm - no meal rate in the cultivation Field. Hostile Artillery less active. Weather fine - improving later.	2us.f.
	7th		The night was quiet with the exception of harassing fire & an increased hostile rate pm. fell heavily all morning. Visibility nil in the forenoon improving later. Enemy Artillery showed slightly increased activity especially against back Areas. ROBECQ was shelled intermittently during the day & the Canal Bank Area. Aircraft more active.	2us.f.

Army Form C. 2118.

WAR DIARY
or
INTELLIGENCE SUMMARY.
(Erase heading not required.)

191

Instructions regarding War Diaries and Intelligence Summaries are contained in F. S. Regs., Part II. and the Staff Manual respectively. Title pages will be prepared in manuscript.

Place	Date	Hour	Summary of Events and Information	Remarks and references to Appendices
Field	1918 May 8th		Harassing fire kept up throughout. Area 99c7d. Q10d & Q15c received general attention. D/256 fired approx. Embankment in PARADIS. Enemy Artillery fire below normal. Visibility was good & aircraft both hostile and our own were very active. Patrols took place in which no E.A. were seen down. Enemy positions were reconnoitred work begun on them.	J.W.J.
	9th		From 11am the usual amount of harassing fire was carried out until 9pm. The enemy morning "searching" searching Roads, Areas & leading up to Brigade Zone. Enemy retaliation was weak & used mainly machine guns from Strainer as to the Enemy. Offensive being received towards morning certain preparations and tanks C/256 moved to new position about 500 to a flank. The position however became unstable owing to continuous shelling. They moved back to the Battery position D/256 sent forward a 4.5" Tank Gun to Q24.658 to meet possible attacks with Tanks. The day was generally quiet. Visibility was good aeroplanes were very active during the day. No photograph registrations.	J.W.J.
			Casualties: No. 224,833 Gr. Evans W.G.74075? Gr. Laley R. C. Bty. wounded	
	10th		Heavy Harassing fire was kept up during the night D/256 carried out mustard gas shoots on Battery Position at Q4c009abb area Q10d a mustard C16 & Q15b & Q16a kept up. The only morning harassment (Shown on Air Photos Q15b & Q16a. The morning generally quiet. Visibility poor. Enemy Artillery quiet. R8ECD & Canal Bank Area not shelled at intervals. Aeroplane inactive	J.W.J.

Army Form C. 2118.

192

WAR DIARY
or
INTELLIGENCE SUMMARY.
(Erase heading not required.)

Instructions regarding War Diaries and Intelligence Summaries are contained in F.S. Regs., Part II. and the Staff Manual respectively. Title pages will be prepared in manuscript.

Place	Date	Hour	Summary of Events and Information	Remarks and references to Appendices
Gidès	1918 July 11		At 2 am this morning 183 Infantry Brigade carried out a minor Operation. The field Artillery covering the 61st Div. (less 255 Bde.) put down a rolling Barrage lasting for 26 minutes. Heavy artillery & T.M. co-operated (see appendices) 183 Bde. front — rolling Barrage. The nature of the Barrage was also suffered heavy losses by running back into own Barrage. There was practically no reply to our Barrage from enemy artillery in addition the usual night firing was done. Visibility good. Steady registration of Calibrations were checked. Enemy artillery chiefly most active during the day calling ROBECQ LES AMUSOIRES, Canal Bank & BUSNES. There was also a marked increase in the use of Gas Shell. Various intervals throughout the day specially in the LES AMUSOIRES - Canal Bank area.	24.A.
	12		13 pm. Our own punishment Anti Tank Guns firing 15 rounds on Carpentier Farm assembly trenches – Q.10.15.76. 18 pm & 4.5 How fired during the night on Carpentier assembly trenches. Visibility fair. Enemy Artillery less active. Aircraft was very active throughout the day. Our Bombing planes were active during the night.	20.2
	13		Night harassing fire was maintained mostly after 2 am until after dawn. Enemy Artillery quiet. Visibility good. Aeroplanes not quite not active.	24.1.

WAR DIARY
or
INTELLIGENCE/SUMMARY

(Erase heading not required.)

Army Form C. 2118.

193

Place	Date	Hour	Summary of Events and Information	Remarks and references to Appendices
Field	1918 May 14		At 11.55 pm. barrage of 355 + 358 Bde. R.F.A. put down a Box Barrage supporting Raid by 1/4 Infantry Bde. on home + orchard at Q14 d 7.4 (see Appendices) The raiding party reached their objective + captured 2 prisoners in the orchard + withdrew without suffering any casualties. Enemy Artillery made little or no reply. Harassing fire carried out as usual. 4.5 How & 17 pdrs carried out general shoots during the day on known Barrages v. with good effect. Enemy direct SOS were obtained + casualties inflicted. Enemy Artillery shown more activity today especially general back areas. Visibility was good all day & aeroplanes were very active particularly between 6 + 9.30 pm. Night bombing was again carried out by us. Casualties killed No 7/3116 S. Welton P(D)	2nd L
	15th		At 11.30 pm. last night a raid was carried out by 1/82 Infantry Bde. on the Steenen in Q2c. 238 Bde Co-Operated in the Barrage. The patrol which went out of the main objective of the attack was found to be empty but prisoners were picked up out of shell hole on the bank of the Stream. The usual harassing fire was maintained. Hostility again good + forced shooting was effectively done on places S.15 — Q22. targets — Q15 + Q16. Enemy Artillery less active. There was a general increase in hostile aerial activity during the day + there was a considerable amount of enemy flying bombing between 9.30 pm — 11.30 pm. Hostile observation balloons were also much in evidence during the day. Casualties 635750 L/Bdr. W. Jones A.B. Bty. wounded at duty.	2nd L

WAR DIARY
or
INTELLIGENCE SUMMARY

Army Form C. 2118.

Place	Date	Hour	Summary of Events and Information	Remarks and references to Appendices
Judé	1918 May 16th		Continuous harassing fire was carried out. Visibility good. Observed shoot on Howrs. Beams etc. was carried out during the day. Enemy artillery fairly quiet. Aircraft active during the afternoon evening. A considerable amount of night bombing by both sides took place. Casualties: 285403 Gr Clark & Y 872 Sr. E Davis D.R. Lee killed. 635958 Gr. Freeman W D. Bty. wounded at duty.	Nil
	17th		Harassing fire & usual retaliatory shoots noting barrage, Enemy artillery quiet during the day except for some shelling by H.V. Guns in Back areas. Hostilities were again very active. A counter "Contact" took place — 6 E.A. reported driven down. Night firing was again carried out.	Nil
	18th	C.1. 3.48 a.m.	This morning a special 5 minute concentration was carried out from 1st Army mobile Artillery Reserve at 5.15 p.m. (see appendices) Visibility fair. Enemy artillery quiet.	S.R.L
	19th		Harassing fire was maintained. Fire selection 5 minute special concentration shoots were carried out 3.10 a.m. & 4.15 p.m. Enemy artillery quiet during the day until 8.30 p.m. when our support Trenches were heavily shelled. There was considerable activity in front of the Division on our right. Hostile planes were very active early this morning firing Verey lights & bombing machineguns. Under instructions from XI Corps 51 Divl. Arty is interchanging with 61 Divl. Arty which at present covering the 4th Division XIII Corps on our right. 255 Bde. located gun with 306 Bde. R.F.A. 256 Bde. " " 307 Bde. R.F.A. 1 am 19.4.20 & 21st inst. gun for Battery changing on east side.	Nil

(A7892). Wt. W12859/M1293. 75,000. 1/17. D.D. & L., Ltd. Forms/C2118-14.

WAR DIARY or INTELLIGENCE SUMMARY

Army Form C. 2118.

Place	Date	Hour	Summary of Events and Information	Remarks and references to Appendices
Field	1918 May 19	7.30p	The interchange of front sections with 306 Bde. took place. Guns were not exchanged.	205
	20		Harrassing fire was maintained during day. Twilight, visibility poor & our own & enemy's aeroplanes were very active. Enemy artillery was quiet.	
		9.30p	The interchange of second sections with 306 Bde. took place.	205
	21		The night was quiet except for rumours from north. Visibility was good. Recy. T. Personnel check at Mines Havrincourt & Hermies Carrying parties.	
	1/-		General of Batteries & Brigade period. Repetitive this morning north of Gouzeaucourt were as follows:-
			A/251. 2 guns V.12c.30.11. 4 guns V.11d.80.30.
			B/251. 6 guns V.11g.80.50.
			C/251. 5 guns V.11c.55.70. 1 gun V.11.6.6.L.
			D/251. 3 Hows. V.11d.65.90. 3 Hows V.12c.81.73.
			H.Q.P. V.10.d.75.75. BUSNETTES.
			Rd. Cr. for Ammn.
			The Cavalry covering the 4th Division was composed as follows:-
			Right Group. Group Commander Lt. Col. Bacon D.S.O.
			32nd Bde. R.F.H. (4 D.A.)
			256. Bde. R.F.A.
			Left Group. Group Commander Lt. Col. W. F. L. Paton D.S.O.
			29th Bde. R.F.A. (4 D.A.)
			255. Bde. R.F.A.

WAR DIARY or INTELLIGENCE SUMMARY

Army Form C. 2118.

Place	Date	Hour	Summary of Events and Information	Remarks and references to Appendices
Lillers	1918 May	21	Regtl Group S.O.S. Lines were as follows:— 52" Bde — Q34d 3550 — Q34c 0095 256 Bde — M7258. Q27c30 — 7060. B7258. Q33b 1560. Q33a 7085 Q7258. Q33a 7085 — Q27c 3090 (2 guns) Q33a 8595. Q29d 4555 (a gun) D7258. mortar targets	
		22nd	Harassing fire was carried out at decreased expenditure in Route Trench vaquelikea. Every Gallery Sault Green at 7.45pm — 10.15pm an enemy M.G. opened fire South. The enemy bombarded the area Q31a & party heavily with mustard gas between 11pm — 9.12 midnight.	No 3
		23rd / 31st	During the period under review nothing unusual happened. Rumours were rife tonight that an entire enemy Regt was in what the 18th Div. considered more or less visibility was poor during this period owing to ground mist. Church in Chapel Mt in PACAUT & PARADIS was carried out. The Brigade Commander M.G. Coys carried on his own accord got two O.Ks — one being an Artillery observer on the march. Mobile artillery were generally quiet — BERNENCHON, BOMMEHEM, Tank Corps intermittently shelled Rusplaun, Rich Hu Kule rounds and active enemy contact took place between Enemy machines were seen down. Night flying bombing was unsuccessful generally. The Batty positions were improved Bagul controlled to D/258 near Wood Vid 6590. Casualties during this period N.L. 17th mounted Brigade 2 W.Hd Sin. 2 O.R. killed. 2 others W. 3 W.H./568 Group at Vid 6590 2 O.R. killed, 2 O.R. W. Wid 8030.	No 4

Army Form C. 2118.

WAR DIARY
or
INTELLIGENCE SUMMARY.
(Erase heading not required.)

Instructions regarding War Diaries and Intelligence Summaries are contained in F.S. Regs., Part II. and the Staff Manual respectively. Title pages will be prepared in manuscript.

Place	Date	Hour	Summary of Events and Information	Remarks and references to Appendices
Field	1918 May 31		The following is a record of the Ammunition expended during the month	197
			18 pdr — 26,915 rds	
			4.5 How — 7,130 BX	
			1,127 Gas Shell	
			Total 35,172 rounds	
			Honours & Awards received during the month.	
			Legion d'Honneur (Chevalier) Lt Col. T.M. Ryan D.S.O — Authority 5I(H) D.R.O. N° 999 dated 28/4/18
			D.S.O. Major R.R. Will B/256 — Authority 5I(H) D.R.O. N°1015 dated 18/5/18
			M.C. 2/Lt. a.B. Twist Queen A Battery } Authority Third Army N° HR
			M.C. 2/Lt H.C. Green A Battery } 1360 g 14/5/18 & 5I(H) D.R.O
			Bar to M.C. 2/Lt a.B. Twist Queen A Battery } N°1869 g 14/5/18
			M.C. 2/Lt D.M. Gordon C Battery } Authority II Corps R.O. N° 248
				g 22/5/19
			Mentioned in Despatches - King's Messenger R.R.Will B Battery
			Birthday Honours Gazette dated Captain H.A Ollett Late g D/256
			June 1918. 4/13633 Sgt. g. Gealy g 8/256
			Bar to M.M. 635694 Cpl Lambley A } Authority XI Corps R.O. N° 184 &g 4/5/18
			M.M. 636113 L.A. Cpl Lefroid g } B Bay. Set. g issued 8/5/18
			D.C.M. 636194 A/L a.f m. Lock B/256 } Authority 3rd Army R° HR/1360 g 14/5/18.
			M.M. 16585 B.S.M g. Z Revie B/256 } - 5I(H) D.R.O. N° 1007 g 17/5/18.
			R.Cdm 4/3090 Gunner Morris W. C/256 } Authority II Corps R.O. N° 248 g 22/5/18
			A.C.M. 4/13633 Sgt g. Gealey D/256 } Authority II Corps R.O.
			N° 4.A. Gibson &/256	
				BFK g 3
				Comdg. 256 Brigade R.F.A
			2/6/18	197

Confidential

War Diary

257 Bde. RFA. (T.F.)

From 1st June 1918 to 30th June 1918

(Volume ---)

Vol 38

Army Form C. 2118.

198

WAR DIARY
INTELLIGENCE/SUMMARY
(Erase heading not required.)

Instructions regarding War Diaries and Intelligence Summaries are contained in F. S. Regs., Part II. and the Staff Manual respectively. Title pages will be prepared in manuscript.

Place	Date	Hour	Summary of Events and Information	Remarks and references to Appendices
Field	1918 June 1/2/3		During the past 3 days nothing unusual happened. Harassing fire was maintained during the night. Wire cutting & special Eno concentration shoots were carried out by 4.5" Hows. Enemy Artillery has been quiet. Visibility good. Aeroplane shewed none activity on both sides. Under instructions received from 4th Division, 57th Divl Arty. are to be relieved on night 3/4 and 4/5th as follows:— 255 Bde. R.F.A. by 65th Army F.A. Bde. ⎫ see Appendices 256 Bde. R.F.A. by 104th Army F.A. Bde. ⎭ Bde. Battery Commanders of 104 Army Bde. visited Bde. & Battery positions today. & arrangements were made for the Relief.	
	4th	10 p.m.	One section of Battery relieved by corresponding section of 104 Bde. Relieved Section withdrew to wagon lines. The usual night firing was kept up. Registration of 104 Bde. Guns in action was completed.	W.J.
	5th	M.30 p.m. 2 a.m.	Relief of remaining sections completed. Relieved section + Bde. Head.qrs. withdrew & Bde. rendezvoused at ALLOUAGNE. Bde. marched to CAUCOURT (N. of AUBIGNY) via MARLES-LES-MINES – BRUAY, HOUDAIN arriving CAUCOURT 7 a.m.	
	6th		Bde. came under XVIII Corps & remained in 1st Army Reserve. Bde. was inspected by Maj. Genl. R.A. 1st Army (Genl Alexander).	W.J.
	7th	3 p.m.	All Brigade Guns + Hows. calibrated at PETEWAWA Calibration Range. E.g. Gony-Serving Brigade Horses & Lines were inspected by 1st Army Commander Genl. Sir H.S. Horne K.C.B. K.C.M.G. along with M. & R.A. 1st Army, G.O.C. 57th Divisn. C.R.A. &	W.J.

WAR DIARY
INTELLIGENCE/SUMMARY
(Erase heading not required.)

Army Form C. 2118.

199

Places	Date	Hour	Summary of Events and Information	Remarks and references to Appendices
field	1918 June 6/14		During this period, the Brigade carried out an organised scheme of Training including Rifle drill, Gun drill, Driving & Riding drill, Battery Staff Rides. Wired signalling also firing at the Rifle Range. Orders received from 51st D.A. to relieve the 15th Divl. Arty. (covering the 51st Division) in the line on nights 16/17th and 17th/18th as follows:—	
			255 Bde. R.F.A. to relieve 71st Bde. on the Right Sector.	App J.
			256 Bde. R.F.A. to relieve 70th Bde. on the Left Sector. (see appendices)	App J.
	15th		Bde. Battery Commanders Reconnt party proceeded to 70 Brigade H.Qrs. (ROELINCOURT). B.C.s reconnoitred Battery Positions. O.Ps & completed arrangements for Relief.	
	16th	3 pm	Brigade marched to ERANT (Amp. - ECOIVRES (P.14 & 66) via CAMBLIGNEUL, CAMBLAIN L'ABBÉ A/Cs arriving ECOIVRES 6 pm.	
		10 pm	3 Subsections per Battery relieved corresponding Sections of 70th Bde. in action. Guns were not exchanged.	
	17th	11 pm	Relief completed. Battery Positions taken over were as follows:—	
			A/256 - 5 guns A30c 8520 &/256. 5 guns A18d 08	
			1 gun B10d 4535 1 gun B7b 00	
			1.15 pdr A.T gun B20b 0440	
			B/256 5 guns A18c 2582 D/256 Howitzers A18d 2582	
			1 gun B19b 1545 2 Hows B13c 5275	
			H.Qrs. were established at A29 a 1.4. Waggon Lines remained at ECOIVRES	Appx K.

The

Army Form C. 2118.

No. 200

WAR DIARY
INTELLIGENCE SUMMARY
(Erase heading not required.)

Place	Date	Hour	Summary of Events and Information	Remarks and references to Appendices
Field	1918 June 17		The disposition of the Artillery covering the 51st Division was as follows:— Right SubGroup – 255 Bde. R.F.A. covering Right Infantry Bde. Left SubGroup – 256 Bde. R.F.A. covering Left Infantry Bde. also 51st D.A. T.M. Batteries (12 6" Newton T.M?) XVII Corps T.M. Battery. (1 – 9.45" T.M) Left H.A. Group United SubGroup also still acted as C.R.A. 57th Div.	as appendices pages 1–
	18		Registration was completed. Visibility was good. Enemy artillery showed little activity	P.W.J. P.W.J.
	19		Observation was poor up to 2 pm. After this it improved. Harassing fire was carried out during the night on Roads Tracks Communication Trenches & in Bde. Zone. A Enemy working Party in C7C was dispersed by C/255 with good results. D/256 fired on suspected T.M. emplacements. Enemy Artillery Quiet. Aircraft active.	P.W.J.
	20		Observation not good today. Enemy Trenches & back areas were harassed during the night. B/255 fired & destroyed new work at B18a 80.85 & B18a 80.45. From 6pm to 7 pm all forms and Guns searched area in B6C. Enemy Artillery Quiet Wagon Lines moved into wagon lines vacated by 15th D.A. of Julian. Napoo Battery rear Lines. Battery wagon lines — F15C & F21A.	
	21	3am	256 Bde. co-operated in Artillery Scheme at MADAGASCAR CORNER. A26c 45.15. White 45th Infantry Bde front. (see appendices) The raid was very successful & resulted in the capture of about 15 prisoners while a large	P.W.J.

(A7092). Wt. W12835/M1293. 750,000. 1/17. D. D. & L., Ltd. Forms/C.2118/14.

Army Form C. 2118.

WAR DIARY
INTELLIGENCE SUMMARY.
(Erase heading not required.)

Instructions regarding War Diaries and Intelligence Summaries are contained in F. S. Regs., Part II. and the Staff Manual respectively. Title pages will be prepared in manuscript.

201

Place	Date	Hour	Summary of Events and Information	Remarks and references to Appendices
Field	1918 June 21		number of the enemy estimated at about 100 were killed. Machine Guns & Trench Mortars destroyed. The Enemy retaliation was slight.	JWJ
	22		Harassing fire was carried out in addition. The day was generally quiet. During early part of day haze prevented good observation. Afternoon very good and forward Guns & Hows active throughout the night. Harassing Parties & Headquarters. Enemy artillery quiet. Aircraft active.	JWJ
	23		Of the enemy were engaged during the day. Enemy artillery quiet. Working Party in Harassing fire maintained during the night. Visibility good today. Enemy artillery slight. B6.6 engaged by forward Guns at 5.45pm & dispersed. Enemy artillery slight activity on B26 d & q BAILLEUL.	JWJ
	24		Visibility good today. Special harassing Scheme carried out in early morning. 4.5 Hows. fired in — destroyed new work in B12 a also on enemy Carpenter T.M. position. Enemy artillery quiet.	JWJ
	25		Observation good this am. 18 pdrs. fired on enemy Trenches, registering junction & offset and working parties engaged. Enemy artillery slightly was intermittent. Shelling of BAILLEUL vicinity also BISCOT heavily shelled with 5.9 from 8.30pm to 8.45pm. Pool	JWJ
	26		Visibility good. Harassing fire carried out all night. Special hostile chart by Br. Km. officer harassed. Enemy artillery quiet. Aircraft active. Several E.M. attempted to cross our lines.	JWJ
	27		Observation carried owing to haze our guns active last night & today. Special harassing fire between 3 & 4 am carried out. Enemy artillery quiet.	JWJ
	28			

WAR DIARY
INTELLIGENCE SUMMARY
(Erase heading not required.)

Army Form C. 2118.

Place	Date	Hour	Summary of Events and Information	Remarks and references to Appendices

Field	1918 June 28/30		Harassing fire maintained on Enemy Trenches, Tracks & communications by night. Many small Enemy working Parties engaged by our ground guns. Instructional shoots to Junior Officers were carried out. Visibility was good during this period. Enemy Artillery active. at 1110 pm on 28th Bde. cooperated in Artillery (support covering) Raid by 1/7th "Black Watch" on Enemy post in B24a (NORTH TYNE ALLEY). The Raiding Party found the Posts unoccupied & returned without suffering any Casualties. (See Appendices) During the period 1st to 3rd June & 17th to 30th June the following amounts of Ammunition were expended.
			
			  1st June to 3rd June. 933. 18 pdr. 188 BX 100 Cars Shell
			  17th June to 30th June. 8206 18 pdr. 2537 BX 100 Cars Shell
			  ───── ──── ─────────
			  9139 18 pdr. 2723 4.5 How. Cars Shell
			
			 Casualties :- Killed Nil
			  Wounded 18/6/18. 23173. Gr Trueman P. B" Bty
			  24/6/18. 660253 Gr. Aitcheson M. " (at duty)
			  29/6/18. 127832 Yr. Shelton M. "
			
			 During the period 20/6/18 to 30/6/18. a fever known as "Three Day" fever broke out in the Brigade. An average of about 40 men per day were affected. Honours.
				See 2
				
				 ML
				
				 ML

Army Form C. 2118.
203

WAR DIARY
INTELLIGENCE SUMMARY.
(Erase heading not required.)

Place	Date	Hour	Summary of Events and Information	Remarks and references to Appendices
Field	1918 June		Honours & awards received during the month for gallantry & devotion to duty during the period from 20th September 1917 to 20th February 1918 in Kings Birthday Honours Gazette dated 1st June 1918.	
			Major J.B. Meikle C/256 — Military Cross	
			Major R.R. Will D.S.O.	
			Captain H.A. Ollett, Late D Battery } mentioned in dispatches	
			Captain R.C. Macpherson late B Battery	
			Bombdr. R. Mackenzie B Battery D.C.M.	
			Sergt. J. McGray C Battery M.S. Medal	
			Sergt. J. Illidge D Battery mentioned in dispatches	W.S.

3/7/18

S.G. ——, Major R.F.A.
Comdg. 256 Bde. R.F.A.

Divisional Artillery

51st (Highland) Division

256th BRIGADE   R. F. A.

J U L Y. 1 9 1 8.

Confidential

War Diary
of
252 Brigade R.F.A. (T.F.)

From 1st July 1918 to 31st July 1918

(Volume ———)

Vol 39

WAR DIARY
INTELLIGENCE SUMMARY
(Erase heading not required.)

Army Form C. 2118.

Place	Date	Hour	Summary of Events and Information	Remarks and references to Appendices
Field	1918 July 1st		Harassing fire carried out on tracks, communication trenches &c throughout the night. Visibility poor. Own aircraft very active. Small parties of hostile enemy engaged. Enemy artillery quiet. Our own enemy aeroplanes active.	Ref J.
	2nd		Harassing fire as usual. Visibility fair throughout the day. Movements were engaged indifferent on B12A58, C13C58 + B13C83. Enemy Artillery channel slightly more activity. Enemy flashes by enemy gun fire. Aeroplanes active. Enemy balloon brought down in flames at 11.30am.	Ref J.
	3rd		Special area harassing fire Scheme carried out. 4.37hrs carried out destructive shoots of enemy new work. Known movement of small enemy working parties now engaged by 18pdrs. Visibility good. Enemy artillery inactive.	Ref J.
	4th		No harassing fire was done during the night. Visibility good. Enemy artillery quiet. E.A. active. 4.37hrs carried out shoot with Aeroplane observation on hostile Battery at B9C8490 with good results - several OKs received.	Ref J.
	5th		Harassing fire vigorously carried out during the night. Visibility fair. Enemy Artillery quiet. Exception shelling of back areas. Enemy are fairly inactive. A/258 exchanged main Battery position with C/255 under arrangements made between Batteries concerned. New Battery position A/256 - A18C7004. No. 188598 P. Jones S. (B) Wounded. 63043 P. Preble A. " "	Ref J.
	6th		In addition to the usual overnight harassing fire opened intentional shoots. Officers + NCOs were carried out. Visibility good. Enemy artillery more active than usual. Many flashes of hostile batteries near positions located.	Ref J.

Army Form C. 2118.

205

WAR DIARY
or
INTELLIGENCE SUMMARY.
(Erase heading not required.)

Instructions regarding War Diaries and Intelligence Summaries are contained in F. S. Regs., Part II. and the Staff Manual respectively. Title pages will be prepared in manuscript.

Place	Date	Hour	Summary of Events and Information	Remarks and references to Appendices
Field	1918 July 7th		No harassing fire was sent during the night. Visibility was poor all day. Enemy artillery had active. Our own harassing planes active throughout the day.	P.W.J.
	8th		Harassing fire carried out throughout the night. Visibility good. Intentional shoots between Observation O/Pos & Bys, taken on by 9our 5/5 How Bat'y, 4.5 How Bat'y, & graphical test of forward Observation Post of enemy. 5.5 How Bat'y carried out destruction shoot on C.T. & front junction with good effect. 1 retaliation of Infantry 92052 Ft. Julio H. 669739 Ft. Samuel L. 18959 Ft. Beach S. 222955 Ft. Clark T. at C.Battery killed.	P.W.J.
	9th	at 12.30 am this morning 258 Bdr. co-operated in Barrage covering Raiding Party of 152 Infantry Bdr. on the enemy trenches in B11c and d. No identifications were obtained. – Harassing fire continued as usual. Hostile aircraft were active. 1 EA brought down at 11.15 a.m. near Italian wood out of a flight of 5. Many flashes of enemy guns seen & positions located.		P.W.J.
	10th		Visibility good during 10th. Our own working party & casualties inflicted. Enemy artillery shewed more activity than 9/ery. Enemy planes again active. 1/30/90 Ft. Norris W. (D) Wounded.	P.W.J.
	11th		Harassing fire as usual. Visibility fair. Rather intentional shoots carried out. Enemy artillery less active than last few days. Our own planes very active during day. Our own flight bombing machines active by night.	P.W.J.
	12th		Harassing fire was kept up during forenoon with more ment of Enemy observed retaliation enemy artillery more active shelling forward back area. Under orders received from D.A. (Rectorn) 9 Batteries were relieved by comprising	P.W.J.

WAR DIARY
or
INTELLIGENCE SUMMARY.
(Erase heading not required.)

Army Form C. 2118.
206.

Place	Date	Hour	Summary of Events and Information	Remarks and references to Appendices
Field	1918 July 12		Sections of 4th Canadian F.A. Brigade Relieved sections without change to wagon lines. (see appendices). Guns were not exchanged.	W.J.
	13.	2.30am	Boo Barrage was carried out covering front opposite Left Bde, Right Batteries co-operated in general barrage firing scheme at Zero plus 1 hour & from 3am to 5am. (see appendices)	W.J.
		10/pm	Remaining sections of Batteries relieved & proceeded to wagon lines. Orders had been received that Brigade on relief would move to EHS starting at 2.30 am 14.d. These orders were however cancelled at 8pm. Instructions received that Batteries would remain amalgamated with relief until further orders. Hqrs. proceeded to ECOIVRES after completion of relief where they were billeted for the night.	W.J.
		11.30pm	Orders received that Divisional Artillery would march to staging area prior to entrainment	W.J.
	14.	9am 2pm	Hqrs. & B/256 marched to BAJUS. A.F.C. Batteries marched to MAGNICOURT. D/256 remained at wagon lines. Orders received that Division was entraining for an unknown destination. (see appendices)	W.J.
	15.d		256 Bde. proceeded to BRIAS & entrained thus as follows:- Hqrs. 2pm, A/256 5pm, B/256 11pm, D/256 proceeded to TINCQUES & entrained there at midnight (see appendices)	W.J.
	16.d	8am	Orders were received en route from front authorities that Bde would detrain at HERME & NOGENT - 60 miles S.E. of PARIS. Hqrs. Train arrived at HERME at 8.30pm after 28 hours journey. Detrainment was complete by 7.30pm.	W.J.

Army Form C. 2118.

WAR DIARY
or
INTELLIGENCE SUMMARY.
(Erase heading not required.)

207

Place	Date	Hour	Summary of Events and Information	Remarks and references to Appendices
Field	1918 July 16	8.35am	Negro. & No. 2 Section D.A.C. marched to MONT/GOTHIER - 10 miles N.E. of HERMÉ. 51st Divisional Hdqrs. was at VILLENEUVE. Batteries on arrival at detraining station received orders to march to the SEZANNE area.	
	17th	10.30am	Hdqrs. & No. 2 Section D.A.C. marched to VILLENEUVE SAINT VISTRE - 6 miles South of SEZANNE.	
		6pm	Orders received for Brigade to proceed to the area NORMÉE & ÉCURY LE RIPOS. (4 miles N.E. & N. of FÉRE-CHAMPENOISE respectively) march to be completed by 12 noon 18th. Batteries to march independently.	
		11pm	Hdqrs. accompanied by No. 2 Section D.A.C. marched to ÉCURY LE RIPOS via SÉZANNE - FÉRE-CHAMPENOISE, arriving ÉCURY LE RIPOS at 8 am. Batteries on arrival were billetted as follows:- A/255 - at NORMÉE. B/ & C Batteries at ÉCURY LE RIPOS where they remained overnight.	R.o.J.
	19th	2pm	Orders received for Brigade to proceed to AY - 2 miles N.E. of ÉPERNAY. Brigade marched to AY via MORRAINS - LE PETIT - VERTUS - MAREUIL S/AY. arriving AY 1 am 20th. R.R. Wilk R/255 had proceeded on ahead earlier in the day to act as Liaison Officer with the 153 Infantry Brigade.	
	20th	5pm	On arrival at AY, Brigade was met by C.R.A. 51st Div. Orders were received that 51st Division were to attack the enemy at 8 am 20th in conjunction with the French & the 62nd Division until 51st Divisional Artillery would march to the in opposition & readiness to support the attack by Zero hour. Bde. proceeded to position of assembly - South Eastern	
		2am	Orders were accordingly issued +	

WAR DIARY
INTELLIGENCE SUMMARY

Army Form C. 2118.

208

Place	Date	Hour	Summary of Events and Information	Remarks and references to Appendices
Field	1918 July 20		Outskirts of BOIS-de-NANTEUIL about 1 Kil. North of the Nlage of NANTEUIL. Bos. arrived there at 6 a.m. Main Support Lines were established at AY	M.J.
		8 a.m.	The attack of the 57th Division was covered by a Barrage from the French Field & Heavy Artillery. 57th D.A. did not take part in the Barrage. The Boundaries of the 57th Division attack were as follows:- Right flank - Ruvu ARDIS - 62nd Division being on the right. Left flank - CHAMPLAT - VILLE EN-TARDENOIS - 14th French Division being on the L/A. Objective. First Objective. Blue line } see Map & Offensive Second Objective. Brown line } Line. Orders were received that after the final artillery Barrage had ceased, the 253rd & 258th Bdes. would support the attack with own fire at the earliest possible moment, moving forward in close support & co-operation with the Infantry Bdes. 253rd Bde. was instructed that with the 154 Infantry Bde. on the Right, 253rd Bde. with the 153rd Infantry Bde. operating on the left. At 10.30, 6/30 acted as Bde. Liaison Officers with 153rd Infantry Bde. & Majors 256 Bdes. were established along side their Hqrs. in Bois de NANTEUIL. The advance of the 153rd Infantry Bde. was very successful knowing prisoners were taken. By 9 a.m. the Battalions began to move	
		9 a.m.	forward in close support. Situation of the 154 Infantry Bde. was very obscure. Officer Patrols when have been pushed forward about 961 Zero reported that the Right flank of the 154 Bde. had been	
		12 noon	unable to push forward owing to the 62nd Division having been held up on the right.	
		12.45 p.m.	Later reported that the German line was only hardly held & that the 153rd Infantry Bde. had gained their first objective completely. Batteries came into action by 11 a.m. 500x Lieut f. POUREY & some of the K. Battery brought down a slow Barrage 100 yards N. of Reed	
		12.30 p.m.	61-12 Superior orders received E W through CHAMPLAT. Fire was immediately opened on the line Pat.f.

Army Form C. 2118.

WAR DIARY
INTELLIGENCE / SUMMARY
(Erase heading not required.)

Instructions regarding War Diaries and Intelligence Summaries are contained in F. S. Regs., Part II. and the Staff Manual respectively. Title pages will be prepared in manuscript.

Place	Date	Hour	Summary of Events and Information	Remarks and references to Appendices
Field	1918 July 20	At 12.55 a.m.	Our Officers Patrols reported that MARFAUX was still held by the enemy. Orders were immediately sent to the Battns to be careful of their right flank & open fire were issued & the Battns to put up by occasional bursts on Bois, etc. FELISSES to the western slopes thereof – 500y beyond Green Line. Battercoss opened fire on these Targets.	
		2 p.m.	Defensive Battery Positions were also reconnoitred in the neighbourhood of Assembly Positions & 2/55 Bde were manoeuvred after a forced march & sent to act NW of CORMOYEUX. Fire was kept up during the afternoon by occasional bursts of fire.	
			As the intention for the night was still to observe Battery, one Battery was ordered to withdraw to Defensive Position previously reconnoitred and Battery left behind was to sit on allocated supports of the infantry from about taking on any "Target" that might present themselves. Batteries accordingly withdrew at 7 p.m. took up positions North of thereabouts.	
			CORMOYEUX. The 153 Infantry Bde were laid out as follows: SOS lines covering Point on the MERVILLE – CHAUMUZY Road where N° 270 E. & W. Grid Line 258 Bde. from Point on trench Road to Point where N° 7 N.-S. grid line cut out. W. three along Road to Point where road from South Western boundary of Wood R.A.C. from that Point thence along round 153 Bde Zone	G.W.R.
	21st	9 p.m.	New SOS lines were ordered as follows: on a line N.E. – N. of MAYLES – Bee Zone. The line remained unchanged of Bde – the 57th Division relieved the enemy in conjunction with the 62 Division &	G.W.R.

A10266) Wt W5300/P713 750,000 2/18 Sch. 58 Forms/Cal18/16.

WAR DIARY
or
INTELLIGENCE SUMMARY

Army Form C. 2118.

2/0

Place	Date	Hour	Summary of Events and Information	Remarks and references to Appendices
Field	1918 July 21		The Artillery supporting the Division was distributed as follows: Covering the 154 Infantry Bde on the Right — 285 Bde RFA, 246 R.A.C. (3 Groups French), the 153 Infantry Bde on the left — 252 Bde RFA, 41 R.A.E. (3 Groups French), 37 R.A.E. (1 Group French). 2 Groups French Heavy Artillery covered the Divisional front. 256 Bde co-operated in the Barrage until entangled wire delayed their advance to take if their places in the Barrage as soon as they got out. Batteries accompanying moved forward on the occasion of PARADIS being captured. On the occasion of BEUVRY-SOUS-CHATILLON it was ascertained however that the trench system in rear of that PARADIS still remained in enemy hands & that forced this Batteries to be withheld to take up their old positions. The place was taken later by the 51st Division through continuous infantry attacks during the day. The enemy artillery has been very active all day, the Railway W. of MONTAGNE engaged targets Enemy Artillery on line Vineyards N. of Red Post Lane 30.S. W. Junction E. of W. through CHAMPLAT. Awaiting 2/Lt J. Henderson killed: 271408 Cpl. R.H. Cunningham (Hyp); 249576 Cpl. Burke H. (H.P.); 2/Lt J.G. Daintyhill (C) 249557 Gnr. J.M. O'Neill (HQ); Wounded 223073 L/Bdr P.A.H... (H.Q); 636125 Gnr G. Todd (C); 99941 Pt. Vickery T.(C); ...	Nil

WAR DIARY
INTELLIGENCE SUMMARY
(Erase heading not required.)

Army Form C. 2118.

Place	Date	Hour	Summary of Events and Information	Remarks and references to Appendices
Field	1918 July 21		Casualties 21st Killed Capt. J.C.T. Taggart (Medical Officer) Wounded 636457 L/Sgt Brown (C) 635499 L/Cpl Cuthill (A) 781460 Pte. Winter W.(A) 622245 Pte Lewis G.(A) 635142 Pte T. Robertson (A) 211264 Cpl Rushbrook J.(A) 645818 S.P. Matheson (A) 638955 D.A. Davidson (A-) 157709 Pte Watts A.B.(C) Pte 101340 Pte Kerr H.(C) Pte 856088 St. Lorenck (C) Pte 232037 St. Mansfield J. (C) Pte 	RNSJ
	22nd		Demur was maintained on the enemy today. At 5 p.m. the 9th French Division attacked with Objectives PARADIS & LA NEUVILLE 153 Infy Brigade co-operated with instructions to push forward immediately with the French PARADIS was bombarded from 3 pm by Heavy & Field Artillery. The French were unable to push forward more than 1/2 up by heavy M.G fire. S.O.S. been remained the same till 9 pm. 256 Bde were established along ridge to Balleau W.L.P. began S.O.S with Keown with 152 Infantry Bde. Enemy Artillery had been very active during the day. The Battalions were subjected to heavy gas bombardment during the night	RNSJ
	23rd		Casualties 22nd Killed Nil Wounded 249553 Pte Shepherd B. (H.Qrs) only. Harassing fire on back areas had been carried out during the night at 5 and 152 Infantry Bde attacked the enemy in conjunction with an attack by the 62 Division on their right. (see appendices) 513 Bde's first on the Barrage:- 256 Bde covering the Zone of the left attacking Battn 255 Bde. The Heavy & Field Artillery co-operated. French Tanks assisted	RNSJ

Army Form C. 2118.

WAR DIARY
or
INTELLIGENCE SUMMARY
(Erase heading not required.)

Place	Date	Hour	Summary of Events and Information	Remarks and references to Appendices
Field	July 23		Our objectives were gained practically along the whole front from line were established as follows: - Western edge of the BOIS de PETIT CHAMP - 600 metres W. of COUTRON 500ᵗ West of MARFAUX - Western edge of the BOIS de H. AULNAY to the east of ESPILLY which still remained in the enemy's hands. Between 200 + 250 prisoners were captured - this operation belonging to 3 different divisions. A + C Batteries moved forward to positions W. of MARFAUX. S.O.S. lines for the night remained on full Protective Barrage Lines. Batteries were again (previously) bombarded with gas shell throughout the night.

Casualties: Wounded: Capt. J.C. McKay M.C. (C)
Lieut. D.m. Gordon M.C. (C)
A.R.S. Taylor (C)
2/Lt. U.H.J. (C) 635100 Dr. Bam C(C) 635031 Gr. Munn W.F. (C) 636459 A/Bdr.
9/Lane (C) 635055 Etc. Jones W. (C) 22129 Gr. Hunt W. (C) 635520 Gr. Cowell D (C)
C/286 { 635768 Gr. Lawn D. (C) 635048 Dr. Potts (C) 97628 Gr. Nailer (C) 78599 Gr. Parker F (C)
635204 Gr. Bennett W. (C) 636532 Dr. Bem J. (C) 945458 Dr. Rigby F. (Gnr.)104708
Dr. Robson A.(C) Gnr. 37189 Dr. Phillips CH. (C) Gnr. 636452 Dr. Rhelock (C) Gnr. 119804
Dr. Metcalfe (C) Gnr. 635308 a F/Sgt. Seagrove E. (C) Gnr. 635768 A/Lieuten W. (C) Gnr.
635148 A/D. Donald G. (Gnr.)(C) 246646 Gr. Crompton E. (C) Gnr. 636180 Gr. Leeler J. (C) Gnr.
955208 Gr. Page L.R. (C) Gnr. 635022 Gr. McDonald A. (C) Gnr. 635146 4/Bdr. Grant B. (C)
A/286 { 122675 4/Bdr. Humboldt W. (A) Gnr. 645831 4/Bdr. Miller T. Gnr. 16687 of Bdr. Palmer FC A/Gnr.
214150 Gnr. Tattersall W. (A) Gnr. 760945 Gr. Hannesak A.R. 152019 Gr. Cane F. (A) Gnr.
94 5054 Gr. Maddox A. (A) Gnr. 66433 Gr. Dawn E. Gnr. 635841 Dr. Roberts E. Gnr. Q.M. | 2/2 |

Place	Date	Hour	Summary of Events and Information	Remarks and references to Appendices
Field	1918 July 23		Casualties 23rd Cnt.?	2/3
		B/25?	635626 Sgt. Hammond W.635614 L/Sgt. D. McDonald 660253 Pr. Gibson 635796 Pr. B. Taylor 935624 Pr. Deakin C. 236612 Pr. S. Jackman 143381 Pr. N. Kininburg 53043 Pr. A. Priddle 635748 Pr. J. Jones 70276 Pr. P. Reid 798262 Pr. Rodgers H. 75362 Pr. J. Smith 213613 Pr. W. Hanrath 21420 Pr. W. Hearn all Gassed. Pr. W. Hanrath 21420 Pr. W. Hearn all Gassed. Pr. H. Wilson 406143 L/Cpl. W. Wood 146194 Pr. W. Young 635352 L/Bdr. Enstaliatz 227781 Pr. S. Hertzel 351527 Pr. J. Shaw 217703 Pr. H. Haywood all gassed	
		Welsh	24,959 L/Cpl. Crichton 249533 Spr. B. Whyherd 267662 Pr. S. Hertzel 351527 Pr. J. Shaw	
	24		153 Infantry Bde. was relieved in the line by the 35th Regiment 14th French Division the left flank of the 51st Division was altered in consequence as follows:- CHANTEREINE Farm - Road through the DE of BOIS - DE - COUTRON - Northern edge of the Bois DE SARBRUGE - Road junction 1 Kilometre East of FORMOYEUX (all inclusive) to BELLEVUE (Exclusive) to 51st Division. The Right flank of the 51st Division remained the same - River ARDRE. The line was held by the 152 Infantry Bde on the Right from the River ARDRE to point 204, 400 metres East of Espilly. By 154 Infantry Bde on the left. The dividing line between Bdes being from point 204 to point 8246 & thence to NANTEUIL. 256 Bde. R.F.A. covered the 154 Infantry Bde. + 255th Bde. R.F.A. covered the 152 Infantry Bde. Bde. Hegrs. moved forward & established new Hegrs. in NANTEUIL leaving 154 Infantry Bde. No attack was made today. The line remained unchanged except that in the Bois de COUTRON our patrols made a little ground by peaceful penetration. C.P.was established communication by horse Manual with Battns + Bde. Hegrs. Officer Patrols + F.O.O.'s went forward as usual + kept in touch with the Infantry of the General situation.	3rd S.

WAR DIARY / INTELLIGENCE SUMMARY

Army Form C. 2118.

Place	Date	Hour	Summary of Events and Information	Remarks and references to Appendices
Juld	1918 July 24		B v D Battery moved forward to Paitons 500ⁿ NW of MONTENIL	
			A Battery moved forward Paiton 200ⁿ N of MONTENIL. B Battery moved to new Position 1200ⁿ N of MONTENIL. The whole of the areas were complete Harassing fire on the enemy back areas was carried out.	
	25		Casualties Killed 746/237035 S. Endrew; A/C. C Bty. Wounded 31499 Sgt. T. Knowlley 45213 Sj W. Wadie 680720 Sj. Morgan J. 232412 Sj. Goodhur T. 636222 Sj. S.E. Trail 930311 Sj. P. Pullen 205889 Sj. Q. Smith 18321 Sj. N. Wilkes 635375 Sj. W. awellatone (only) [bracket] 125732 Bdr. Crust 643646 L/B. G. Easton 636404 D. E.A. Robertson 138053 Dr. Brady J. 0816 D. J.G. Smith 165919 Dr. R.W. Wilas 178637 Dr. A. Litherland 635383 Dr. G. Wertz 1/781 1741 C.J. Cathik 236714 Dr. G.J. Pickering 79591 Dr. J. McCartney 765374 Dr. W. Zadall 67440 Sj. Snow 246543 Sj. N. Butler 633409 Sj. F. ...ward A 436662 Sj. J. Holland 1/781 370 F. Elliott 1235012 Dr. J. Lyppl. Shiria D.R. Raven 234827 Dr. W. Payne 636435 Dr. P. Kelly 489643 D. Acford 109048 D. J. Just 193728 D. J. Popp 185362 Dr. H.... 32480 Dr. Hinterby Gassed	Not J.
		9/5a	B/236- 9/556-29 G/df. Prayer 6	
	26ᵗʰ		The line remained unchanged. No attack was made today. Batteries carried out ... shoots on back areas & target of enemy position. Harassing fire on Roads tracks & centres of activity was vigorously carried out by any tactics. Casualties Gassed 232738 Sj. J. Ryley 155266 Sj. H.W. Greener 334769 Sj. M.H. Conley 635409 Gk. C. Edwards. 636464 Sj. J. Hollan	W. J.
	26		The line held by us remained the same. The Tank Corps on our left attacked the morning & advanced their line. They also captured a number of prisoners. Several shots were carried out by Batteries during the day. At 7:30 pm Batteries replied to an SOS. No enemy attack took place, firing slackened into a slow ordinary Harassing fire forward & back areas. especially BELL along the ANDRE Valley 635752 P.B. Shanks 635377 Sj. London 635687 Sj. G. Crippole 636182 Sj. Robertson 223179 Sj. T. Collinio 635792 Bdr. S. Robertson 635727 Sj. S. Kelp 221244 Sj. C. Wattinson acc D/256.	W. J.

Army Form C. 2118.

WAR DIARY
or
INTELLIGENCE SUMMARY.
(Erase heading not required.)

2/5

Place	Date	Hour	Summary of Events and Information	Remarks and references to Appendices
Field	1918 July 27		At 6 am this morning the 153 Infantry Bde & the 187 Infantry Bde (62nd Division) attacked on the front BOIS D'AULNAY to the main Ridge in the BOIS de COURTON in conjunction with an attack by the Corps on our left. 51st Div. Artillery covered the advance with a creeping barrage which henry of left Artillery also co-operated. French tanks also took part in the assault. Officers Patrols pushed forward as usual at the commencement. Both attacks met the enemy pickets, and heavy barrages of the enemy was laid down. W & NAKES – 2188. 2704 was reported as having been received by 10 am the final objectives along the line W & NAKES – 2173. 2684 – Boo metres all along the line. By 10 am the final objective Infantry advanced with very little infantry opposition. By 10 am the Infantry reached what eventually the large N edge of BOIS des ECLISSES W of CHAUMUZY. Moulin de CHAUMUZY, SE corner of BOIS de COURTON. SE corner of Bois des ECLISSES with the Right of Bois also pushed forward as the N edge of the Bois de ECLISSES with the Right of taking of a defensive line on the Western edges. The advance of the 153 Infantry Bde was supported by 258 Bde. The enemy fire had was practically absent at 10 am. but became heavy on the Northern advance of CHAUMUZY & the W edges of the BOIS DE REIMS giving particular attention. Batteries moved forward at 3 am from 8 N.E. corner of BOIS de L'AULNAY. A/258 C/258 New Pounts No. 8 N.E. corner of BOIS de L'AULNAY. B/258 & D/258 Limbo Road 200x E of Pointe road below the 4 of BULLIN & A/258 Batteries BULLIN. Batteries silenced immediately they opened fire on Pt.–1.00 x N of the mill. Hdqrs were established at Mill de ARDRE on Spur. Pt.–1.00 x N of the mill. 153 Infantry Bde & Hdqrs between 400 South of LES GARINETTES transmission established with them. 153 Infantry Bde Patrols pushed onwards Officers Patrols reported that the Bois des ECLISSES was	

WAR DIARY or INTELLIGENCE SUMMARY

Army Form C. 2118.

Place: Field
Date: 1918 July 23

and a Bde. of 62nd Division on this night with orders to pushing & establishing a line MICHAEL RENAUT FARM & high ground N. of CHAMBRECY. No artillery support (beyond the back area) was wanted as the position of the French was uncertain. Attempts were made during the night to advance to within 500x from Infantry but owing to heavy shelling & the exposed nature of the Valley the enemy M.G. fire it was found impossible to come into action.

The advance made some progress but was held up by M.G. fire & a few prisoners were captured. S.O.S. lines for the night were put down on a line running through MICHAEL RENAUT FARM to point 128.9.

154 Infantry Bde. relieved 153 & 152 Infantry Bdes. in the main line & withdrew to the ridge south of CHAMBRECY Bois & ECLISSES & the ravine west of CHAMBRECY both being maintained with the 62nd Division on right & French on left 152 Infy. Bde. moved to area South of BULLIN Farm & 153 Bde. to area named NAPPES.

During the night the Regt. put up a heavy harassing fire on all roads & tracks routes of activity to the ARCY Road, and villages though our front were engaged with Heavy artillery during the night. The Enemy made systematic use of gas shells – shelling Bois de ECLISSES & the Valley of the ARDRE.

Casualties: Killed 680594 Gunner T. Whittle C.B{y?}
Wounded 202602 Cpl. H. Lodge (C) 635046 Gr. A. Grains (C) 926074 St. G. Mills (C) 233641 St. J. Thurney (C) 645722 St. J. Kirkwood H.Q (early) 635431 Gr. W. Burick (A) 636209 Gr. J. Logan (A) 645754 Gr. J. Franer (A) 635917 4 Bde 9 Mess (B)
Hurt H.B. Cardwell B/253
Gassed 774004 4/Bde J. Oliver (A)

P.W.L
P.W.J

24. No further attack was made today, but positions gained were improved. Patrols pushed forward & our line was slightly advanced. Harassing fire by my tonight was kept

WAR DIARY
INTELLIGENCE SUMMARY
(Erase heading not required.)

Army Form C. 2118.

Place	Date	Hour	Summary of Events and Information	Remarks and references to Appendices
Field	1918 July 27		Clear of the Enemy. Main Boche I and Infantry seemingly hesitant forward to support the old trench line (Colour Redan trap) West of the BOIS des ECLISSES. SOS lines were put down as a precautionary measure during any line. Harassing fire on back areas was carried out during the night. Casualties Nr. 44/258 O.R. D. Mid (A) Wounded. 44/258 Tr. Kitchens. 44425 Tr. Kitchen. Buried 782417 4/Bde. Gatling out 64494. 0911 W. Kitchen. A/258	Ref.
	28		Mounted Patrols went forward at dawn & found the line held to be last night. Battalies moved forward in close support & new position taken up as follows:— D/258 at 11am in Dukes Post 500° S.W. of CHAUMUZY — Negro were established F/258 at 11 am ... at S. of CHAUMUZY along side D/258 A/258 + C/258 12 noon in Valley 1000x one S. of CHAUMUZY. In nothing forward the Batteries came under direct observation MARFAUX + CHAUMUZY were engaged by the Enemy. They had to push forward rapidly over 1/2 mile of exposed country before coming under cover of the BOIS des ECLISSES. They also sustained a ... rate B/258 in moving forward was also hindered by Enemy Aeroplanes which dropped numerous ... bombs on chopped site round them but no casualties were sustained. The Infantry continued to push forward Patrols during the morning. 62 Division on our right attacked MONTAGNE de BLIGNY this morning & captured Officers + 60 O.R. The Batt are in complete possession of the southern & south eastern slopes while the enemy hold the northern slopes — 153 Infantry Bde hang in touch with the French on their left south of CHAMBRECY. ago and established in the Northern edge of the Bois de ECLISSES. Telephone communication was maintained throughout in addition to Liaison mounted Patrols at 1.30pm 153 Infantry Bde advanced in conjunction with the 14th French Division on their left. Ref.

Army Form C. 2118.

WAR DIARY
or
INTELLIGENCE SUMMARY
(Erase heading not required.)

Place	Date	Hour	Summary of Events and Information	Remarks and references to Appendices
Field	1918 July 29		Up on back areas. Casualties Killed 645897 Pte M Wyllie (B) 223260 Pte S.E. Walmsley 168211 Pte L. Moore (B) 672031 Pte D. Blackey (B) 640773 Fr. Ackerley (B) Wounded Gassed 635077 Pte W. Ritchie	218
	30		No further advance was made today. Observed shoots were carried out on back areas. 1/236 took on silenced a hostile Battery which was firing on & fading on the front system. Regular harassing fire was also kept up during the night. Orders were received that 57th Divl. Artillery would be relieved by tom morrow night & that A.D. (Tr. Bk.) today as follows. 253 Bde. hfto 1/pm → 236 Bde. at 6 am 31.7. 314 gpm. Bellona replaced by 505 on Right. Battalion front. No other known Casualties Nil	
	31.	6am	236 Bde. withdrew to Wagon Lines & took no further part in the Operations all the Ammunition on hand had been expended during the previous 24 hours. The Battery Positions were cleared up and all surplus cartridge cases returned to dumps. The total ammunition expended during the Operation was as follows. 16,838 18 pdr 4,577 4.5 How Casualties Gassed 193283 Gr K. McPherson (B) The total casualties sustained by the Brigade during the Operations were as follows:-	Pul

Army Form C. 2118.

WAR DIARY
or
INTELLIGENCE SUMMARY.
(Erase heading not required.)

Place	Date	Hour	Summary of Events and Information	Remarks and references to Appendices

Field	1918 July 31		As follows:
			
			      Officers Other Ranks
			Killed 1 8
			Wounded 7 (2 at duty) 32
			Gassed 2 84
			      —— ——
			Total 10 148
			
			The number of Horses lost in the 3 actions were as follows:
			    Killed 24
			    Wounded 46
			    Gassed 51
			        ——
			    Total 121
			
			Orders were received that 51st Divl. Arty. would proceed by Train today & tomorrow to First Army Area (see appendices) entraining (entraining time table) Negro 256 Bde marched to entraining station – AVIZE S – 8 miles S.E. of EPERNAY & strained at 3 pm. Batteries marched independently to entraining station – times of entraining being as follows:
			1/18/18 A/256 7.30 am. B/256 3 pm. C/256 11 pm
			5/8/18 D/256 7.30 am.
				219

5/8/18

2n Johnston Capt a/Lieut Col
B 256 Bde. RFA.
Comdg. 256 Bde. R.F.A.

Confidential.

98 40

War Diary

256 Brigade R.F.A.(T.F.) (51st Div)

From 1st August 1918 to 31st August 1918.

(Volume No.   )

Army Form C. 2118.

WAR DIARY
INTELLIGENCE/SUMMARY.
(Erase heading not required.)

220

Place	Date	Hour	Summary of Events and Information	Remarks and references to Appendices
Field	1918 August 1st		'A' 'B' 'C' Batteries entrained at AVIZES - 8 miles S.E. of EPERNAY - as follows :- A/256 - 7.30 a.m. B/256 3 p.m. (EPERNAY Station) C/256 - 11 p.m.	P.v.J.
	2nd		D/256 entrained at AVIZES at 7.30 a.m.	
	2nd/3rd		Hdqrs. & Batteries detrained at CALONNE on arrival & marched independently to ACQ.	P.v.J.
	3rd/10		Divisional Artillery came under the orders of the XVII Corps 1st Army. During the period under review Brigade personnel at rest in ACQ. Batteries were reorganised & reequipped. Reinforcements received & gun cmts. & workshops for overhaul. A general scheme of training was begun.	
	8th		His Majesty the King visited First Army Area. The Brigade was formed up on the ECOIVRES - ACQ Road - & welcomed the King as he passed.	P.v.J.
	9th		51st (H) Division came under the command of the XXII Corps & remained in G.H.Q. Reserve ready to move at 24 hours notice	P.v.J.
	9/15th		The Scheme of training was vigorously carried out - including Riding Drill, musketry, signalling, Battery driving drill, Battery Staff Rides, V.C. & Competition was held between Batteries of 255, 256 Bdes. 5th Div. on Gun ms/gun drill & Teams complete & resulted as follows :- 1st A/255 2nd A/256 3rd D/256. Absolute/matched pairs of horses 1st D/256 2nd A/255 & B/255 equal.	P.v.J.

WAR DIARY
INTELLIGENCE SUMMARY
(Erase heading not required.)

Army Form C. 2118.
221.

Place	Date	Hour	Summary of Events and Information	Remarks and references to Appendices
Field	1918 August 13th	12	Orders were received that 51st (H) Division would be prepared to relieve the 52nd (Lowland) Division in the line forthwith. Later orders were received that 51st Divisional Artillery would relieve 52nd D.A. in the line on the nights 14/15th & 15/16th. (see Appendices) Orders issued accordingly & arrangements made for B.C's to reconnoitre positions of 9 a.m. tomorrow.	
		12 midnight	Orders received that 252 Bde. would stand fast & that other arrangements were being made.	P.M.D.
	14th		Orders received that 256 Bde would relieve a Brigade of 57th D.A. in the line North of the SCARPE on nights 16/17th & 17/18th. This rendered necessary owing to a re-adjustment of the line. Battery Positions of 285 Bde R.F.A. (57 Div Arty) reconnoitred by B.C's	
	15th	10 pm	Two sections per Battery relieved corresponding sections of (57 D.A.)	P.M.D.
	16th	10 pm	Relief completed (see Appendices) The positions taken over were as follows:— A/256 4 guns {H7.a.0889 2 guns {H7.c.6727 C/256 4 guns {H7.a.6010 2 guns {H13.c.2525 Wagon lines ANZIN Area. B/256 4 guns {H1.d.2734 2 guns {H1.b.4090 D/256 4 Hows {H7.d.55 2 guns {I3.c.a.2530 Bde Hdqrs were established at. H7.a.12	P.M.D.

Army Form C. 2118.
222

WAR DIARY
INTELLIGENCE SUMMARY
(Erase heading not required.)

Place	Date	Hour	Summary of Events and Information	Remarks and references to Appendices
Field	1918 Aug. 18		The 57th (H) Division commanded the sectors of the XVIIth Corps. The line was taken over as follows:— The Division relieved the Right Subsector (N. of GAVRELLE) of the 52nd Div. on 16th. In relieving the Centre & Left (Subsectors) (N. of Right SCARPE) of the 57th Division. In addition the Right Bde. 57th Division (S. of SCARPE) remained in the line & came under the G.O.C. 57th Div. The line is being held as follows:— 170 Infantry Bde. (57th Div.) on the Right South of the SCARPE, covered by 177 Bde. R.F.A.	
			152 — Dº — 51st Div. on the Right Centre from SCARPE to H11C85150 covered by 186 Bde RFA	
			153 — Dº — Dº on the Left Centre from H11C85150 to B29C3535 covered by 256 Bde RFA	
			154 — Dº — Dº on the Left from B29C3535 to B23b65 covered by 255 Bde. RFA.	
			Regtl. 153 Infantry Bde. were established at C12 b 83 (beside 238 Bde. Hdqrs.). Harassing fire was carried out. Throughout the night a prisoner captured by 57th Div. late night south of the SCARPE reported that enemy had withdrawn bulk of troops to general line BIACHE – PELVES – MONCHY leaving only a few machine guns in his front line as a screen & during the capturing the enemy's outposts South of the River SCARPE. The attack was unsuccessful 5 prisoners & a machine gun being captured.	P.S.L.
	19th	1 am	2/256 co-operated in a Barrage supporting an attack by 170 Infantry Bde. with the object	ref.

WAR DIARY
INTELLIGENCE SUMMARY

Army Form C. 2118.
223

Place	Date	Hour	Summary of Events and Information	Remarks and references to Appendices
In the Field	1918 Aug 19th		Throughout the day observed shoots were effectively carried out. Visibility was good.	
	20"		Harassing fire was vigorously carried out throughout the night & enemy's back areas & approaches. Batteries moved their detached sections to man Battery Positions. Special harassing fire shoots were also done during the day. Enemy Artillery more active shelling our new positions south of the SCARPE constantly.	Inf.
	21"	1.30am	2 Col 1 Bn. Span RH, 4 MDA 2 MGR H. 2sger RH, and BP 2 & Bn. bn. in support of Brigades 232 Bde. concentrated in a Barrage covering an attack by the 152 Infantry Bde on enemy French immediately N. of FAMPOUX (see Appendices). The operation was successful, the enemy being driven out of the village & an enemy man captured.	
		1.35 am	395 gas projectors were successfully fired upon the enemy trenches opposite 153 Infantry Bde. front.	
		4.55 am & 6.55 am	256 Bde. carried out a 2 hours bombardment in co-operation with operations South of the SCARPE by Canadian Corps (see Appendices). During the day Batteries continued their Harassing fire programme. In addition B/256 effectively cut Enemy wire opposite 153 Bde. front.	Inf.
	22"		During the day our 18 pdrs + the 3" How. were engaged in registration & wire cutting. Whilst Artillery quiet. Our planes were active during the day. Visibility good.	Inf.

Army Form C. 2118.
224

WAR DIARY
or
INTELLIGENCE SUMMARY.
(Erase heading not required.)

Instructions regarding War Diaries and Intelligence Summaries are contained in F. S. Regs., Part II. and the Staff Manual respectively. Title pages will be prepared in manuscript.

Place	Date	Hour	Summary of Events and Information	Remarks and references to Appendices
Field	1918 Aug 23		Harassing fire was kept up as usual on enemy tracks, C.T. approaches, O/25B fired a special gas shoot. Batteries were engaged during the day in wire cutting. Hostile Artillery quiet throughout the day. Our aircraft was very active. Visibility good. 51st Division came under the orders of the Canadian Corps at 12 noon today.	2nd/
	24		Increased harassing fire was done by Batteries during the night.	
		4.30 am	An attack was carried out this morning by 153 Infantry Bde on the Enemy front trenches with a view to establishing the line Zion Alley – HYDERABAD slag support line to H5-d.91. 256 Bde. Co-Operated in the Barrage covering the attack (see Appendices). The attack was successful except on the left flank where considerable bombing was encountered inside a pocket of the Enemy held out. A few prisoners were captured. Wire Cutting was continued by Batteries who opened barrage put down at zeroehr hold by Enemy most were captured this morning. Hostile Artillery quiet. Aeroplanes active. Forward Battery Positions were reconnoitred in view of an advance.	M.L. 2nd/
	25		The usual harassing fire was maintained.	

WAR DIARY
INTELLIGENCE SUMMARY
(Erase heading not required.)

Army Form C. 2118.
225

Place	Date	Hour	Summary of Events and Information	Remarks and references to Appendices
Field	1918 Aug/ 25.	4.10am to 5.10am	Batteries replied to an SOS & beat off a hostile attack on new positions gained y'day. The attacking party was beaten off by M.G. & Rifle fire brought in our Barrage.	
		6am	253 Bde. O. Spotted in a creeping Barrage covering an attack made by 153 Infantry Bde. with a view to extending the line captured y'day. The attack had been fixed to take place at 5am but owing to the hostile attack between 4 and 5 am, it was postponed until 6am. The attack was again very successful all objectives being gained & a few prisoners captured. Batteries fired during the day on enemy movement & bombarded Enemy O.P.s. Harassing fire was maintained until midnight.	
	26	3am	Canadian Corps (part of the SCARPE) on our Right attacked the Enemy positions south of the SCARPE. 51.(H) Division co-operated North of the SCARPE but did not attack until later. The attack was carried out by 2nd & 3rd Canadian Divisions – 3rd Canadian Division being on the left between the SCARPE & the ARRAS – CAMBRAI ROAD. The field Artillery covering the 3rd Canadian Division was disposed as follows:–	
			9 Bde. C.F.A. Rotators group. 52nd AFA Bde. 180 Bde. RFA 57th A.A. group	
			10th Bde. C.F.A. 126th AFA Bde. 253 Bde. RFA	

WAR DIARY
INTELLIGENCE SUMMARY

Army Form C. 2118.

226

Place	Date	Hour	Summary of Events and Information	Remarks and references to Appendices
Field	1918 Aug 26		The Field Artillery cooperated by putting down a creeping Barrage (see Barrage Map & Appendices) The attack was completely successful. We have captured MONCHY LE PREUX, ORANGE HILL & Area E. of BOIS du SART, GUEMAPPE WANCOURT, HENINEL, the high ground S. of the latter place. Over 500 prisoners were captured & several guns. Orders were received that in the event of the operations of the Canadian Corps being successful, the 51st Division would attack & in rising the line from CORDITE trench through CAKE Avenue, CHICKEN Reserve to Tony Alley.	
		10 am	The attack took place at 10 am by the 153 Infantry Bde. & was covered by a Barrage put down by 237 Bde. RFA. 255 Bde. RFA. 180 Bde. RFA. (see Appendices) At the same time 152 Infantry Bde. were to undertake operations between the Railway & the SCARPE & were covered by 177 Bde. These attacks were successful. The Germans first defensive system S. of GAVRELLE being carried & the Chemical Works being captured & outskirts of ROEUX reached. GAVRELLE was reported clear of the enemy.	
		7pm	at 7 pm 153 Infantry Bde attacked GREENLAND HILL under a Barrage covered by 236, 255, 180 Brigades R.F.A. The attack was again successful & our 2nd.	

Army Form C. 2118.

Army Form C. 2118.

227.

WAR DIARY
or
INTELLIGENCE SUMMARY.
(Erase heading not required.)

Instructions regarding War Diaries and Intelligence Summaries are contained in F. S. Regs., Part II. and the Staff Manual respectively. Title pages will be prepared in manuscript.

Place	Date	Hour	Summary of Events and Information	Remarks and references to Appendices
Field	1918 Aug 26		Infantry succeeded in reaching the crest of the hill. Harassing fire was maintained vigourously kept up throughout the night. New Battery Positions were reconnoitred further forward.	
	27	10 a.m.	The Advance of our Infantry was continued today. 153 Infantry Bde again attacked this morning, the objectives being the Northern & Eastern edges of Greenlock Hill. The attack was covered by 255, 256, 180 & 177 Bdes R.F.A. F.O.O. Liaison officers were sent forward as usual. The Infantry met considerable resistance & bombing by the Enemy in the Railway Cutting which up a line WISPER & CARVE Trenches. The Batteries moved forward & came into action in previously reconnoitred positions as follows:— A/256 H15 8 80.75. B/256 H16 a 19. C/256 H15 d 80.75. D/256 H10 c 20.15. E/256 H15 6.75.	J.H.S.
		2.30pm	At 2.30pm a further attack was launched between the Railway & the River by 152 Infantry Bde & was covered by 255, 256, 177 & 180 Bdes R.F.A. The attack was carried forward to Church Trench (west of HANSA & DELBAR Woods) between checked there by the resistance of the Enemy M. Guns. Patrols and troops were compelled to withdraw. P.T.O.	

(A9175) Wt. W2358/P360 600,000 12/17 D. D. & L. Sch. 82a. Forms/C2118/15.

Army Form C. 2118.

WAR DIARY
INTELLIGENCE SUMMARY.
(Erase heading not required.)

Place	Date	Hour	Summary of Events and Information	Remarks and references to Appendices
Field	1918 Aug 27		to withdraw to the line of Quent, Chico & CARVE owing to Enemy Troops being in force in the Railway Cutting. During there attacks the enemy retaliation was weak. S.O.S. lines fixed through went put down on a line I.9.d.o.4 along the Green Line to I.9.b.o.5 - I.3.d.o.5. Harassing fire was vigorously engaged in throughout the night. Enemy Troops & approaches to	N.S.
	28"		No Operations was carried out today beyond Infantry Patrols pushing forward. Batteries carried out observed shoots & special area shoots at the request of the 153 Infantry Bde. This was continuously and not especially on sunken Roads + trenches in I.9.c. where the enemy were strongly holding out also in GAVRELLE Support & Count Avenue in C.26.c.+d.	
	3/pm		Bde. Hqrs moved forward to new Hqrs. beside 153 Infantry Bde. at I.10.c.39. forward Battery positions were reconnoitred & positions prepared	
	4/pm		It was reported that the HANSA & DELBAR Works were clear of the enemy & Infantry Patrols were accordingly pushed forward. In order to keep in touch with these patrols a Brigade patrol consisting of 12 men under 2/Lt. McNEILL M/256 was sent forward, the patrol proceeded forward carried touch with forward Patrols established a sub-service of 2 Lewis Guns + Rifle	J.A.S.

WAR DIARY
INTELLIGENCE SUMMARY
(Erase heading not required.)

Army Form C. 2118.
329

Instructions regarding War Diaries and Intelligence Summaries are contained in F. S. Regs., Part II. and the Staff Manual respectively. Title pages will be prepared in manuscript.

Place	Date	Hour	Summary of Events and Information	Remarks and references to Appendices
Field	1918 Augt. 28	7.30 pm	153 Infantry Bde. reported that Enemy were again bunching down C.T. on our flank in I2a. A Heavy Barrage was put down on these trenches & fire kept up throughout the night. D/258 bombarded SQUARE WOOD & HOLLOW COPSE with Gas Shell. Special harassing fire scheme including two transport Barrages between 3.30 am & 3.55 am. 4.30 am & 4.56 am were carried out.	
			153 Infantry Bde. were relieved in the line by the 154 Infantry Bde. & the Northern Divisional Boundaries readjusted (see Appendices). S.O.S. lines for the night covering the 154 Infantry Bde. were put down as follows:— 252 Bde. I15a 3055 – I9c14 – L9c04 – L27c04. 253 Bde. I13c00 – L27c00. 177 – 180 Bdes. R.F.A. covered the 152 Infantry Bde. on the Right.	
			Casualties 67/244 Pr. Wilson Q. 172033 Pr. J.A. Wains 224/312 Pr. Morris P. C/258 wounded. 646 803 Pr. Walters Q. A/258 (gassed) 1416 Bdr. Bird W. 228268 H/Bdr. Ward S. D/258 wounded.	J.M.C.
	29	6.30 am	At 6.30 am 154 Infantry Bde. attacked the enemy positions with a view to capturing the line (Old French K I15a 36 – I9c15 thence along WALK & WILLOW TRENCH to WHISPER TRENCH	J.M.C.

WAR DIARY
INTELLIGENCE SUMMARY
(Erase heading not required.)

Army Form C. 2118.
230

Place	Date	Hour	Summary of Events and Information	Remarks and references to Appendices
Field	1918 Aug 27		The attack was supported by 253, 256, 177 & 180 Bde RFA also 2nd Canadian Bde R.G.A	
			The attack was successful, all the objectives being gained by 8am & a number of prisoners captured	
		10 a.m.	A & C Batteries moved forward to previously reconnoitred positions West of the Chemical Works - A/256 - H.18.d.45.30 C/256 H.18.b.8.4 & were in action by 11:30am	
			4.5 Hows in cooperation with Heavy Artillery bombarded HAISH & DELBAR Woods from 12 n to 1pm & thereafter lifted to & kept up a steady fire on CRIB Trench from I.15.d.0.3 southwards. Our Patrols pushed forward & passed through the woods & occupied CARAVAN Trench beyond.	
		4:30pm	B & D Batteries moved forward beside A & C Batteries & came into action B/256 - H.18.d.0.5 D/256 H.18.d.15.30	
			Registration was carried out. D.P. established in GREENLAND HILL. 51st Division came under command of 22nd Corps at 12 noon. Zones were rearranged as follows:- 177 Bde. R.F.A. to cover 152 Infantry Bde. 180 & 255 Bdes to cover 154 Infantry Bde. 256 Bde superimposed over 180 Bde Zone with orders to be prepared to switch on to any part of the Divisional front. No harassing	Ses

WAR DIARY
INTELLIGENCE SUMMARY

Army Form C. 2118.
231.

Place	Date	Hour	Summary of Events and Information	Remarks and references to Appendices
Field	1918 Aug. 29		Fire was carried out by 252 Bde. during the night. Ammunition was got up to new Positions. The night was quiet.	
	30		Observed shoots were carried out during the day. Infantry Patrols were pushed forward & Posts established well forward. Emergency SOS lines were put further back on the Enemy FRESNES-ROUVROY line of defence. Two aeroplane shoots were carried out by D/256 with good results. Enemy Artillery was fairly quiet. Visibility good. Casualties: 635233 Gr. Mills W. in 52725 L/Bdr. J. Tinkler 33406 Gr. Williamson A 20184 Gr. Cargyl killed W.B. 970546 A/Cpl. Conlin & Dvr A/256 wounded	
	31.		Harassing fire on Roads & Approaches to FRESNES-ROUVROY line was continuously kept up during the night. In addition D/256 fired gas shell in GLOUCESTER Wood Area. During the day Batteries engaged Dispersed all movement seen. Enemy Artillery more active - Casualties: 925989 Bdr. B/256 wounded.	
			The following amounts of Ammunition were expended by Brigade for period from 16/8/18 to 31/8/18 :- 18pdrs 33,070 A & AX 185 Smoke 4.5 How 6744 BX 517 Smoke 553 Gas Shell Total 33,255 rds 18pdrs. 7 7,764 rds 4.5" Hows	

2/9/18.

B. Major R.F.A.
Comdg. 256. RFA

Confidential

War Diary

235 Brigade R.F.A. (T.F.)

From 1st September 1918 to 30th Sept 1918

(Volume -)

Army Form C. 2118.
232

WAR DIARY
or
INTELLIGENCE SUMMARY.
(Erase heading not required.)

Place	Date	Hour	Summary of Events and Information	Remarks and references to Appendices
Field	1918 Sept 1		During the day Batteries registered new Zero lines & in the afternoon movement was engaged & dispersed during the night. Harassing fire was carried out on S.T. Knock Junction, Roads & Tracks leading to the FRESNES - RONY ROY Line. Hostile Artillery showed increased activity. FAMPOUX Area being heavily gas shelled. Visibility good.	
			4. Cpl Aiscaud D.S.O. became attached to Bde. Hdqr.	N.I.
		2	During the day various Enemy movements & targets were successfully engaged. Batteries put down a concentrated fire on Enemy's front line in retaliation to heavy bombardment of our Lines. Hostile Artillery again active. Our Battery positions were shelled with H.E. mixed with Gas. Harassing fire was kept up throughout the night. 8/256 N bombarded BIACHE with Gas Shell. The following Honours & Rewards were gained for work done during the MARNE Operations.	
			633373 Sgt W Waddington } Awarded M.M. by 38455 " T Linsley } 22nd Corps 21/8/18 633203 Cpl R Stacks }	
			671244 Gunner W Austin } "A" Battery } {-Do-} {-Do-} 635160 Sgt Hastings C } "C" Battery 2/Lt E J Dalziel B Battery - Military Cross - 31/8/18.	N.I.

Army Form C. 2118.

WAR DIARY
or
INTELLIGENCE SUMMARY.
(Erase heading not required.)

233

Place	Date	Hour	Summary of Events and Information	Remarks and references to Appendices
Field	1918 Sept 2		Honours & Rewards Cont. 637626 Sjt W Mourant "B" Battery} D.C.M. 41537 B.S.M. Ryan "A" Battery } 30/8/18. 637626 Sjt W Mourant "B" Battery. Mentioned in Fifth Army (French) General order No 363 of 9/8/18.	w.d. w.d.
	3		Various retaliatory concentrations on selected points in Y.E. of the FRESNES-ROZYROY Line were carried out. Considerable movement was reported at dawn in D25 C+D + an intense harassing fire was accordingly put down on Roads C.T.P. leading to Enemys front system. Enemy artillery again very active particularly during the night. "B" Battery positions & rampart area were again heavily shelled with gas shell. Enemy aircraft very active. Lt Col L.M. Ryan D.S.O. (who had been acting as C.R.A.) proceeded home on 3 months tour of duty.	
	4		Observed shoots were carried out during the day. At 2.2.5 pm + 3 pm 18 pdrs + 4.5 How put down a concentration on Enemys trenches. Hostile artillery continued active especially in Greenland Hill & Fampoux areas. Casualties: Captain J.C.D. Mackie (Gas) Wounded. Lieut E.N. Bagshawe & Lt. J. McNeill 2/Lt. Ryson C/236 Injured. 3" C.M. B/236 + D.I.	w.d. w.d.

WAR DIARY
INTELLIGENCE SUMMARY
(Erase heading not required.)

Army Form C. 2118.
2344

Place	Date	Hour	Summary of Events and Information	Remarks and references to Appendices
Field	1918 Sept. 4		Lt. Col. J.H. Nickle R.H.A assumed Command of the Brigade from this date.	
	5		Harassing fire was kept up during the night on selected targets. Slight enemy movement observed during the day engaged by our 18 pdr. Mobile Artillery again active shelling Battery Positions & Transport Lines.	
			180 Bde R.F.A. were relieved in the line on the night 4/5th by 176th Army Bde RFA.	
			The left Group covering the 51st Div. now consists of :-	
			236 Bde. R.F.A. } Bdes commanded Lt.Col. J.H. Nickle R.H.A.	
			175 Army Bde R.F.A. }	
	6		Casualties :- 26 O.R. D Bty. gassed. 7 O.R. C Bty. gassed. 10 O.R. D Bty gassed. Vigorous harassing fire was maintained during the night. Various targets were fired on during the day. At 10-15 p.m. enemy transport reported in BIACHE was fired on by 18 pdrs. r.4.5 How. - Casualties 22 O.R. gassed. D Battery 1 O.R 'A' Bty. gassed.	
	7		The usual harassing fire programme was carried out. A number of special concentrations were fired down on selected targets. During the day retaliation shoots were carried out at the request of the Infantry. Hostile A. activities especial activities good. D/236 were withdrawn to wagon lines.	
			Artillery quiet. Visibility good. D/236 were withdrawn to wagon lines.	
	8		Casualties :- 2 O.R 'D' Battery (gassed)	J.N.J

Army Form C. 2118.
235

WAR DIARY
or
INTELLIGENCE SUMMARY.
(Erase heading not required.)

Place	Date	Hour	Summary of Events and Information	Remarks and references to Appendices
Field	1918 Sept 8		Special harassing fire schemes were carried out during the night including concentration on hostile Battery positions reported active. During the day our fire was confined to registration & destroying individual movement. Little Artillery active. Casualties 1 O.R. C Bty. 1 O.R. B Bty. wounded (gas)	N.I.
	9		Harassing fire was kept up. Registration or destructive fire was carried out during the day. Enemy movement was engaged including concentrations at the request of the Infantry over front down. Casualties 2 O.R. (gassed) D Bty. 5 O.R. Sargent C By.	N.I.
	10		During the night all troops approaches to the FRESNES-ROUVROY Line, little Batteries reported active. Enemy's rear communications harassed. Movement was observed engaged on I.10 a & b – casualties inflicted. Hostile artillery quiet. Casualties. 2 O.R. 9236 Wounded Gas. B/236 withdrawn H. Guns to Wagon lines. The remaining Section was lightened.	N.I.
	11		Action to go on with harassing fire Y.C. The usual harassing fire programme was carried out during the day, bursts of fire were put down on the FRESNES-ROUVROY Line at request of Infantry.	N.I.

Army Form C. 2118.
236

WAR DIARY
or
INTELLIGENCE (SUMMARY).
(Erase heading not required.)

Instructions regarding War Diaries and Intelligence Summaries are contained in F.S. Regs., Part II. and the Staff Manual respectively. Title pages will be prepared in manuscript.

Place	Date	Hour	Summary of Events and Information	Remarks and references to Appendices
Field	1918 Sept 11		Hostile Artillery quieter. Forward Battery & Bate positions were reconnoitred & trenches made leading thereto. Casualties: 1 O.R. G/256 (Gassed) 2nr J.T. McNeill D/256 (died of wounds recd)	
	12		Usual harassing fire was maintained. Visibility was poor throughout the day. Enemy Artillery fairly active. Orders were received that the 51st Division would be relieved on the line by the 49th Division – the Divisional Artillery being relieved on the nights 12/13th and 13/14th. One section on the first night & the remainder on the 2nd night. 255th Bde. R.F.A. to be relieved by 246 Bde. R.F.A. and 256 Bde. R.F.A. by 246 Bde. R.F.A. Orders also received that 51st Div. Arty would move to ACQ & TREVIN. CAPELLE when relieved.	
	13	8.30p	Relief of one section of B Battery by corresponding section of 246 Bde. R.F.A. carried out. Relieved section withdrew to Wagon Lines. Casualties: 1 O.R. B/256 Wounded 1 O.R. B/256 Wounded (Gas) In addition to the usual harassing fire scheme – 187th D. Battery co-operated with Infantry Patrol at 12 midnight. Registration & was carried out during the day. Wagon Lines moved to ACQ at 15 aaw.	M.J. M.J.

Army Form C. 2118.
237

WAR DIARY
INTELLIGENCE SUMMARY
(Erase heading not required.)

Instructions regarding War Diaries and Intelligence Summaries are contained in F. S. Regs., Part II. and the Staff Manual respectively. Title pages will be prepared in manuscript.

Place	Date	Hour	Summary of Events and Information	Remarks and references to Appendices
Field	1918 Sept. 13	8 am	Remaining sections were relieved by 246 Bde. R.F.A. & withdrawn to Wagon Lines at ACQ. command passed to 246 Bde. R.F.A.	
			Ammunition expended from 1st to 13th inclusive	
			13,824 - 18 pdr. 905 4.5 How. 1882 4.5 How Gas Shell	
			Casualties from 1st to 13th inclusive	
				O.R.
			Killed	1
			Wounded	5
			Gassed 4	90
			Total 4	95	R.S.
	14/21		During the period under review the Batteries were reorganised & re-equipped. Reinforcements received & Guns sent to Workshops for general overhaul. Intense training was carried out by all Batteries which included Gun drill, Laying & tying setting, Rifle drill, Box Respirator drill, Driving drill, Marching & Saluting drill. In addition special drill Calif. schemes were carried out every afternoon which included Anti Tank Gun defence with Mobile sections, Co-operation & Communication between Batteries & Aeroplanes, Infantry attack under Artillery Barrage & Artillery co-operation to counter-attacking Machine Gun Sch. &c. Lectures were also given by the C.R.A. (see appendices)	237.

Army Form C. 2118.

WAR DIARY
or
INTELLIGENCE SUMMARY.
(Erase heading not required.)

Instructions regarding War Diaries and Intelligence Summaries are contained in F. S. Regs., Part II. and the Staff Manual respectively. Title pages will be prepared in manuscript.

Place	Date	Hour	Summary of Events and Information	Remarks and references to Appendices
Field	Sept. 21st	10.30 p.m.	Orders were received that 51st Division would relieve the 49th Division in the line & that the Divisional Artillery would relieve the 49th Div Arty on the nights 22/23rd & 23/24th. The 285th Bde relieving the 245th Bde covering PLOUVAIN Section & the 256th Bde relieving the 246th Bde covering GREENLAND HILL Section.	
	22d		255th Bde received orders that their move was postponed for two days.	ARMQ
	23rd		The 256th Bde calibrated at First Army Calibration Range PETEWAWA during the day & then moved up into action in the evening.	ARMQ
Field		9 p.m.	Relief completed & Batteries had taken over the following positions:- HQ. 256 Bde. H.16.d. 3.8. A/256. H.18.d. 42.50 B/256. H.18.b. 6.8. with wagon lines in MUSKETRY VALLEY. C/256 H.18.d. 15.59. D/256. (2 Hows) H.12.d. 20.25.	
		10.30 p.m.	Batteries carried out Counter Preparation for half an hour on order received from Brig. Gen. Comdg. 148 Inf. Bde, on Trenches from I.14.a.25.00 - T.10.a.85.65. Repeated at 5 a.m.	
		11.4 p.m.	Batteries opened on S.O.S. lines in response to S.O.S. Rocket & fired after first 20 mins at a slow rate until 11.54 when orders to cease firing were received from G.O.C. Batteries of 5 p.m. & 8 a.m. Batteries carried out harassing fire between	

WAR DIARY or INTELLIGENCE SUMMARY.

Army Form C. 2118.

Place	Date	Hour	Summary of Events and Information	Remarks and references to Appendices
Field			fire on trenches & approaches to FRESNES – ROUVROY Line. Visibility fair throughout the day.	OVB m.o. Q
	24th	5 am	Counter preparation was carried out by batteries on the FRESNES line until 5.30 am. During the day Registration was carried out. 18 pdrs harassed trenches & tracks in T.4 & T.5 – I.10 throughout the day & night. 4.5 Hows continued wire cutting in T.4 & C. Enemy artillery showed considerable activity about our front system. Visibility good throughout the day. E.A. active doing 9am bombing H.15. Casualties 1 O.R. wounded at being 300. 15th 2nd Bde. 8am. Counter preparation carried out by batteries until 5 am at request of 300. 15th 2nd Bde. 18 pdrs carried out registration & engaged movement during the day. 4.5 Hows continued wire cutting. Usual harassing fire carried out on FRESNES – ROUVROY line. Enemy artillery active on FAMPOUX area & Battery positions. 30 as shell fired on the latter area. Little movement observed during the day. Visibility poor until afternoon when it improved. Bde. received thanks of G.O.C. 4th Div. for its very efficient help on night 23/24th. A/256 withdrawn 15 wagon lines. 1 O.R. B/256 wounded whilst	AP & m Q CW R & Q
	26th		B/Batteries engaged enemy movement during the day & 4.5 Hows continued wire cutting	

WAR DIARY
or
INTELLIGENCE SUMMARY

Army Form C. 2118.

Instructions regarding War Diaries and Intelligence Summaries are contained in F. S. Regs., Part II. and the Staff Manual respectively. Title pages will be prepared in manuscript.

(Erase heading not required.)

Place	Date	Hour	Summary of Events and Information	Remarks and references to Appendices
Field	26th		At night the usual Harassing fire was kept up on the FRESNES — ROUVROY by & track approaches to it. Hostile artillery was throughout the day quiet in GREENLAND HILL area in front of 158th Bde. Visibility good after 10 am.	A8ME Q.
	27th	5.30am	Battery fired a harassing approximate with a Johnson attack by the Divisions (51st D.A. Order No. 155) (Number of Rds fired 1700 18th 146 4.5 Hows) Enemy movement was engaged by 18 pdrs during the day & 4.5 Hows continued to act some in front of the FRESNES line. During the night the usual harassing fire was carried out, special attention being paid to enemy M.G. & T.M. emplacements, situated in & near the FRESNES — ROUVROY. Enemy artillery showed increased activity. 300 rds 4.2 were fired into our front angles in I.14.b. F.A.M. P.8. v.x. was shelled intermittently throughout the day, a number of gas shell were fired into I.14.d. (Rly. Embankment) Much movement was noticed between VITRY & FRESNES — BRÉBIÈRES road. Enemy balloons were very numerous & stayed up all day. Visibility was good.	A8ME Q

WAR DIARY
or
INTELLIGENCE SUMMARY
(Erase heading not required.)

Army Form C. 2118.

Place	Date	Hour	Summary of Events and Information	Remarks and references to Appendices
Field	Sept 28th		Batteries engaged enemy movement during the day. H.S Hours continued wire-cutting. Harassing fire was carried out as usual on trenches, tracks & approaches to FRESNES – ROUVROY line, special attention being paid to enemy posts, T.M.G. emplacements. Enemy artillery fairly active especially on our trenches in the GREENLAND HILL area. A lot of movement was observed around GLOSTER WOOD & on the road from VITRY to this wood. Enemy aircraft very quiet during the day but were very active at night bombing. Visibility poor during morning, improving later.	W.B. in Q.
	29th		Registration of zero lines was carried out by Batteries. 18 pdrs & H.S Hours continued cutting wire in front of the FRESNES line. At 5.24 pm "D" By engaged a hostile RFA in C 29 d. 18 pdrs engaged enemy MG emplacements in the afternoon. At night harassing fire was carried out on tracks & approaches to the FRESNES – ROUVROY line. Hostile shelling was about normal & Q active. H Balloons observed during the morning. Visibility during morning good, but only four in the afternoon.	W.B. in Q.

Army Form C. 2118.

WAR DIARY
or
INTELLIGENCE SUMMARY.
(Erase heading not required.)

Place	Date	Hour	Summary of Events and Information	Remarks and references to Appendices
Front	Sept 30th		During the day Battery engaged enemy movement, fired on M.G. emplacement & also continued wire cutting in the FRESNES line. At night harassing fire was continued on roads & tracks approaching FRESNES — ROUVROY line. Hostile artillery activity was below normal & all seemed to be from long range, a few gas shell were fired into our outpost line about SQUARE WOOD. Enemy movement was very slight. Weather fine. Ammunition expended from 23rd inst to 30th inclusive :— 8,989 — 18 Pdr. 1501 — 4.5 How. (45 Gas shell incl.) Casualties from 23rd to 30th inclusive	

	Officers	O.R.
Killed	—	—
Wounded	—	2
Gassed	—	1
Total	—	3

Alex. BrMQueen Lieut.
Major. 256 Bde R.F.A.

256th BRIGADE.
R.F.A.
Date 30/9/18

Confidential   Vol 42

War Diary
of Brigade R.F.A. (T.F.)
236 (H) Brigade R.F.A. (T.F)
From 1st October 1918 to 31st October 1918

(Volume —)

Army Form C. 2118.

243

WAR DIARY
INTELLIGENCE SUMMARY.
(Erase heading not required).

Instructions regarding War Diaries and Intelligence Summaries are contained in F. S. Regs., Part II. and the Staff Manual respectively. Title pages will be prepared in manuscript.

Place	Date	Hour	Summary of Events and Information	Remarks and references to Appendices
Field.	1/10/18.		Registeration of Zero Lines by 18-pounders, and wire cutting by 4.5.Hows: was carried out during the day. Batteries also engaged and dispersed enemy movement between the hours of 20.00. and 06.00. Fire was maintained on roads and tracks approaching the FRESNES Line, special attention being paid to enemy M.G. and T.M. emplacements. Hostile Artillery was noticably quiet. Visibility was good throughout the day, but little movement was observed.	J.W.J.
	2.nd.	0030.	All Batteries cooperated in a barrage in conjunction with a raid by the 152nd.Inf.Bde. as per Divisional Artillery Order No.156. Ammunition expended, 1540.- 18-pdrs. and 550.- 4.5.Hows: During the day Batteries fired on, and dispersed enemy movement, and continued wire cutting. All night harassing fire was kept up on roads, tracks, and approaches to the FRESNES Line. Hostile Artillery was very quiet. A good deal of movement was noticed in enemy lines throughout the day. Visibility fair. Orders received that Divisional Artillery would be relieved in the Line, 255th. Bde RFA. by 33rd. Bde. on 2/3rd. and 256th.Bde.RFA. to withdraw on 3/4th.	J.W.J.
	3rd.		Batteries continued wire-cutting, and engaged and dispersed enemy movement. Hostile Artillery showed increased activity, especially on Battery Positions. Visibility was fair. At 18.30.hrs.- Batteries had withdrawn from the Line in accordance with 51st.D.A. Order No.157. to their wagon Lines in MUSKETRY VALLEY. Orders also received that Brigade (with exception of "A"Battery	

Army Form C. 2118.

244

WAR DIARY
INTELLIGENCE SUMMARY
(Erase heading not required.)

Instructions regarding War Diaries and Intelligence Summaries are contained in F. S. Regs., Part II. and the Staff Manual respectively. Title pages will be prepared in manuscript.

Place	Date	Hour	Summary of Events and Information	Remarks and references to Appendices
Field.	Oct.3rd.		to ACQ) would move on the 4th.inst. to HABARCQ from Wagon Lines. Ammunition expended from 1st. to 4th.October, inclusive. 3828.rds. - 18-pdr. and 1064.rds. - 4.5.Hows:	
	4th.	0900.	Brigade moved from Wagon Lines to HABARCQ. (A/256. to ACQ. attached to 152nd.Infy.Bde.)	
		2100.	Orders received that Divisional Artillery would move on the 5th.inst. to relieve 3rd.Canadian Div: Artillery. ad go into action on night of 6/7th.October.	
	5th.	0900.	Brigade moved to staging area at CAGNICOURT.	
	6th.	1000.	Orders received from C.R.A. 3rd.Canadian Div: that 51st.Div: Artillery would not relieve 13th. and 14th. C.F.A.Brigades, but would be superimposed on the front of these Brigades. A/256. and B/256. went into action at 1900.hrs.	
	7th.		C/256, and D/256. in action. Batteries had taken up positions as follows:- A/256.-F.10.b.2070. B/256.-F.10.c.0580. C/256.-F.9.b.2525. D/256.-F.3.b.5220. Wagon Lines at INCHY-EN-ARTOIS. Headquarters at,- F.15.a.9080. Hostile Artillery was considerably active throughout the day. E.A. were not as active as usual. Visibility good. At night Battery Positions were bombed, and one O.R. of C/256 was wounded at duty.	
	8th.	0430.	256th.Bde. less "D" Battery, fired a barrage in conjunction with the 39th.D.A. Order No.103. Ammunition expended 240.rds. per Gun. - 50% "A" and 50% "AX"	

Army Form C. 2118.

245

WAR DIARY
or
INTELLIGENCE SUMMARY.
(Erase heading not required.)

Place	Date	Hour	Summary of Events and Information	Remarks and references to Appendices
Field.	Oct. 8th.	1210.	Orders received from 39th.D.A. that A/256. and B/256. would be placed tactically at the disposal of O.C. 8th.Army Bde.C.F.A. for purpose of supporting attack by 8th.Canadian Infy.Bde. E.A. very active bombing at night, the vicinity of Brigade Headquarters was heavily bombed, and subjected to a slow rate of fire from a H.V.Gun. One O.R. D/256.wounded at duty.	
		1430.	Orders received by 'phone from the 39th.D.A. that forward positions for "B" and "D" Batteries were to be selected in order to assist in Artillery cooperation with the 4th.Can.Infy.Bde. for an effective protective barrage on their front. These positions were accordingly selected, and were as follows:- D/256.- A.2.b.50.30. and B256.- A.2.b.50.40. with one Gun at,A.13.b.9005. to infilade main street in CAMBRAI.	J.W.F.
	9th.		Forward positions were occupied before daylight, D/256. cooperated with the 128th.Bty. in a protective barrage on the line B.8.b.50.50. - B.14.d.80.10.	
		0732.	Orders from 39th.D.A. that A/256. and C/256. would revert to command of 256th.Bde. and that forward positions would be reconnoitred, and occupied as soos as possible. These positions were accordingly occupied about 14.15.hrs. C/256. xxx at S.29.a.75.15. and A/256. at A.18.a.central. This Brigade was the first RFA. Brigade tocome into action on the eastern edge of CAMBRAI. C/256. cooperated with the 5th.Can: Infy: Bde. in an attack on NAVES.	J.W.F.

Army Form C. 2118.

246

WAR DIARY
INTELLIGENCE SUMMARY.
(Erase heading not required.)

Instructions regarding War Diaries and Intelligence Summaries are contained in F. S. Regs., Part II. and the Staff Manual respectively. Title pages will be prepared in manuscript.

Place	Date 1918.	Hour	Summary of Events and Information	Remarks and references to Appendices
Field.	Oct. 9th.	1700.	Orders received from 39th.D.A. that Brigade would remain in position of observation with following defensive zone held by the 9th.Can.Infy.Bde. - A.12.central. to A.6.central.	JW/
	10th.	0745.	Orders from 51st.D.A. that 51st.Div.Artillery would be transferred from noon Oct.10th.1918. to Canadian Corps Reserve, and would remain in Wagon Lines pending further orders. The Brigade was accordingly withdrawn from the position of observation, and bivouacked in the area A.2.c. Hostile H.V.Gun shelled the valley in the vicinity of D/256. former position. Casualties:- one O.R.wounded.	JW/
		1900.	Brigade was placed under three hours notice to move.	JW/
	11th.		On the morning of the 11th.Oct.1918. 256.Brigade RFA. were bivouacked North West of CAMBRAI after having taken part in the barrage covering the attack of the 4th.Canadian Division on CAMBRAI on the 9th.inst.	
		1100.	Orders were received from the C.R.A. 51st.D.A. that 51st.Division would relieve the 2nd.Can: Division in the line tonight. The line held by the Canadians extended from the canal DE L' ESCAUT to just North of IWUY.	
		1200.	The C.O.visited Canadian Divisional Headquarters, and received instructions as to disposal of the line.	JW/

WAR DIARY
INTELLIGENCE SUMMARY
(Erase heading not required.)

Army Form C. 2118.

247.

Place	Date	Hour	Summary of Events and Information	Remarks and references to Appendices
Field.	1918. Oct. 11th.	1430.	Brigade moved forward from present bivouacking area to position of assembly in T.14.c. & d. Brigade Commander, Adjutant, and B.C's. went on ahead to get in touch with 5th.Can:Artillery Bde.(2nd.Canadian Division.) and reconnoitred positions.	
		1730.	Batteries moved forward and took up positions as follows:- A/256.-T.9.a.40.00. B/256.- T.9.b.50.20. C/256.-T.15.b.71.25. and D/256.-T.9.b.5030.	
		1830.	All Batteries were in action. Headquarters were established with Canadian Infantry Bde. and arrangements made with B.G. Commanding 154th.Infy.Bde.(51st.Division) as to Liaison with them on their taking over the line. The Artillery covering the 6th.Canadian Infy.Bde. was as follows:- 285th. and 286th.Bdes.RFA.(57th.Division)-Cook's Sub-Group. and the 256th.Bde.RFA. The line held by the 6th.Canadian Infy.Bde. ran approximately as follows:- From Canal DE ESCAUT N.28.b.34. - N.29.44. - N.30.d.45. and S.O.S.Lines covering this line were ordered as follows:- N.22.d.10.- along Grid Line to N.24.c.50. - N.30.b.74. These S.O.S.Lines having been put down by 256th.Bde.RFA. The 5th.Canadian Bde.C.F.A. withdrew from the line. Liaison Officers were ordered to join Battalions in line viz. 4th.Seaforths, and 7th.A.& S.H. Vigorous harassing fire was carried out between midnight and dawn.	
		0500.	The night was generally quiet and the Infantry relief was completed by 05.00.hrs.Casualties.NIL.	

Army Form C. 2118.

248

WAR DIARY
INTELLIGENCE SUMMARY.
(Erase heading not required.)

Place	Date	Hour	Summary of Events and Information	Remarks and references to Appendices
Field.	1918. Oct. 12th.	0430.	Orders were received that the 51st. Division were to attack the enemy today, in conjunction with the 49th. Division on the Right, and the 2nd. Canadian Division on the Left. The first objectives being:- AVESNES-LE-SEC. - LA MN BLANCHE Fm. thence to LA PAVE D'HORDAIN. The Artillery supporting the attack of the 51st. Division being as follows:- RIGHT GROUP.- Brig:General W.G.Thompson D.S.O. C.R.A. Commanding.- 174th. and 186th.Army Brigades RFA. and the 255th. Bde.RFA. LEFT GROUP.- Lt.Col.J.Hamilton Meikle.R.H.A. Commanding.- 256.Bde.RFA.- 285. Bde.RFA. and the 286. Bde.RFA.	
		0800.	Batteries moved forward to new positions to be able to carry out the whole barrage. The positions taken up were as follows:- A/256.-N.36.d.27. B/256.-T.5.b.62. C/256.-T.5.b.12. and D/256.-T.4.d.24.	
		1200.	The attack took place at 12.00 hrs. and proved very successful. Little opposition was encountered, and by 14.00 hrs. all the objectives were gained. Two Mobile 18-pdr.Sections proceeded forward and followed closely behind the Infantry, one Section following each Battalion. The special tasks of these Sections were to engage Tanks, and Machine Guns, in accordance with special instructions issued by Battalion Commanders. The Section of A/256. under LT.Gillispie followed closely behind the first Infantry wave, and came into action in the	

Army Form C. 2118.

249.

WAR DIARY
INTELLIGENCE SUMMARY.
(Erase heading not required.)

Instructions regarding War Diaries and Intelligence
Summaries are contained in F. S. Regs., Part II.
and the Staff Manual respectively. Title pages
will be prepared in manuscript.

Place	Date	Hour	Summary of Events and Information	Remarks and references to Appendices
Field.	Oct. 1918. 12th.	1200.	open against M.G's. in LIEU ST AMAND. He succeeded in silencing two M.G's. that were located but many more were firing from concealed positions. This Section was engaged by an Enemy 8" How: Battery, and the Detachments were withdrawn. One of the Infantry Commanders of the 7th. A.& S.H. told Lt.Gillispie that they were to advance on LIEU ST AMAND. Lt Gillispie brought his Section up into action, and opened fire on the village, in conjunction with other Artillery The Section was again taken on by Enemy 8" Hows: and his task being complete he again withdrew his Detachments. One of the Firing Battery Wagons was set on fire, and Lt.Gillispie regardless of personal risk at once put this out. He displayed great courage and coolness in pushing forward his Section in face of heavy M.G. fire, and handled his Section boldly and skilfully. He was of real practical assistance to the Infantry. The General Officer Commanding 154th.Infy. Brigade.(General Buchanan.) - Lt.Col.Gartside. 1/7th.A.& S.H. and Lt.Fergusson. 7th.A.& S.H. all spoke very highly of the work done by this Section. The other Mobile Section under Lt. Simkins. A/256. followed up in close support of the Infantry. As they however, had little opposition, and were nowhere held up, the Section was not called upon to give covering assistance. After the barrage ceased the attack was further exploited, and more progress made. A special concentration was put on the village of LIEU ST AMAND. from 17.00.hrs. to 17.30.hrs. as many	J.M.J.

Army Form C. 2118.

250

WAR DIARY
INTELLIGENCE SUMMARY
(Erase heading not required.)

Instructions regarding War Diaries and Intelligence Summaries are contained in F. S. Regs., Part II. and the Staff Manual respectively. Title pages will be prepared in manuscript.

Place	Date 1918.	Hour	Summary of Events and Information	Remarks and references to Appendices
Field.	Oct. 12th.		Machine Guns were located there.	
		1500	Batteries moved forward and took up new positions in the Calvigny Valley as follows:- A/256.- O.19.a.35. B/256.-O.31.c.96. C/256.-N.24.c.39. and D/256.-O.19.a.93. Meantime Brigade Headquarters moved with 154th.Infty.Bde. and established new Headquarters in IWUY. at N.36.c.51. Orders were received from D.A. that the 77th. and 189th.Army Bdes.RFA. would relieve 57th.D.A. in the line tonight.	M.J.
		1730.	Brigade Commander, and B.C's. of the 189th.Army Bde.RFA. reported, and situation was explained to them, and instructions issued to them to take up positions in the Calviguy Valley, the 77th. Army Bde.RFA. did not report until 04.00 hrs. similar instructions were given to them. These reliefs were completed by dawn, and orders were issued to 285th. and 286th.Bds.RFA. to withdraw to their Wagon Lines. S.O.S. Lines for the night were ordered to be put down on a line.- H.36.b.90.00.- O.2.b.10.80. and O.3.d.99.40. The night was generally quiet. Harassing fire was carried out during the hours of darkness. Casualties.- 1.O.R.wounded D/256.	
	13th.		Orders were issued to Brigades, and Batteries, that the 154th.Infy.Bde.were to attack the enemy lines, in conjunction with the 152nd.Infy.Bde. The first objective of the 154th.Infy.Bde. was to be the village of LIEU ST AMAND. and Station buildings at PAVE DE VALENCOENNES. The second	M.J.

Army Form C. 2118.

251.

WAR DIARY
INTELLIGENCE SUMMARY.

(Erase heading not required.)

Instructions regarding War Diaries and Intelligence Summaries are contained in F. S. Regs., Part II. and the Staff Manual respectively. Title pages will be prepared in manuscript.

Place	Date 1918.	Hour	Summary of Events and Information	Remarks and references to Appendices
Field.	Oct. 13th.		objective being NOYELLES. The Artillery programme for attack on the first objectives was a rolling barrage over the objectives covering the attack, supported by:- LEFT GROUP. Lt.Col.J.Hamilton Meikle.R.H.A. Commanding. - 256th.Bde.RFA. 189th. and 77th.Army Brigades RFA. Heavy artillery also co-operated. The Artillery programme for the attack on NOYELLES. was to consist of a heavy bombardment of the village until Zero plus 105. in which Field and Heavy Artillery co-operated. A Mobile 18.pdr. Section of C/256. was ordered to accompany the advance of the 4th.Seaforths. to engage hostile Tanks, and M.G's. The attack took place at 09.00.hrs. little progress was made owing to heavy M.G. fire from the railway and LIEU ST AMAND. Various flanking movements were tried to capture the village, but these were unsuccess- -ful. The Infantry accordingly took up the line they held previous to the attack. S.O.S.Lines covering this line were put down on a line from: - 0.9.c.70.80. - 0.6.c.60.40. - Zones being allotted so that the 189th.Army Bde.RFA.covered Left Half, and the 77th.Army.Bde.RFA.Right Half. 256th.Bde.RFA. superimposed over whole Zone. Firing was kept up and all Targets reported were engaged. In addition certain heavy Sections. (34th.Bde.RGA.) reported, and Targets were given them to engage. During the barrage 2/Lt.J.M.Smith.(since wounded) of D/256. displayed great gallantry, and devotion to duty in serving his Guns, one Howitzer was disabled, and he went	

Army Form C. 2118.

252

WAR DIARY
INTELLIGENCE SUMMARY.
(Erase heading not required.)

Instructions regarding War Diaries and Intelligence Summaries are contained in F. S. Regs., Part II. and the Staff Manual respectively. Title pages will be prepared in manuscript.

Place	Date	Hour	Summary of Events and Information	Remarks and references to Appendices
Field.	1918. Oct. 13th.		and took the breech-block off, and put it on another Gun which was temporarily out of action, owing to breech-mechanism trouble. The area around the Battery positions was continuously, and heavily shelled, with H.E. and Gas. This Officer by his example and personal supervision kept the Guns going throughout the barrage. Instructions were received from C.R.A. 51st.D.A. that the main purpose of the Division was mainly that of securing the left of the main operations further South, and that ordinary defence arrangements would at once come into force. Arrangements were therefore made to have Guns distributed in depth. 256th.Brigade RFA.accordingly withdrew, one at a time,and took up positions as follows:- A/256. - N.36.d.99. B/256. -T.5.b.91. C/256.N.36.d.65.80. and D/256.-N.36.d.74. These withdrawals were carried out under heavy shelling, as the whole Calviguy Valley had been subjected to continuous heavy hostile shelling the whole day. The 189th. and 777th. Army Brigades also withdrew and took up positions on the outskirts N.E. of IWUY. These moves were all completed by dusk. Harassing fire was ordered to be carried out on Roads, Tracks, and approaches to Brigade front. Targets were also given to the Heavies.	
		1900.	New S.O.S. Lines were ordered to be put down on a Line.- O.9.c.06. - O.3.c.99. - N.12.a.46. Zones being covered as before. Enemy Artillery was quiet during the night,but towards dawn	

Army Form C. 2118.

WAR DIARY
INTELLIGENCE SUMMARY.
(Erase heading not required.)

253

Place	Date	Hour	Summary of Events and Information	Remarks and references to Appendices
Field.	1918. Oct. 13th.	1900.	became very lively, shelling both forward and back areas. Casualties:- 2/Lt.G.M.Smith. D/256, wounded. 3.O.R's.Wounded. A/256. - 1.O.R.Killed, and 5.O.R's. Wounded. B/256. - 2.O.R's. Killed, 12.O.R's Wounded, and 1.O.R.Gassed. C/256. - 3.O.R's.Killed, and 13.O.R's.Wounded.D/256.	M.S.
	14.th.		Special Artillery Shoots were arranged to take place throughout the day in co-operation with a series of 154th.Infty.Bde. Patrols. who were to continue keeping pressure on the enemy with a view to ascertaining if the enemy was holding his front as actively as formerly. The Left Group co-operated by engaging, and concentrating on suspected M.G.Nests, at various times during the day. Two Mobile Sections from A/256. and C/256. were sent forward to the Calvigny Valley the former by covering Right Battalion, and the latter the Left Battalion. The positions taken up were as follows:- A/256. - O.19.a.54. C/256. - N.24.a.15.05. These Sections were at the disposal of the respective Battalion Commanders, ready to engage Tanks, and M.G.Nests.etc. Various M.G.were located by O.P's. and engaged. A special observed shoot was carried out at the request of B.G. 154th.Infy.Brigade. by C/256. on enemy trench system, and M.G.Post in O.8.a. The shoot was carried out by 2/Lt.Gay who laid a wire out to advanced O.P. under M.G.fire, and very successfully engaged the Target, 255 rounds were fired in all. Targets were given and engaged by the Heavy Artillery. S.O.S. Lines for the night remained the same. Harassing fire	M.S.

Army Form C. 2118.

254

WAR DIARY
INTELLIGENCE SUMMARY.
(Erase heading not required.)

Instructions regarding War Diaries and Intelligence Summaries are contained in F. S. Regs., Part II. and the Staff Manual respectively. Title pages will be prepared in manuscript.

Place	Date	Hour	Summary of Events and Information	Remarks and references to Appendices
Field.	1918. Oct. 14th.		schemes for Field and Heavy Artillery were arranged and carried out during the night. Casualties :- 2/Lt.Young. D/256. Killed.	M.T.
	15th.		Enemy Artillery was more active this morning shelling both forward, and back areas heavily with a good proportion of Gas Shells. During the day visibility was bad, but notwithstanding many Targets were engaged. Left Group co-operated with Heavy Artillery in a bombardment of Southern houses in LIEU ST AMAND. where enemy M.G's. were located. A working party in O.8.b. was successfully engaged by C/256. and casualties inflicted, while an enemy working party digging party S. of road in O.7.a.& b. reported by Infantry, was dispersed. In addition suspected M.G. Nests were shelled. During the night harassing fire was vigourously maintained on Targets specially arranged with Infantry Brigade. Wagon Lines moved back to T.14.c. & d. Casualties :- 4 O.R's. Wounded. Headquarters.	M.T.
	16th.		Enemy Artillery again very active in early morning. Harassing shoots were carried out throughout the night. Visibility was poor during the day. Various observed shoots were carried out, one by C/256. on M.G.Posts in O.8.c. Direct hits were observed and posts appeared to be considerably damaged, 6 men were seen to run away during the shoot, 3 of them were hit, a shell dropping directly on to them. A working party in O.8.a. was also engaged, and dispersed, and	M.T.

Army Form C. 2118.
255

WAR DIARY
INTELLIGENCE SUMMARY.
(Erase heading not required.)

Instructions regarding War Diaries and Intelligence Summaries are contained in F. S. Regs., Part II. and the Staff Manual respectively. Title pages will be prepared in manuscript.

Place	Date	Hour	Summary of Events and Information	Remarks and references to Appendices
Field.	1918. Oct. 16th.		casualties inflicted. Enemy Artillery less active. Our own and enemy planes inactive. Casualties:- Nil.	J.W.J.
	17th.		Harassing fire was kept up during the night, in conjunction with Heavy Artillery, various retaliation shoots on enemy's front system, and back areas were carried out during the day at the request of the Infantry. 4.5.Hows: carried out destructive shoots on M.G.Posts, Strong Points, etc. Visibility was poor during the day. Enemy Artillery more active shelling forward areas with H.E. and Gas Shells. Our own and Heavy Artillery was very active throughout the night, harassing all roads, tracks, and approaches, as well as enemy's front line, posts, etc. Casualties:- Nil.	J.W.J.
	18th.		Visibility this morning very poor, improving in the afternoon. Batteries were engaged on special shoots during the day. Destructive shoots were carried out by B/256. in conjunction with 6" Hows: on enemy posts in O.7.b. and O.1.d. and strong points in O.2.a. & c. with excellent results, many direct hits were obtained. The shoot was carried out from an advanced O.P. in the front line of posts, from where excellent observation was obtained. 4.5.Hows: engaged enemy front line system, and strong points, with short bursts at irregular intervals. Enemy Artillery less active. Aircraft active during the clear spells. Harassing fire	J.W.J.

Army Form C. 2118.
256.

WAR DIARY
INTELLIGENCE SUMMARY
(Erase heading not required.)

Instructions regarding War Diaries and Intelligence Summaries are contained in F. S. Regs., Part II. and the Staff Manual respectively. Title pages will be prepared in manuscript.

Place	Date	Hour	Summary of Events and Information	Remarks and references to Appendices
Field.	1918. Oct. 18th.		was kept up as usual throughout the night. Brigade Headquarters moved with the 153rd.Infty.Bde. Headquarters to N.35.b.26. Casualties:- Nil.	M.J.
	19th.		Orders were received that an operation was to be carried out by XXII.Corps. The 4th.Division were to attack on the right of the 51st.Division, to gain an objective running through P.23.a. and b. - P.22.central. - P.8.c.80. - P.8.a.02. and 0.12.b.34. To protect the flanks of the 4th.Division. the 51st.Dibision was to attack at the same time with an objective running through O.9.a.& b. The attack of the 51st.Division to be carried out by the 154th.Infty. Brigade on the right, and the 153rd.Infty.Brigade on the left. For the operation the Field Artillery covering the 51st.Divisional front, was to be organised as follows:- RIGHT GROUP.- Brig: General N.T. Thompson.D.S,O. C.R.A. 39th.D.A. commanding, covering the 154th.Infy.Bde. 174th.186th.777th. and 189th.Army Brigades RFA. and the 255th.Brigade R.F.A. LEFT GROUP. - Lt.Col.J.Hamilton Meikle.R.H.A. commanding, covering the 153rd.Infty.Brigade. 256th.Brigade RFA. and 2.Brigades CFA. 2nd.Canadian Division. The 22nd. Corps. heavy artillerywere to co-operate, also the Canadian Corps. heavy artillery. Arrangements were made accordingly. During the forenoon Patrols were out towards LIEU SR AMAND. but reported presence of enemy.	
		1230.	It was reported that the Canadians on out left were pushing forward towards BOUCHAIN and	M.J.

Army Form C. 2118.

257.

WAR DIARY
INTELLIGENCE SUMMARY.
(Erase heading not required.)

Instructions regarding War Diaries and Intelligence Summaries are contained in F. S. Regs., Part II. and the Staff Manual respectively. Title pages will be prepared in manuscript.

Place	Date	Hour	Summary of Events and Information	Remarks and references to Appendices
Field.	1918. Oct. 19th.	1230.	ROEULX. Infantry patrols were again pushed forward, and by 14.00.hrs. it was reported that they had reached the Southern outskirts of LIEU ST AMAND. The 154th.Infantry Bde. also pushed forward patrols keeping in touch with the 153rd.Infty.Bde. on the left.	
		1500.	It was reported that the Canadians had reached ROEULX.NEUVILLE. Orders were issued cancelling the operation tonight. New positions were reconnoitred in the vicinity of LIEU ST AMAND. as it was now reported that the Infantry were through LIEU ST AMAND. and were advancing in the direction of DOUCHY and NOYELLES.	JW
		1730.	256th.Brigade RFA. moved forward and came into action, covering the 153rd.Infantry Bde. in O.7.a. & b. Orders were issued to 77th.and 189th. Army Brigades RFA. to reconnoitre new positions. These Brigades moved forward, and came into action as follows:- 77th. Army Brigade RFA. - N.12.a. and the 189th.Army Bde.RFA. - N.12.a. Orders were issued for the Division to continue the advance throughout the night, with a view to establishing a line FLEURY.-O.6.c. NOYELLES SUR SELLE.- DOUCHY CANAL.-I.15.b. The 153rd.Infantry Bde. were to advance in three bounds. 6th.A.& S.H. on right, and 7th.Black Watch on left. First bound.- The NEUVILLE-SUR-L'ESCANT. - NOYELLES-SUR-SELLE Road running through FRETE-AU-POIRIER. at I.27.b.23. Second bound.- Line of railway I.28.d.d. and at I.22.c. - T.21.b. - I.15.d. Third bound.-I.15.b.	JW

Army Form C. 2118.

WAR DIARY
INTELLIGENCE SUMMARY.
(Erase heading not required.)

Instructions regarding War Diaries and Intelligence Summaries are contained in F. S. Regs., Part II. and the Staff Manual respectively. Title pages will be prepared in manuscript.

Place	Date	Hour	Summary of Events and Information	Remarks and references to Appendices
Field.	Oct. 1918. 19th.	1730.	East of DOUCHY.- I.29.central.	258
		1900.	The Right Battalion, 4th.Canadian Infty.Bde. were reported at 19.00.hrs. to be in NEUVILLE-SUR-L'ESCAUT. and it was arranged that as soon as the 7th.Black Watch passed through NEUVILLE, the 4th.Canadian Infty.Bde. would be squeezed out, and a Brigade of the 4th.Canadian Division would be on the left of the 7th.Black Watch. These advances were all carried out without much opposition, DOUCHY and NEUVILLE being captured. Many French civilians were liberated from these villages. S.O.S. Lines covering the final objectives were put down as follows:- 189th. Army Bde.RFA.-I.29.b.00.- I.23.a.47. 77th.Army Bde.RFA.-I.23.a.47.-I.16.a.89.-I.16.c.37. 256th.Bde.RFA.--superimposed over whole zone. The 256th.Brigade Headquarters moved with 153rd.	
		0200.	Infty.Bde.Headquarters 02.00.hrs. to PAVE DE VALENCIENNES. -N.6.a. The final objectives having been reached, cyclist patrols were pushed forward to the high ground North of DOUCHY.	
			Casualties:- Nil.	
	20th.		Orders had been issued that the 153rd.Infty.Bde. would continue to advance towards the canal.	*[initials]*
		0600.	Orders were issued to 256th.Bde. RFA. to reconnoitre new Battery positions in I.26.a & b. (S.of NEUVILLE) for three Brigades at 0600.hrs. Positions accordingly reconnoitred, and Batteries 256th.Bde.RFA. moved forward, and took up positions N.of NEUVILLE as follows:-	*[initials]*

Army Form C. 2118.

259

WAR DIARY
INTELLIGENCE SUMMARY.
(Erase heading not required.)

Instructions regarding War Diaries and Intelligence Summaries are contained in F. S. Regs., Part II. and the Staff Manual respectively. Title pages will be prepared in manuscript.

Place	Date	Hour	Summary of Events and Information	Remarks and references to Appendices
Field.	1918 Oct. 20th.	0600.	A/256.-I.20.d.1550. B/256.-I.26.a.88. C/256.-I.26.a.9095. and D/256.-I.26.a.58.	
			Meantime however it was reported that our Infantry were being held up by M.G. fire from the wood in I.17. and a M.G. at the cross roads in I.24.a. Arrangements were made for a 15 minutes concentration, one Battery on each Target. "C" and "D" Batteries(were stopped by the Adjutant (Captain P.W.Johnston.) who had ridden to the Batteries with the orders, as Telephone communication had broken down owing to shelling.) on the point of limbering up, and carried	
		0915.	out the concentration at 09.15.hrs. The Infantry, however, were still unable to push forward, and another 15.minutes shoot was arranged to take place at 10.45.hrs.	JWJ.
		1045.	The 4 Batteries 256th.Bde,RFA. carried out this concentration, "B" and "D" Batteries from new positions, and "A" and "C" Batteries from a point at I.26.c. off the main DOUCHY Road while moving forward to new positions. The shoot was carried out with excellent results, and to the satisfaction of the Infantry. The forward Mobile Sections co-operated on their own initiative	
		1100.	and obtained direct hits. The Infantry advanced on the wood, and the Cross Roads at 11.00.hrs. when the concentration ceased, and had no difficulty in capturing them. A Mounted Officer's Patrol was sent forward to keep in touch with the Infantry, and keep us informed of the general situation. The 77th. and 189th.Army Bdes.RFA. were ordered to move forward to new positions	JWJ.

Army Form C. 2118.

WAR DIARY
INTELLIGENCE SUMMARY.
(Erase heading not required.)

Place	Date	Hour	Summary of Events and Information	Remarks and references to Appendices
Field.	1918. Oct. 20th.		S.of NEUVILLE. in I.26. They accordingly moved forward and were in action by 10.30.hrs. The advance of the 153rd.Infty.Bde.continued satisfactorily, and did not meet with much opposition. New positions just West of DOUCHY were reconnoitred for the 3 Brigades. The 256th.Bde. RFA.	
		1400.	moved forward at 14.00.hrs. to new positions as follows:- A/256. - I.21.b.94. B/256.-I.21.b.75. C/256. - I.22.c.15.80. D/256.- I.22.c.18. Wagon Lines moved to N.19.d. West	
		1500	of NEUVILLE. The Batteries were in action by 15.00.hrs. and the 189th.Brigade RFA. then moved forward and took up positions as follows:- 34th.Battery.- I.21.d.65.85. B/189.-I.21.b.	
		1700.	55. C/189.- I.21.b.69. D/189. - I.21.d.95.90. and were in action by 17.00.hrs. The 77th.Army Brigade RFA. moved forward and took up positions as follows:- A/77. - I.21.d.95.	
		1800.	B/77. - I.27.b.25. C/77. - I.27.b.38. D/77. - I.27.b.47. and were in action by 18.00. During the day over 4,000 French civilians were liberated from NEUVILLE and DOUCHY. During these operations the Mobile Sections were of much assistance to the Infantry. The Mobile Section of C/256. under 2/Lt.J.P.Hardern, had followed up close in rear of the 1/7th. Black Watch keeping in touch with the Battalion and Company Commanders. He took up a position of readiness at I.27.b.25. S.W. of DOUCHY. At 09.00.hrs. M.G's. in a house at I.24.a.24. and small wood I.17. central. were reported to him by C.O. 1/7th. Black Watch. As however, the bridges over the	

Army Form C. 2118.

261.

WAR DIARY
INTELLIGENCE/SUMMARY
(Erase heading not required.)

Instructions regarding War Diaries and Intelligence Summaries are contained in F. S. Regs., Part II. and the Staff Manual respectively. Title pages will be prepared in manuscript.

Place	Date	Hour	Summary of Events and Information	Remarks and references to Appendices
Field.	1918. Oct. 20th.		River were impassable, he engaged these Targets with direct observation, and voice control, from a good position, and obtained direct hits on the house, and fired about 50.rounds into the wood. The other Mobile Section of A/256. under Lt.A.Simkins. was attached to the 6th.A.& S.H. and had followed up in close support since the 19th.inst. At 08.00.hrs. on the 20th. he was informed that the Infantry were being held up by M.G's. near house at I.24.a.24. The Section moved forward and engaged this Target over open sights, and secured direct hits. Lt.Col.Coats 6th.A.& S.H. observed this shoot with Lt.Simkins, and expressed his appreciation. Their were civilians in the cellar of the house, and they afterwards told Lt.Simkins that an enemy Machine Gunner was badly wounded. At 11.30.hrs. Lt. Simkins went forward with Lt.Col.Coates, but were met with M.G.fire. The Section was brought forward and the Targets engaged. Infantry Patrols reported that the shelling caused casualties, and silenced the M.G's. At 15.00.hrs. this Section moved across the canal, and took up a position at I.23.a.56. covering THIANT. where it remained for the night. During these operations this Section fired 110.Rounds.	
		2400.	256.Brigade Headquarters moved forward with the 153rd.Infty.Brigade Headquarters to new Headquarters at DOUCHY. Casualties:- Nil.	
	21st.		During the night our Patrols continued to push forward, and reached the Line of the Ecaillon	

Army Form C. 2118.

WAR DIARY
INTELLIGENCE SUMMARY.
(Erase heading not required.)

Instructions regarding War Diaries and Intelligence Summaries are contained in F. S. Regs., Part II. and the Staff Manual respectively. Title pages will be prepared in manuscript.

Place	Date	Hour	Summary of Events and Information	Remarks and references to Appendices
Field.	Oct. 21.st. 1918		River. Orders were issued by the 153rd.Infty.Bde. that as soon as the 10th.Canadian Infty.Bde. on the right on the left were known to occupy ROUVIQUES and PRONOY. and the 154th.Infty Bde. on the right occupied the Rubber Factory- I.15.b. and were in touch with the Canadians, the 153rd.Infty.Bde. would withdraw. This was accomplished by the late afternoon. Meantime orders were issued that the 77th.189th.and 256th.Brigades RFA. would advance and take up new positions West of THIANT. The 256th.Bde.RFA. moved forward first and took up positions as follows :- A/256. - J.13.d.30.	
		1200.	B/256.- J.14.d.54. C/256.-J.14.d.63. and D/256.-J.13.b.93. and were in action by 12.00.hrs.	
		1100.	The 77th.Army Bde.RFA. moved forward, and came into action at J.19.d. and J.20.a. at 14.00.hrs. The 189th.Army Bde.RFA. moved forward and came into action at J.14.a. at 14.00.hrs. The front of the 51st.Division after the withdrawal of the 153rd.Infty.Bde. was now being held by the 154th.Infty.Bde. The Divisional Artillery covering the 154th.Infty.Bde. consisted of :- RIGHT GROUP. -O.C. 255th.Bde.RFA. Commanding:- 174th.and 186th.Army Bdes.RFA.(39th.D.A.) 255th.Bde.RFA. and the 147th.Army Bde.RFA. LEFT GROUP. - O.C. 256th.Bde.RFA. Commanding.- 256th.Bde.RFA.- 77th. and 189th.Army Bdes. RFA. The Right Group covered the Right Battalion, and the Left Group covered the Left Battalion. The 34th.Bde.R.G.A. also covered the Divisional Front.	

Army Form C. 2118.

263

WAR DIARY
INTELLIGENCE SUMMARY.
(Erase heading not required.)

Instructions regarding War Diaries and Intelligence Summaries are contained in F. S. Regs., Part II. and the Staff Manual respectively. Title pages will be prepared in manuscript.

Place	Date 1918	Hour	Summary of Events and Information	Remarks and references to Appendices
Field.	Oct. 21st.		S.O.S. Lines covering the 154th.Infty Brigade were put down as follows:- From J.29.c.50. due North to J.11.c.50. Harassing fire was carried out throughout the night. The two Mobile Sections remained with the Infantry, but were not called upon for any assistance during the day. Casualties:- Nil.	M.
	22nd.		Our Line remained unchanged and was as follows:- From North to South.- Rubber Factory J.15.b.- THIANT. West of the Escaillon River (inclusive) along the road through - J.21.d. - J.27.b. & d. Patrols reported the East Bank of the River strongly held by the enemy. A series of Chinese Barrages were carried out during the day by Left Group, and Right Group, in conjunction with Heavy Artillery, at 06.45.hrs. - 09.00.hrs. - 11.30.hrs. and 16.00.hrs. These barrages were very effective, and many casualties were caused. Numbers of enemy stretcher-bearer parties were seen afterwards. Enemy Artillery activity increased since yesterday. Hostile reply to our Chinese Barrages was not very strong. Visibility and weather bad. Harassing fire was carried out on Roads, Trcks, etc. by night. Casualties:- Nil.	M.
	23rd.		Chinese Barrages were repeated today at 05.00.hrs.- 15.00.hrs.- 15.45.hrs. and 23.45.hrs. In addition various observed shoots were carried out, and Batteries registered their Lines,etc. Enemy Artillery quiet. This afternoon indications pointed to the possibility of the enemy	M.

Army Form C. 2118.

WAR DIARY
INTELLIGENCE SUMMARY
(Erase heading not required.)

264

Instructions regarding War Diaries and Intelligence Summaries are contained in F. S. Regs., Part II. and the Staff Manual respectively. Title pages will be prepared in manuscript.

Place	Date	Hour	Summary of Events and Information	Remarks and references to Appendices
Field.	1918 Oct. 23rd.		having withdrawn. Infantry Patrols were at once pushed forward and reached the West bank of the River, they however came under fire from THIANT. and the cemetery in H.22.a.	JW
		1800.	Orders were received that the XXII.Corps. would carry out an operation on the 24th.inst. in conjunction with XVII.Corps. The 51st.Division were to attack on the left of the XXII.Corps. with the 4th.Division on the right. The attack of the 51st.Division was to be carried out by the 153rd.Infty.Bde. with 2 Battalions. The minimum objective of the 51st.Division was the high ground in J.30. and the village of MAING. The Artillery covering the 153rd.Infty.Bde. was as follows:- Field Artillery-Right Group.- O.C.255th.Brigade RFA.Commanding.- 255th.Bde.RFA. 174th.186th.and 147th.Army Brigades RFA. Left Group. O.C.256th.Brigade RFA.commanding.- 256th.Bde.RFA. - 77th. and 189th.Army Bdes.RFA. Heavy Artillery.- 34th.Brigade RGA. and in addition the XXII.Corps Heavy Artillery. Casualties:- Nil.	JW
	24th.	0400.	The attack was launched at 04.00.hrs. and our Infantry crossed the Escaillon River. The attack on the 153rd.Infty.Bde. front met with considerable resistance from enemy M.G's. and Trench Mortars, but these were overcome and rapid progress made. Detached Section under 2/Lt.H.C. Inkson. B/256. proceeded across the first pontoon bridge over the Escaillon River at 11.00.hrs. and went forward in close support of the 7th.Black Watch. and took up a half-cock position	JW

Army Form C. 2118.

WAR DIARY
INTELLIGENCE SUMMARY.
(Erase heading not required.)

Instructions regarding War Diaries and Intelligence Summaries are contained in F. S. Regs., Part II. and the Staff Manual respectively. Title pages will be prepared in manuscript.

Place	Date	Hour	Summary of Events and Information	Remarks and references to Appendices
Field.	1918. Oct. 24th.		at J.17.a.41. commanding by voice from a distance of 25 yards. Targets were engaged such as:- M.G's. firing from positions on high ground in J.7. - J.13. and J.19. The effect of the fire was excellent, and was commented upon by Major D.R.Keir. of the 7th.Black Watch. The Section was under heavy hostile shelling for 4 hours, but no casualties were sustained. The Section rejoined its Battery after dark, having expended all its ammunition. 2/Lt.Moore acted as Liaison Officer with the 7th.Black Watch and repeatedly sent in valuable information as to the progress of the Battle. Orders were received that as soon as the Bridges over the Escaillon River, were ready Brigades would advance at once in the following order:- 255th.Bde.RFA.- 256th.Bde.RFA.- 77th.Army Bde.RFA.-and the 189th.Bde. RFA. to new positions East of THIANT. and that 39th.D.A. (174th.and 186th.Bdes.RFA. - Right Group, would drop out, as soon as 189th. Army Bde.RFA. moved forward. Positions were accordingly reconnoitred, and 256th.Bde.RFA. stood ready to advance as soon as bridges were ready. The Royal Engineers, however, experienced great difficulty in getting the bridges put up owing to very heavy enemy shelling, and the work	
		1100.	was much delayed. By 11.00.hrs. the first pontoon bridge was reported reday for Field Artillery. 256th.Bde.RFA. immediately went forward. The bridges, and whole river bank including the village of THIANT were being continuously shelled with a result that fairly heavy	

WAR DIARY
INTELLIGENCE SUMMARY.
(Erase heading not required.)

Army Form C. 2118.

Place	Date	Hour	Summary of Events and Information	Remarks and references to Appendices
Field.	1918. Oct. 24th.		casualties to personnel, and horses were sustained. C/256. under Major Hawker.M.C. and Lt. Hunter displayed great steadiness and gallantry, in getting through the village and across the bridge, although they received the following casualties:- one O.R.Killed, 11.O.R's.Wounded and 18 casualties amongst the horses. The Batteries took up positions previously reconnoitred	
		1400.	East of THIANT in square - J.22.c. and were all in action by 14.00.hrs. Ammunition was dumped and Wagons sent back, these got across without a casualty. In the meantime it was reported that had taken place in the village of MAING, and that the 7th.Black Watch had captured most of the village, but they were still meeting considerable resistance. A good	
		1700.	number of prisoners were taken. At 17.00.hrs. it was reported that Divisional Front Line ran approximately as follows:- J.30. d.78. along road to cross road.- J.24.a.25. along main street of MAING. -to Cross Roads J.18.d.16.thence North along road J.18.a.67. Orders were received at 15.30.hrs. that the 77th. and 189th.Army Brigades RFA.-Left Group.- would not move to new positions across E/caillon River, but would take up position close to Western bank. These moves were accordingly carried out and Brigades took up positions as follows:- 77th.Army Bde.RFA. - J.21.d. and J.27.b. and 189th.Army Bde.RFA.-J.15.d. and J.16.a.7.c.(North of THIANT) S.O.S.Lines covering the left Battalion were put down as follows:- K.13.c.35. -K.13.a.26.	

Army Form C. 2118.

267/

WAR DIARY
INTELLIGENCE SUMMARY.
(Erase heading not required.)

Instructions regarding War Diaries and Intelligence Summaries are contained in F. S. Regs., Part II. and the Staff Manual respectively. Title pages will be prepared in manuscript.

Place	Date	Hour	Summary of Events and Information	Remarks and references to Appendices
Field.	1918. Oct. 24th.		- J.12.a.80. - J.12.a.82. Harassing fire was carried out throughout the night on roads, tracks, etc. in Group Zone. Orders were received that Divisional Front would be re-organised, and that the 153rd.Infty.Bde. would be relieved in the right sub-sector, of the Divisional Front by the 152nd.Infty Bde. on the night of the 24/25th. In consequence of this change the Infantry Brigade Boundary would be the MAING-FAMARS ROAD inclusive to the 153rd.Infty.Bde. Orders were received later that the attack of the XXII.Corps. would be continued tomorrow the 25th.inst. The 51st.Division would attack on the left of the 4th.Division, with the 152nd. Infty.Bde. on the right. (2 Battalions) and the 153rd.Infty.Bde. on the left. (one Battalion) The objectives of the 51st.Division were to capture Caumont Farm- La Batterrave Farm, @ Rouge Mont. and thence to K.7.c.53. Artillery available for the support of the attack was re-grouped as follows:- Right Group. - covering the 152nd.Infty.Bde.- O.C. 255th.Bde.RFA. commanding.- 255th.Bde.RFA. - 174th. and 186th.Bdes.RFA. 39th.D.A. - 77th. and 147th. Army Brigades RFA. Left Group. - covering the 153rd.Infty.Bde.-O.C. 256th.Bde.RFA. commanding:- 256th.Bde.RFA. - 189th.Army Bde.RFA. In addition the 34th. Army Brigade R.G.A. and the 22nd.Corps. heavy Artillery would co-operate. Casualties:- 1.O.R.-Killed. 11. O.R's.-Wounded, and 3 O.R's. -Gassed. "C" Battery, and 1. O.R. Wounded "D"Battery.	

Army Form C. 2118.

WAR DIARY
INTELLIGENCE SUMMARY.
(Erase heading not required.)

Instructions regarding War Diaries and Intelligence Summaries are contained in F. S. Regs., Part II. and the Staff Manual respectively. Title pages will be prepared in manuscript.

Place	Date	Hour	Summary of Events and Information	Remarks and references to Appendices
Field.	1918 Oct. 25th.	0700.	The attack was launched at 07.00.hrs. and again made excellent progress, all the objectives were reached in face of heavy fighting, and a large number of prisoners were taken. The attack of the 153rd.Infy.Bde. was carried out by the 6th.A.& S.H. with the 6th.Seaforths (152nd.Infy.Bde.). 2/Lt.Moore acted as Liaison Officer, and 2/Lt.Dalziel as F.O.O. Major J.B.Meikle. on right. C/256.went to act as Brigade Liaison Officer with the 153rd.Infy.Bde. whose Headquarters were at NOYELLES. The 6th.A. & S.H. pushed forward after the final objective was reached, and established posts on the railway in K.7.b.& d. and South of FONTENELLE Wood. A Section of 4.5. Hows: under Lt. McMaster.M.C. -D/256. was attached to the 6th.A.& S.H. and followed up in close support of the Infantry. During the afternoon M.G's.in LA FONTENELLE.-J.1.a, and also at POIRIER Farm. in K.1.d. were engaged from a position in J.17.d. with direct observation, and with good results, the enemy being seen to run about in all directions. These Targets were kept under fire at the request of the Infantry, also the Southern houses in the village of FAMARS. where M.G's. were located that were giving considerable trouble. Fire was kept up until after dark, and after having used up all its ammunition, the Section rejoined its Battery for the night. At 16.30.hrs. Batteries replied to an S.O.S. on Right Companys Front of 6th.A.& S.H. O.P.reported that our fire was very accurate, and that the enemy who had attempted to	

Army Form C. 2118.

WAR DIARY
INTELLIGENCE SUMMARY.
(Erase heading not required.)

Instructions regarding War Diaries and Intelligence Summaries are contained in F. S. Regs., Part II. and the Staff Manual respectively. Title pages will be prepared in manuscript.

269.

Place	Date	Hour	Summary of Events and Information	Remarks and references to Appendices
Field.	1918. Oct. 25th.	1630.	counter-attack in numbers from the village of FAMARS. was caught in our Barrage and suffered heavy casualties. Another counter-attack was attempted by the enemy at 18.00.hrs. but the 6th.	
		1800.	A.& S.H. met them with the bayonet, and inflicted heavy casualties on them, and took a number of prisoners, also a Minenwerfer, and several M.G's. They also advanced their line to East of the Railway. Meantime after the conclusion of the barrage the 189th.Army Bde.RFA.were ordered to move forward to new positions West of MAING. The Brigade accordingly moved forward and took up positions in J.23.b. immediately West of MAING. All Batteries were in action by	
		1700.hrs.	Their B/189. remained in action North of the canal de L'ESCAUT. in J.4.b.	
		1400.	Brigade Headquarters moved forward to new Headquarters in THIANT alongside the 153rd.Infty.Bde. Bursts of fire were put down on MONY HOUY and POIRIER Farm at the request of the Infantry. S.O.S. Lines covering the 153rd.Infy.Bde. for the night were put down as follows:- K.14.a.6570. - K.8.a.2540. - J.6.d.8515. Casualties:- 1.O.R.Wounded B/256. and 2. O.R's.Wounded D/256.	W.J.
	26th.		Orders were received that the 22nd.Corps. would continue the attack today the 26th.Inst. The 51st. Division would attack with the 152nd.Infy.Bde. on the right (one Battalion) and the 153rd.Infy.Bde. on the left (one battalion) The objective of the 51st.Division was to capture the ridge FAMARS-MONT-HOUY. which commands the valley of the riverRhonelle. The attack of the	W.J.

Army Form C. 2118.

WAR DIARY
INTELLIGENCE SUMMARY.
(Erase heading not required.)

270'

Place	Date	Hour	Summary of Events and Information	Remarks and references to Appendices
Field.	1918. Oct. 26th.		153rd.Infy Bde.was to be made by the 6th.Black Watch, and by the 4th.Gordons.(152nd.Infy Bde.) on their right. The Artillery covering the attack would be - Right Group.- covering the 152nd. Infy.Bde.- O.C.255th.Bde.R.F.A.commanding.- 255th.Brigade R.F.A.- 77th. and 147th. Army Bds.RFA. Left Group.- covering 153rd.Infy.Bde.- O.C.256th.Brigade RFA. commanding: - 256th.Bde.RFA. and the 189th.Army Bde.RFA. The 34th.Brigade R.G.A. also to co-operate. Orders were issued to Batteries. Bursts of fire were kept up on FONTENELLE Wood in K.7.b. from 05.30. to Zero hour-10.00.hrs.	
		1000.	The attack was launched at 10.00.hrs. Lt Moore continued to act as Liaison Officer with the 6th.Black Watch. Lt.McMaster was in charge of Mobile Section of 4.5.Hows: with the Infantry. 2/Lt.Jones acted as F.O.O. The attack was again successful although stiff opposition was met with in FAMARS. by the 152nd.Infy.Bde. and on the slopes of MONT HOUY by the 6th.Black Watch.	
		1400.	It was reported that the 4th.Gordons had captured the village of FAMARS after stiff fighting and that the 6th.Black Watch had captured FONTENELLE and the ground in K.1.including POIRIER Farm. The enemy's artillery response was heavy. He made several counter-attacks in the afternoon and evening, but these were all broken up by our Artillery and M.G. Fire. The Mobile	

Army Form C. 2118.

27/1

WAR DIARY
INTELLIGENCE SUMMARY.
(Erase heading not required.)

Instructions regarding War Diaries and Intelligence Summaries are contained in F. S. Regs., Part II. and the Staff Manual respectively. Title pages will be prepared in manuscript.

Place	Date	Hour	Summary of Events and Information	Remarks and references to Appendices
Field.	1918. Oct. 26th.	1400.	Section under Lt.McMaster again did good work. It came into action between the front, and support lines of the attacking Infantry at J.13.a.26. at 09.45.hrs. Targets were engaged including a M.G. at J.7.b.9590. which was holding up our Infantry at 13.45.hrs. This Target was successfully dealt with. Other suspected M.G! Nests at LA FONTENELLE. and high ground round MONY HOUY, and LA POIRIER Station also Wood at K.2.c.38. were engaged with direct observation. All his ammunition was expended on the Targets. New Battery positions were reconnoitred further forward during the day. During the afternoon (in cooperation with Heavy Artillery). SOS lines for the night were put down and evening enemy concentrations were put down as follows:- K.8.b.2045.- K.2.c.80. - K.2.c.50.25.- -K.2.c.15.60. - K.2.a.10.30. About 800 French civilians were liberated during the day night from FAMARS, they had been in the cellars for two days, and many of them were gassed as a result of the enemy having bombarded the village during the afternoon with Gas Shells. The whole forward area was intermittedly shelled with Yellow Cross gas shells. The night was generally quiet. The 153rd.Infy.Bde. was relieved in the line by the 154th.Infy.Bde. - the 4th.Seaforths, relieving the 6th.Black Watch. Casualties:- Nil.	JM
	27th.		The line this morning remained unchanged. No attack was made today. A series of Chinese Barrages were arranged and carried out at 14.30.hrs.-15.50.hrs.-17.-10.hrs.21.30.hrs.-22.30.hrs.	JM

Army Form C. 2118.

WAR DIARY
INTELLIGENCE SUMMARY
(Erase heading not required.)

Instructions regarding War Diaries and Intelligence Summaries are contained in F. S. Regs., Part II. and the Staff Manual respectively. Title pages will be prepared in manuscript.

Place	Date	Hour	Summary of Events and Information	Remarks and references to Appendices
Field.	1918. Oct. 27th.		in which Heavy Artillery co-operated. The enemy counter-attacked our positions in FAMARS at noon, and penetrated the Northern portion of the village, but we at once counter-attacked and after heavy street fighting in which many of the enemy were killed, our line was completely restored. All Batteries fired in reply to the S.O.S. call. Our line ran approximately.- K.1.b.14. - K.1.b.50.- K.1.d.61. - K.8.central. FAMARS inclusive K.15.b.30. along sunken road to K.22.d.43. In addition to the Chinese Barrages vigorous harassing fire was carried out on all approaches. Hostile artillery was very active, and our forward areas, and Battery positions were heavily shelled in connection with the enemy's counter-attack. During the night the Chinese Barrages were repeated at 02.30.hrs.-03.50.hrs. in which the heavies co-operated, in addition the 34th.Bde.RGA.in conjunction with Field Artillery, kept up a vigorous harassing fire on back areas, and sunken roads. New Battery positions were reconnoitred during the day and Batteries moved forward and took up positions as follows:- B/256. -J.17.d.83. - C/256.-	
		1700.	J.17.d.73. and D/256.-J.17.c.75. They were in action by 17.00.hrs. and ammunition dumped. A/256.provided the Mobile Section under 2/Lt.Beard. and the remainder of "A"Battery Guns were handed over to "B" and "C"Batteries to complete them. The 189th.Army Bde.RFA. also moved forward to new positions in J.23.b. Bde. H.Q.remained at THIANT beside the 154.In.Bde.HQ.Casualties-Nil.	

WAR DIARY
or
INTELLIGENCE SUMMARY.
(Erase heading not required.)

Army Form C. 2118.

273

Place	Date	Hour	Summary of Events and Information	Remarks and references to Appendices
Field.	1918. Oct. 28th.		Orders were received that the attack would be continued today by the 154th.In.Bde. with the object of capturing MONT HOUY. The Artillery available for the support of the attack being:-	
			Right Group. - O.C.255th.Brigade RFA.commanding.- 255th.Bde.RFA. 77th. and 147th.Army Bde RFA	
			Left Group. - O.C.256th.Brigade RFA.commanding.- 256th.Bde.RFA. 189th.Army Brigade R.F.A.	
			The 34th.Brigade RGA. and the Corps. Heavies were to co-operate.	WJ
		05.15.	The attack was launched at 05.15.hrs. Lt.Col.J.Hamilton Meikle.R.H.A. acted as Liaison Officer with the 154th.Infy.Bde. 2/Lt.Moore. continued to act as Liaison Officer with the Infantry attacking Battalion, the 4th.Seaforths. 2/Lt.Stonehewer. D/256. acted as F.O.O. The attack was again successful, and the final objective. viz.Sunken road in E.26.c. & d. and	
		0900.	K.3.a. were reached by 09.00.hrs. and a number of prisoners taken. The Left Company of the 4th.Seaforths encountered stiff opposition about LE POIRIER Station, and houses immediately North of the Station, and fierce fighting continued in that area during the day. Special concentration shoots and searching fire was put down at the request of the Infantry on areas were enemy were reported to be trickling forward. The 34th.Bde.RGA. co-operated in these shoots. *from the Sunken Road to Mont Houy owing to heavy M.G. fire from*	WJ
		1500.	At 15.00.hrs. it was reported that our Infantry had fallen back from the Southern Houses AULNOY. in K.3.a. & b. and from where enemy were reported to be trickling forward and counter-attacking.	WJ

Army Form C. 2118.

WAR DIARY
INTELLIGENCE SUMMARY.
(Erase heading not required.)

Instructions regarding War Diaries and Intelligence
Summaries are contained in F. S. Regs., Part II.
and the Staff Manual respectively. Title pages
will be prepared in manuscript.

274

Place	Date	Hour	Summary of Events and Information	Remarks and references to Appendices
Field.	1918. Oct. 28th.		Searching fire was continued on those areas also on E.26.c. and E.27.c. & d. By nightfall the position was very obscure as it was reported that the enemy had gained possession of the commaning ground in MONT HOUY. The Mobile Section under 2/Lt. Beard. A/256. engaged many Targets during the day. It took up a position of readiness near the Report Centre if the 4th. Seaforths at J.18.b.83. at dusk on the 27/10/13. but owing to heavy shelling had to move up to road in K.13.a.3580. Acting on instructions from Major Henderson. C.O. 4th.Seaforths, it moved forward at 4.am. and took upa position just behind the Infantry jumping off ground at K.7.b.79. During the barrage it fired on Quarry at K.2.c.35.85. where enemy M.G's. were holding up the advance. The fire had excellent effect.	
		1400.	The road from K.9.a.38. to K.3.c.89.was engaged at the request of the C.O. 4th.Seaforths. As it was found impossible to take the Setion over the ridge, owing to intense M.G.Fire. 2/Lt.Beard ran his Guns back, and observed from Tower in K.7.b.77.59. About 50.rounds were fired, but owing to heavy enemy shelling the fire had to be discontinued.	
		1530.	About 15.30.hrs. the situation was very obscure, and as our Infantry were falling back,2/Lt.Beard got his Guns ready to take the enemy on over open sights. The Infantry held on however. He tried to get into touch with Companys but found this impossible. The Guns remained in position until	

Army Form C. 2118.

275

WAR DIARY
INTELLIGENCE SUMMARY.
(Erase heading not required.)

Instructions regarding War Diaries and Intelligence Summaries are contained in F. S. Regs., Part II. and the Staff Manual respectively. Title pages will be prepared in manuscript.

Place	Date	Hour	Summary of Events and Information	Remarks and references to Appendices
Field.	1918. Oct. 28th.		dusk, and were then withdrawn under cover of darkness. During the day new Battery positions were reconnoitred East of THIANT in K.13.c. Batteries moved forward by Sections, and took up positions as follows:- "A" and "B" 256. -K.13.c.15.35. - C/256.-K.13.c.15. - and D/256.-K.13.c.03. These moves were carried out by Sections, and Batteries were all in action by 15.30.hours. The 189th.Army Bde.RFA. were instructed to move forward to new positions in K.24.c. S.E. of MAING. they moved at 16.00.hrs. and were in action by 17.30.hrs. The line at 18.00.hrs. was reported to run approximately as follows:- from POIRIER Station (inclusive) Quarry in Q.2.a. (inclusive)S.outskirts of MONT HOUY Wood.-K.8.b.92. thence to FAMARS inclusive. About 130 prisoners were captured during the day. S.O.S.Lines covering the 154th.Infy.Bde. were put down as follows:- K.3.c.50.15. - K.2.b.62. - E.26.c.28. Orders were received earlier in the day that the 51st.Division would be relieved in the line by the 49th.Division, and the 4th.Canadian Division tonight. As, however the situation on the 154th.Infy.Bde. front was somewhat obscure their relief was postponed for 24 hours. The 255th. and 256th.Brigades RFA. remained in action. Vigorous harassing fire was kept up during the night in which the heavies co-operated. A Section of A/256. was detached for doing harassing fire, and this Section took up a position at B/256. old Battery position at	JW. JW.

WAR DIARY
INTELLIGENCE SUMMARY
(Erase heading not required.)

Army Form C. 2118.

276

Place	Date	Hour	Summary of Events and Information	Remarks and references to Appendices
Field.	1918. Oct. 28th.		Casualties:- 2/Lt.H.Stonehewer. Wounded. D/256. 2 O.R's. Wounded-D/256. at J.17.d.83.	Jn.J.
	29th.		The line this morning was reported unchanged. The 152nd.Infy.Bde. on the right had been relieved in the line during the night, by the 146th. and 147th. Infy Bdes. (49th.Div.) During the morning arrangements were made for allotting and securing Battery Positions for 4 additional Brigades of Artillery for the next operation. These Brigades consisted of:- 245th. and 246th. Bdes RFA. (49th.Division) and 174th. and 186th.Bdes RFA. (39th.Division). These Brigades reported in the morning. Positions allotted were reconoitred and arrangements made for going into action. A re-grouping of the Brigades was made as follows:- LEFT GROUP. covering the 154th.Infy.Bde.(51st.Div) and part of the 146th.Infy.Bde.(49th.Div.) Officer Commanding.- Lt.Col.J.Hamilton Meikle.R.H.A. --- 256th.Bde.RFA.(51st.D.A.) - 245th.Bde.RFA.(49th.D.A.) -- 189th. and 147th.Army Brigades RFA. RIGHT GROUP. covering the 147th. and part of the 146th.Infy.Bdes.(49th.Division) ---255th. Bde.RFA. (51st.Division) 174th.and 186th.Bdes RFA.(39th.D.A.) and the 77th.Army Bde.RFA.	
		09.00.	S.O.S.Lines covering the 154th. and 146th.Inft. Bdes. were re-arranged and put down as follows:- K.9.a.80.85. - K.2.d.30.65. -K.2.b.30.75. - E.25.b.75.10. During the day all enemy movements were engaged by Batteries. An O.P. was established at J.12.a.68. which had been	Jn.J.

WAR DIARY
INTELLIGENCE SUMMARY.
(Erase heading not required.)

Army Form C. 2118.

Place	Date	Hour	Summary of Events and Information	Remarks and references to Appendices
Field.	1918. Oct. 29th.		used by us on previous day, and good observed shooting was carried out by the Detached Section of A/256. Various combined shoots with Heavies were arranged and carried out during the day.	
		1530.	An S.O.S. call at 15.30.hrs. was replied to by all Brigades of the Left Group. A Counter-attack was reported. The enemy put down a heavy barrage but little if any Infantry action developed, and at 17.00.hrs. the situation became quieter. Enemy artillery was very active in the forward areas, and Battery positions being consistently shelled. The Command of the Artillery covering	
		1000.	the 154th.Infty.Bde. and the 49th.Division, passed to the C.R.A. 49th.Division at 10.00.hrs. Orders were received from the 49th.Division that the attack would be resumed on the 30th.Inst. Orders were received later that the attack was postponed for 24 hours. The necessary ammunition was got up to new positions. The 154th.Infy.Bde. were relieved in the line by the 10th.	
		2130.	Canadian Bde. (4th.Canadian Division) the relief was completed by 21.30.hrs. The Left Group Artillery which covered the 154th.Infy.Bde. continued to cover the 10th.Canadian Bde. pending the 4th.Canadian Divisional Artillery getting into action.	JW J.
			Lt.Col.J.Hamilton Meikle.R.H.A. on completion of relief, of the 154th. Infty. Bde. proceeded as Group Commander and Liaison Officer with the 10th.Canadian Bde. (Headquarters THIANT) The night was fairly quiet. Harassing fire was kept up.	JW J.

Army Form C. 2118.

278

WAR DIARY
INTELLIGENCE SUMMARY.
(Erase heading not required.)

Instructions regarding War Diaries and Intelligence Summaries are contained in F. S. Regs., Part II. and the Staff Manual respectively. Title pages will be prepared in manuscript.

Place	Date	Hour	Summary of Events and Information	Remarks and references to Appendices
Field.	1918. Oct. 29th.		About midnight it was reported that an enemy Infantry Relief was taking place opposite the Canadian, and 49th.Divisional Fronts. Orders were immediately given to all Brigades, including the 34th.Brigade R.G.A. and an increased harassing programme was vigorously carried out. It was also reported that enemy tanks had been seen moving South from VALENCIENNES. Orders were given that one Section of 245th.Brigade RFA. would move forward and be in a position of readiness at	
		0600.	06.00.hrs. ready to engage any tanks should the enemy attack. No attack, however took place Casualties:- 1.O.R. Gassed.-C/256.	JWJ
	30th.		The line remained unchanged. Visibility was good today, and observed shoots from detached Sections were carried out. Targets received from the 10th.Canadian Bde. were fired on, in which the 34th.Brigade RGA. Co-operated. The forward Batteries remained silent, all the firing being done by the detached Sections.	
		1300.	Orders were received that the General Officer Commanding 4th.Canadian Divisional Artillery, would take over the defence of the front held by the 10th.Canadian Bde. and that the Left Group 49th.D.A. would come under the command of the O.C.245th.Brigade RFA.(49th.D.A.) covering the 146th.Infy.Bde.	
		1500.	The re-arrangement was carried out and the Command of the Left Group passed from Lt.Col.J.Hamilton -Meikle.R.H.A.	JWJ

Army Form C. 2118.

279

WAR DIARY
INTELLIGENCE SUMMARY
(Erase heading not required.)

Instructions regarding War Diaries and Intelligence Summaries are contained in F.S. Regs., Part II. and the Staff Manual respectively. Title pages will be prepared in manuscript.

Place	Date	Hour	Summary of Events and Information	Remarks and references to Appendices
Field.	1918. Oct. 30th.		to Lt.Col.W.F.Lucey.D.S.O. The Artillery covering the 49th.Div. was now grouped as follows:-	
			Left Group. - covering the 146th. Infy. Bde. - Group Commander Lt.Col.W.F.Lucey.D.S.O. RFA. 244th. and 256th.Brigades R.F.A. and the 189th. and 147th. Army Brigades RFA.	
			Right Group.- covering the 147th.Infy.Brigade-Group Commander- Lt.Col.Duncan.D.S.O.RFA. 246th.Bde.RFA.-255th.Bde.RFA.- 174th.Bde.RFA.-186th.Bde.RFA. and the 777th.Army Bde.RFA.	
			New S.O.S. Lines were laid out covering the 146th.Infy.Bde. as follows:- K.15.b.45.90. - K.9.d.45.80. - K.9.b.00.40. Orders were received that the attack was postponed another 24 hours. The night was quiet. Harassing fire was kept up from detached Section.	
			The Brigade Commander was presented to His Royal Highness the Prince of Wales, who called at the 10th.Canadian Infantry Headquarters, and spent some time, and evinced great interest in the Artillery arrangements of this Group, and in the coming operations.	
			Casualties:- 1.O.R.Wounded B/256. and 7.O.R's.Wounded D/256.	
	31st.		Nothing unusual happened during the night. The Line remained unchanged. In view of the forthcoming attack new Battery Positions were reconnoitred East of the Railway in K.8. in the event of a further advance. Harassing fire was carried out as usual during the day and night.	

Army Form C. 2118.

280

WAR DIARY
INTELLIGENCE SUMMARY.
(Erase heading not required.)

Instructions regarding War Diaries and Intelligence Summaries are contained in F. S. Regs., Part II. and the Staff Manual respectively. Title pages will be prepared in manuscript.

Place	Date	Hour	Summary of Events and Information	Remarks and references to Appendices
Field.	1918. Oct.		The following is a note of the casualties sustained by the Brigade during the month.	
			OFFICERS. OTHER RANKS.	
			Killed. 1. 7.	
			Wounded. 2. 64.	
			Gassed. - 5.	
			Total. 3. 74.	
			The following is a note of the Ammunition expended by the Brigade during the month:-	
			18-pounder. 4.5.Hows:	
			From 1st.Oct.to 4th. (Scarpe operations) 3828. 1064.	
			From 8th.to 9th.Oct. (Cambrai operations) 3408. 672.	
			From 11th.to 31st.Oct. 36683. 8740.	
			Total for month. 43919. 10476.	

Commdg. 232 Brigade R.F.A.
Lieut. Col. R.H.A.

Army Form C. 2118.

281

WAR DIARY
INTELLIGENCE SUMMARY.
(Erase heading not required.)

Instructions regarding War Diaries and Intelligence Summaries are contained in F. S. Regs., Part II. and the Staff Manual respectively. Title pages will be prepared in manuscript.

Place	Date	Hour	Summary of Events and Information	Remarks and references to Appendices
Field.	1918. Nov. 1st.	05.15.	Batteries co-operated in a barrage covering an attack by the 49th.Division , in conjunction with the 4th.Division on the right, and a Canadian Division on the left.	
			The objective of the attack was the PRESEAU-VALENCIENNES Road.	
			The Artillery supporting the attack was disposed as follows:-	
			RIGHT GROUP.- covering the 147th.Infantry Brigade.- Lt.Col.K.Duncan.D.S.O. Commanding.-	
			246th.Brigade R.F.A.- 255th.Brigade R.F.A.- 174th.Brigade RFA. -	
			186th.Brigade RFA. - and the 77th.Army Brigade RFA.	
			LEFT GROUP.- covering the 146th.Infantry Brigade.- Lt.Col.W.F.Lucey.D.S.O. RFA.Commanding.-	
			245th.Brigade RFA. - 256th.Brigade RFA. - 189th.Army Brigade RFA.	
			and the 147th.Army Brigade RFA. (see appendices)	
			The attack was successful, and over 800 prisoners were captured in the early stages of the Battle. The crossing of the River RHONELLE was accomplished although stiff opposition was met.	W.J.
			New Battery Positions were reconnoitred (at the conclusion of the barrage) South of FAMARS.	
		1640.	At 16.40.hrs. the enemy counter-attacked against the whole of the Divisional Front, forcing our Line back slightly. The Line was, however, restored during the night.	W.J.

Army Form C. 2118.

282

WAR DIARY
or
INTELLIGENCE SUMMARY.
(Erase heading not required.)

Instructions regarding War Diaries and Intelligence Summaries are contained in F. S. Regs., Part II. and the Staff Manual respectively. Title pages will be prepared in manuscript.

Place	Date	Hour	Summary of Events and Information	Remarks and references to Appendices
Field.	1918. Nov. 1st.	1800.	Batteries moved forward at 18.00.hrs. to New Positions South of FAMARS in K.15.a. and were all in action by 19.00.hrs. Ammunition had been dumped at these positions earlier in the day. Afternoon in view of the attack being continued early tomorrow. S.O.S. Lines remained on the final protective barrage Line, covering final objective of today's operation. The night was quiet and nothing unusual happened.	
		2000.	Brigade Headquarters moved forward to new Headquarters at MAING at 20.00.hrs. Casualties:- 2.O.R's. Wounded. "D"Battery.	M.J.
	2nd.		The Line remained unchanged our troops holding the PRESEAU-VALENCIENNES Road throughout, and were in touch with the 4th.Division on the right, and the Canadians on the left. No attack was made by us today.	M.J.
		12.30.	It was reported that the enemy were massing in the village of SAULTAIN, and the Wood in E.24.d. Intense concentrations were put down in which the Batteries co-operated. These concentrations were repeated at various times between 13.00.hrs. and 14.00.hrs.	
		1430.	Orders were received that the 49th.Division were to exploit the attack of yesterday, and that the Infantry were to advance at 15.00.hrs. covered by a barrage, their objective being a line	M.J.

(A9173) Wt W4355/P360 600,000 12/17 D. D. & L. Sch. 52a. Forms/C1118/15.

Army Form C. 2118.
283

WAR DIARY
INTELLIGENCE SUMMARY.
(Erase heading not required.)

Place	Date	Hour	Summary of Events and Information	Remarks and references to Appendices
Field.	1918. Nov. 2nd.		about 200 yards East of the present Line. 256th.Brigade RFA. co-operated in the barrage, some little progress was made, and forward posts established.	
		1500.	The C.O. attended a Conference at Left Group Headquarters, when orders were received that the attack was to be continued on the 4th.inst.	
			The 56th.Division relieved the 49th.Division in the Line during the night, and the artillery covering the Divisional Front was re-grouped as follows:-	
			RIGHT GROUP.	
			280th.Brigade RFA. - 246th.Brigade RFA. - and the 77th.Army Brigade RFA.	
			LEFT GROUP.	
			281st.Brigade RFA. -245th.Brigade RFA. - and 147th.Army Brigade RFA.	
			An INDEPENDENT GROUP consisting of :-	
			255th. and 256Th. Brigades RFA.	
			For the attack on the 4th.inst. this Independent Group was to take up advanced positions (about 300 yards behind the jumping off point) the night prior to the attack, and co-operate in the barrage, after the first objective had been reached. Casualties:- NIL.	
			Harassing fire was carried out as usual.	

Army Form C. 2118.

WAR DIARY
INTELLIGENCE SUMMARY
(Erase heading not required.)

Place	Date	Hour	Summary of Events and Information	Remarks and references to Appendices
Field.	1918. Nov. 3rd.	0430	Batteries co-operated in a Counter Preparation Scheme consisting of a rolling barrage covering the 56th.Divisional Front. In view of the attack tomorrow Battery Positions immediately behind our front line were reconnoitred by the C.O. and B.C's. and arrangements made for getting up ammunition etc.	
		1000.	It was reported that a Canadian Patrol on the left of the 56th.Division had pushed forward and were encountering little opposition, and had already reached the Sunken Road in F.3.central. The 56th.Division accordingly pushed forward and made considerable progress. Orders were received from the 56th. Division that the 256th.Brigade RFA. would remain for the time being in present positions. Orders were received later that 256th Brigade RFA. were now in Corps Reserve, and that all ammunition at old positions should be collected and dumped. This was duly carried out. Casualties:- 2. O.R's. -Wounded - "B" Battery.	W.J.
	4th.		Orders were received from XXII Corps, that from midday today the 49th. and 51st.Divisional Artillery would be formed into one group, under orders of Lt.Col.J.Hamilton Meikle R.H.A. mainly for the purpose of salving all ammunition from old positions, within a radius of 3000 yards from FAMARS. This salving of ammunition was accordingly begun, and a Dump formed on the	W.J.

Army Form C. 2118.

WAR DIARY
INTELLIGENCE SUMMARY.
(Erase heading not required.)

285

Place	Date	Hour	Summary of Events and Information	Remarks and references to Appendices
Field.	1918. Nov. 4th.		main FAMARS Road. Casualties:- NIL.	
	5th.		Batteries remained in same positions and continued the salvage of ammunition. Orders were received from XXII Corps that the 51st. Divisional Artillery would move to SAULTAIN-ESTRAUX Area. Casualties:- NIL.	
	6th.	06.00.	256th. Brigade RFA. marched to ESTRAUX. On arrival Brigade Commander, and Adjutant reported to the C.R.A. 56th.D.A. at SAULTAIN, and received orders to the effect that the 51st.Divisional Artillery were to go into action forthwith, and cover a Brigade of the 63rd.(RN)Division. who were relieving in the line, the Left Infantry Brigade of the 56th.Division.	
		1130.	Brigade Commander and B.C's. proceeded to reconnoitre Battery positions, first receiving instructions from 281st.Brigade RFA. as to disposition of the line.	
		1530.	Batteries moved forward and took up positions as follows:- West of the ANNELLE River - West of SEBOURQUIAX. Orders were received that the XXII Corps were to attack tomorrow morning, 56th.Division on Right, and 63rd.(RN)Division on Left.	

Army Form C. 2118.

WAR DIARY
or
INTELLIGENCE SUMMARY.
(Erase heading not required.)

Place	Date	Hour	Summary of Events and Information	Remarks and references to Appendices
Field.	1918. Nov. 6th.		The Artillery covering the attack was re-grouped as follows:-	
			56TH.GROUP. -covering the Infantry Brigade 56th.Division.- under Lt.Col.C.C.Macdowell.D.S.O.	
			230th.Brigade RFA.- 281st.Brigade RFA. - 246th.Brigade RFA.- 245th.Brigade RFA.	
			with the 32nd.Brigade RFA. In reserve.	
			63RD.GROUP. -covering the 189th.Infantry Brigade.-under Lt.Col.J.Hamilton Meikle.R.H.A.-	
			255th.Brigade RFA. - 256th.Brigade RFA. - 175th.Army Brigade RFA. -147th.Army Brigade RFA.	
			with the 29th.Brigade RFA. in reserve.	
		1800.	Orders were received from the G.O.C. 63rd.(RN)Division that Brigades must take up positions East of the ANNELLE River, for the attack. These instructions were accordingly carried out and Brigade took up positions East of SEBOURQUIAX in A.15.a. and c. These moves were all carried out under very adverse weather conditions. The ANNELLE River had to be crossed by Ford, the bridges having been blown up, and owing to heavy rains the crossing over the Ford was no easy task. Batteries, however, were in action by 21.30.hours, and ammunition dumped. Brigade Headquarters were established alongside the 189th.Infantry Brigade Headquarters in SEBOURQUIAX.	

Army Form C. 2118.

WAR DIARY
INTELLIGENCE SUMMARY.
(Erase heading not required.)

Instructions regarding War Diaries and Intelligence Summaries are contained in F. S. Regs., Part II. and the Staff Manual respectively. Title pages will be prepared in manuscript.

28/

Place	Date	Hour	Summary of Events and Information	Remarks and references to Appendices
Field.	1918. Nov. 6th.		The relief of the 168th.Infantry Brigade (56th.Division) was carried out by the 189th.Infantry Brigade (63rd.(RN)Division) during the early morning.	
			Casualties:- Wounded- a/Major T.Hawker M.C. "C" Battery.	
	7th.	0900.	The attack took place at 09.00.hrs. under a creeping barrage (see appendices)	
			The attack of the 189th.Infantry Brigade was carried out by the Hawke Battalion on right, Hood Battalion on Left, and the Drake Battalion in support.	
			The first objective running from B.1.b.99. - T.25.b.91.- T.13.c.84. was gained, and the advance on the 2nd. objective to a line East of AUDREGNIES was continued.	
			B/256. under Captain G.C.Coull, acted in close support of the Left Battalion during the attack and engaged many targets throughout he day.	
		1050	At 10.50.hrs. the line from S.24.a.central. thence S.E. along Sunken Road to Brigade Boundary.	
			Orders were issued to the 29th.Brigade RFA. to move forward, and take up positions in the area A.4. and A.5. West of the village of ANGRE.	
		1400.	By 14.00.hrs. our Infantry had reached, and held the following line:-	
			T.15.b. -T.51.b.48. - T.51.c.63. - and were in touch with ~~he touch with~~ left Battalion 167th.Infty Brigade. in T.15.d.	

Army Form C. 2118.

288

WAR DIARY
INTELLIGENCE SUMMARY.
(Erase heading not required.)

Instructions regarding War Diaries and Intelligence Summaries are contained in F. S. Regs., Part II. and the Staff Manual respectively. Title pages will be prepared in manuscript.

Place	Date	Hour	Summary of Events and Information	Remarks and references to Appendices
Field.	1918. Nov. 7th.			
		1330.	Group Headquarters moved forward along with the 189th.Infantry Brigade Headquarters to ANGRE.	M.J.
			Instructions were issued to the 147th. and 175th.Brigades RFA. to advance and take up new positions in A.12.b. and S.30.d. respectively, S.E. of ANGRE. These moves were all carried out and both the 147th. and 175th. Brigades RFA. were in action by 18.00.hrs.	
			Between 16.00.hrs. and 18.00.hrs. various concentrations were put down by the 29th. and 175th. Brigades at the request of the Infantry.	
			S.O.S.Lines covering the the 189th.Infantry Brigade were put down as follows:-	
			From T.27.b.00. - T.22.c.37. - T.16.c.7.9.	
			These Lines were covered as follows:-	
			175th.Brigade RFA. on the Right Half.	
			147th. do on the Left Half.	
			29th.)	
			255th.)Bdes.RFA. Superimposed over the whole Zone.	
			256th.)	
			Orders were issued to the 255th. and 256th.Brigades RFA. to move forward to a position of Assembly in S.30. North East of ANGRE tomorrow morning. Brigades to be in position by 08.00.hrs.	M.J.

Army Form C. 2118.

289.

WAR DIARY
INTELLIGENCE SUMMARY.
(Erase heading not required.)

Instructions regarding War Diaries and Intelligence Summaries are contained in F. S. Regs., Part II. and the Staff Manual respectively. Title pages will be prepared in manuscript.

Place	Date	Hour	Summary of Events and Information	Remarks and references to Appendices
Field.	1918. Nov. 7th.		Night firing was carried out by Brigades on specially selected targets arranged with the Infantry.	
			Casualties:- Wounded –at duty.- Lieut.R.A.Hunter. "C" Battery.	
	8th.		The advance was continued today by the 63rd.(RN)Division in conjunction with the 56th.Division on Right, and the 2nd.Canadian Division on Left. The first objective being of the 189th. Infantry Brigade who continued the advance, was a line running East of AULREGNIES.- T.27.d.60.- T.27.b.54. - T.28.c.00. - T.16.b.60.	
			The 2nd. objective being High Ground in B.4.a.- T.28.central.- T.23.a.99. including the village of WITHERIES.	
			In connection with these operations special concentrations, or area bombardments were arranged to take place as follows:-	
			29th.Brigade RFA. - Road from T.22.c.46. - T.16.c.58. from 06.00.hrs. to 06.15.hrs.	
			The 175th.Army Brigade RFA. to co-operate, 60-pounders searched and swept the Spur in T.28.central to East of WITHERIES, and the High Ground in T.17.c. from 06.00.hrs. to 07.00.hrs. 147th.Army Brigade RFA. to search and sweep the area T.27.b. between the hours of 06.00.hrs. and 07.00.hrs.	
			Orders were issued accordingly. Owing, however, to certain Infantry re-arrangements the Artillery programme was postponed for two hours.	

(A9175) Wt W2358/P360 600,000 12/17 D. D. & L. Sch. 52a. Forms/C2118/15.

Army Form C. 2118.

290.

WAR DIARY
INTELLIGENCE SUMMARY.
(Erase heading not required.)

Instructions regarding War Diaries and Intelligence Summaries are contained in F. S. Regs., Part II. and the Staff Manual respectively. Title pages will be prepared in manuscript.

Place	Date	Hour	Summary of Events and Information	Remarks and references to Appendices
Field.	1918 Nov. 8th.	08.00.	Information was received that the 189th.Infantry Brigade had reached the area T.27.b. The 147th.Brigade Shoot was accordingly cancelled.	
			The advance continued satisfactorily little opposition being met, and by 10.00.hrs. the 189th. Infantry Brigade had reached a Line - Sunken Road running through T.24.a. - T.24.c. -T.30.a.& c.	
			Instructions were received that the advance would be continued the next objective being - Road Y.20.a. & c. and the village of BLAUGIES, and if little opposition was met, and this objective reached, the advance would be pushed on to the line - U.22.b. - U.28.b.- 0.4.b. & d.	
			During the advance the 255th.and 256th.Brigades RFA. pushed on in close support of the Infantry, the 29th.Brigade RFA. following in reserve.	
			Instructions were issued to the 255th. and 256th.Brigades RFA. to take up positions about T.23. and T.28.b. respectively.	
			Group Headquarters moved with the 189th.Infantry Brigade Headquarters from ANGRE to WITHERIES at 11.00.hrs.	
			Orders were issued to the 147th.and 175th.Army Brigades RFA. to remain in their present positions.	
			The advance met with success and by nightfall the Infantry had reached a Line-U.20.and U.26.	w.j.

Army Form C. 2118.

291

WAR DIARY
INTELLIGENCE SUMMARY

(Erase heading not required.)

Instructions regarding War Diaries and Intelligence Summaries are contained in F. S. Regs., Part II. and the Staff Manual respectively. Title pages will be prepared in manuscript.

Place	Date	Hour	Summary of Events and Information	Remarks and references to Appendices
Field.	1918. Nov. 8th.		including the village of BLAUGIES.	
			S.O.S. Lines for the night were put down on a Line namely.-	
			U.21.central. - U.27.central.- and C.3.central, within the Brigade Boundary.	
			The night was generally quiet.	
			Harassing fire on enemy Roads was carried out.	
			Casualties:- NIL.	
	9th.		Orders were received that the advance would be continued today by the 189th.Infantry Brigade	
			The first objective being the western edge of BOIS DE MONTREUIL. The second objective being	
			the SARS-LA-BRUYARE-EUGIES Road running through square V.26. and V.20.	
			The attack was carried out with the 1st.Artists on Right, and the 7th.Royal Fusiliers on Left,	
			the 4th.Bedfords being in support.	
			The 255th. 256th. and 29th.Brigades RFA. co-operated in the attack, by putting down bursts of fire	
			on selected areas. 256th.Brigade RFA. in order to carry out their task, moved forward to	
			positions in U.19. and U.20. and were in action by 08.30.hours.	
		0930.	The attack commenced at 09.30.hrs. and again met with little opposition. Rapid progress was	
			made. Orders were issued for the 255th. and 256th. Brigades RFA. to follow up in close	

Army Form C. 2118.

292

WAR DIARY
INTELLIGENCE SUMMARY.
(Erase heading not required.)

Instructions regarding War Diaries and Intelligence Summaries are contained in F. S. Regs., Part II. and the Staff Manual respectively. Title pages will be prepared in manuscript.

Place	Date	Hour	Summary of Events and Information	Remarks and references to Appendices
Field.	1918. Nov. 9th.		support of the Infantry. The final objective the SARS-LA-BRUYARE-EUGIES-Road, including the village of SARS-LA-BRUYARE was reached by 10.30.hrs. and the advance was continued towards the Railway in V.23. - V.29. and on to the main MAUBEUGE - MONS Road in W.20. and W.26.	
			The 256th.Brigade RFA. followed up throughout the advance, in close support of the Battalion and passed through SARS-LA-BRUYARE with the first wave of the Infantry.	
			A/256.provided a Mobile Section which co-operated with the 7th.Royal Fusiliers in the attack, The Section was under the command of 2/Lt.McQueen. who acted on many occasions on his own initiative, and went forward with the first wave of the Infantry, engaging successfully M.G's. at close range.	McJ.
		1830.	At 18.30.hrs. our Infantry were reported to be holding an Outpost Line from E.3.central, to W.23.a.50. 255th. and 256th.Brigades RFA.came into action in V.24.d. - V.30.d. covering this Line. Meantime orders had been issued to the 29th. and 175th.Brigades RFA. to move forward and take up positions in support of the 255th.and 256th.Brigades RFA.	McJ.
		1830.	At 18.30.hrs. the disposition of the Line was as follows :- Our Infantry held Outpost Line -E.3.central.- W.23.a.50. The 255th. and 256th.Brigades RFA. in action covering this Line in -V.30.d. - and V.24.d.	McJ.

Army Form C. 2118.

293

WAR DIARY
INTELLIGENCE SUMMARY.
(Erase heading not required.)

Instructions regarding War Diaries and Intelligence Summaries are contained in F. S. Regs., Part II. and the Staff Manual respectively. Title pages will be prepared in manuscript.

Place	Date	Hour	Summary of Events and Information	Remarks and references to Appendices
Field.	1918. Nov. 9th.	1830.	respectively, with the 29th.Brigade RFA. and the 175th.Army Brigade RFA. in action in V.24.c. and V.30.c.	
			S.O.S. Lines covering this line were put down as follows:-	
			255th.Brigade RFA. - E.4.a.00. - W.28.b.70.	
			256th. do - W.28.b.70.- W.23.b.30.	
			175th.Army Bde.RFA. - Superimposed over 255th.Zone.	
			29th.Brigade RFA. - Superimposed over 256th.Zone.	
			The 147th.Army Brigade RFA. was relieved earlier in the day under orders received from the XXII Corps. by the 277th.Army Brigade RFA. This Brigade reported to the Group Commander about midday, and orders were given them to take up positions of assembly in U.29.a. Orders were also issued to the 29th. and 175th. Army Brigades RFA. that the advance would be continued tomorrow, and that these Brigades would follow up in close support of the Infantry, with the 255th. and 256th. Brigades RFA. in reserve.	
			Casualties:- NIL.	In.
	10th.		The attack was again continued this morning the 29th. and 175th.Brigades RFA. following up in close support. More opposition was met with, and stiff fighting took place about the Chalk-Pits.	In.

Army Form C. 2118.

294

WAR DIARY
INTELLIGENCE SUMMARY
(Erase heading not required.)

Instructions regarding War Diaries and Intelligence Summaries are contained in F. S. Regs., Part II. and the Staff Manual respectively. Title pages will be prepared in manuscript.

Place	Date	Hour	Summary of Events and Information	Remarks and references to Appendices
Field.	1918 Nov. 10th.		in Q.28.c.	
			The Mobile Section from the 175th.Army Brigade RFA. covering the right Battalion did good work and engaged at close range enemy M.G's. located there, and enabled the Infantry to go forward.	
			Enemy Guns were also active throughout the day shelling especially the village of ASQUILLIES.	
			The Infantry continued the advance but were held up by M.G. fire from the main GIVRY-MONS Road also from Sunken Road running South through Q.24. and Q.30. These Roads were kept under fire by 29th.Brigade RFA. and 175th.Army Brigade RFA. while D/256. carried out a special shoot on the Sunken Road running North from the Old Colliery from R.31.a. to R.19.c. at 16.00.hrs. to 16.30.hrs.	J.W.T.
		2000.	By 20.00.hrs. our Infantry had reached the main GIVRY-MONS Road. Meantime 255th. and 256th. had advanced and taken up positions in close support East of ASQUILLIES in W.8.b.8d. and W.9.c.	
			Brigade Headquarters moved forward with the 190th.Infantry Brigade Headquarters to ASQUILLIES at 16.00.hours.	
			S.O.S. Lines covering the 190th.Infantry Brigade were put down as follows:-	
			From Q.30.c.72. to Q.30.a.25.	J.W.T.

Army Form C. 2118.

WAR DIARY
or
INTELLIGENCE SUMMARY.
(Erase heading not required.)

Instructions regarding War Diaries and Intelligence Summaries are contained in F. S. Regs., Part II. and the Staff Manual respectively. Title pages will be prepared in manuscript.

Place	Date	Hour.	Summary of Events and Information	Remarks and references to Appendices
Field.	1918. Nov. 10th.	2100.	At 21.00.hrs. orders were received that the 63rd.(RN)Division were to take over the whole Corps Front, as the advance guard of the XXII Corps. and that the Artillery would be re-grouped as follows:-	
			RIGHT GROUP. - covering the 189th.Infantry Brigade.-Commander Lt.Col.J.Hamilton Meikle R.H.A.	
			255th.Brigade RFA.	
			256th.Brigade RFA.	
			LEFT GROUP. - covering the 188th.Infantry Brigade.- Commander Lt.Col.W.Furnavall.D.S.O.(175.Bde RFA)	
			175th.Army Brigade RFA.	
			29th.Brigade RFA.	
			The XXII Corps Boundaries were to be as follows:-	
			NORTHERN. - V.23.a.30. - W.2.a.64. - Q23.central.	
			SOUTHERN. - GIVRY - BINCHE Road.	
			The 189th.Infatry Brigade Boundaries being:-	
			On the Right - the GIVRY - BINCHE Road.	
			On the Left - W.23.central - W.18.central. - X.7.central. - X.3.central to BRAY in M.20.d.	
			In consequence of this change, orders were issued to 255th. and 256th.Brigades RFA. to be	

Army Form C. 2118.

WAR DIARY
INTELLIGENCE SUMMARY

(Erase heading not required.)

Instructions regarding War Diaries and Intelligence Summaries are contained in F. S. Regs., Part II. and the Staff Manual respectively. Title pages will be prepared in manuscript.

396

Place	Date	Hour	Summary of Events and Information	Remarks and references to Appendices
Field.	1918. Nov. 10th.		prepared to move to a position of assembly in W.30. and W.24. The night was generally quiet. Harassing fire was carried out on enemy roads and approaches in Brigade Zone. Casualties:- Wounded. - 2.O.R's. "C" Battery.	M.J.
	11th.	0700.	255th. and 256th.Brigades RFA. marched to positions of assembly in W.24. Meantime the C.O. had ridden on to Headquarters of the 139th.Infantry Brigade, and received instructions as to the disposition of the line held by them.	
		1000.	Intimation had been received that an Armistice had been declared, and would come into force at 11.00.hours after which time there would be no firing. The advance of the 139th.Infantry Brigade was continued, and the 255th. and 256th.Brigades RFA. followed up in close support. 256th.Brigade RFA. took up positions South East of HARMIGNIES by midday as follows:-	
			A/256. - X.1.c.45. C/256. - X.7.c.42.	
			B/256. - X.7.c.31. D/256. - W.12.d.61.	
			All troops were ordered to stand fast in the Line at which they had reached at 11.00.hrs. and that all defensive precautions would be maintained, and an Outpost Line established. Orders	M.J.

Army Form C. 2118.

WAR DIARY
INTELLIGENCE SUMMARY
(Erase heading not required.)

Instructions regarding War Diaries and Intelligence Summaries are contained in F. S. Regs., Part II. and the Staff Manual respectively. Title pages will be prepared in manuscript.

Place	Date	Hour	Summary of Events and Information	Remarks and references to Appendices
Field.	1918. Nov. 11th.		were also issued that there would be no parlying with the enemy, and that if he attempted to come over he would be immediately sent back.	297
			The Line reached by the 188th.Infantry Brigade and held by them at 11.00.hours. was as follows:-	
			Line of MONS - BINCHE Railway running through X.4.11. and 18. with outposts about 200 yards in front.	
			S.O.S. Lines were put out 300 yards plus of this Line, and the Brigade remained in action covering this Line.	
			During the advance from the 7th. the Brigade met with great receptions in the Villages captured and liberated. The Enemy in some cases had left only about an hour previous to the entry of the Batteries, which advanced on this occasion immediately behind the leading waves of the Infantry attack.	
			Casualties:- Wounded - O.R's. - one. - "D" Battery.	
	12th.		Batteries remained in the same positions. Full advantage was taken of the present Armistice to re-organise and re-equip Batteries.	
			Orders were received that the 51st.(Highland) Division was about to march forward into Germany as one of the Divisions of the XXII Corps.	

Army Form C. 2118.
298.

WAR DIARY
INTELLIGENCE SUMMARY

(Erase heading not required.)

Place	Date	Hour	Summary of Events and Information	Remarks and references to Appendices
Field.	1918 Nov. 12th.		AMMUNITION EXPENDED FROM 1ST. NOVEMBER to 12TH. NOVEMBER 1918.	
			18-pounders. ... ... 7,143. Rounds.	
			4.5.Hows: ... ... 1,871. Rounds.	
	12th/18th.		During the period under review the Brigade remained at GIVRY. Batteries were re-organised and re-equipped and a general scheme of training carried out, with guns still in action covering the outpost line.	JWJ
	18th.		Orders were received that the 63rd Division now ceased to be responsible for the front and that the outposts would be withdrawn and that batteries could be withdrawn from action. Orders were accordingly issued to batteries that guns need not now be kept in action.	JWJ
	18th/27th.		The scheme of training including general recreation was continued. Musketry practice was carried out by all men in the Brigade. Orders were received on the 24th inst. that the composition of Armies and Corps proceeding to Germany had been reorganised and that to meet the re-allotment, the 22nd Corps (4th,51st,52nd and 56th Divisions) was transferred from Second Army to First Army at noon 22nd inst., and would accordingly not now proceed to Germany. A Soup Kitchen for the benefit of the poor of the village of HARMIGNIES and also for the refugees was augurated by the Brigade on 22nd inst. at HARMIGNIES. An average of 200 people were fed daily. The scheme was very much appreciated by the Civil Administration.	JWJ

WAR DIARY
or
INTELLIGENCE SUMMARY.

(Erase heading not required.)

Army Form C. 2118.

Place	Date	Hour	Summary of Events and Information	Remarks and references to Appendices
	28th		51st Divisional Artillery moved to ROEULX and MIGNAULT area - 10 miles N.E. of MONS - 256th Brigade maoved to ROEULX. Before laeving GIVRY the Communal Administration of GIVRY through the medium of the Burgmaster presented the Brigade with a Belgium National flag suitably embroidered and a letter of appreciation and thanks for the deliverance of the Town and as a souvenir of our entry to the town on the 11/11/18 when the Armistice came into effect.	
	29/30th.		The Brigade remained at ROEULX and arrangements were made for the scheme of training and recreation being continued.	
			The following Honours and Awards were gained by the Brigade during the month :-	
			BAR TO THE MILITARY CROSS.	
			Lieut.J.Gillespie,M.C. -------- "A" Battery.	
			THE MILITARY CROSS.	
			T/2/Lieut. G.M.Smith,-------- "B" Battery. (Since died of wounds.)	
			THE MILITARY MEDAL.	
			249573 Sapper T.McDougall, H.Q.	
			406127 Cpl.W.M.McCrae,R.E.,H.Q.	
			63570 Bdr.G.Bruce, "A" Battery.	
			81078 L/Bdr.W.J.Howarth,"A" Battery.	
			635067 Bdr.J.Wright, "B"Battery.	
			6172 L/Bdr.J.Baker, "B" "	
			635671 Dr.J.Leslie, "B" "	
			59185 Gr.P.Newport, "B" Battery.	
			72470 Bdr. W.Stark, "C" "	
			149079 " G.Head, "C" "	
			96209 Gr.G.F.Fulford. "C" "	
			44748 Dr.P.Neave. "D" "	
			L/36410 Gr.S.Simmons. "D" "	
			148688 " F.Terry. "D" "	

3/12/18.

Lt. Col. R.H.A.
Comdg. 256 (H) Brigade R.F.A. F.

Confidential

98 4 3

War Diary
of
256 (Highland) Brigade R.F.A. T.F.
From 1st November 1918 to 30th November 1918

(Volume No. — — —)

Confidential

Vol 44

War Diary
of
257 Bde RFA (TF)

From 1st December 1918 to 31st December 1918

(Volume N° -)

Army Form C. 2118.

WAR DIARY
INTELLIGENCE SUMMARY.
(Erase heading not required.)

Instructions regarding War Diaries and Intelligence Summaries are contained in F. S. Regs., Part II. and the Staff Manual respectively. Title pages will be prepared in manuscript.

Place	Date	Hour	Summary of Events and Information	Remarks and references to Appendices

Field	Decr.1918.		The Brigade remained stationed at ROEULX. During the month the general scheme of training, Education and recreation was continued - the forenoons being devoted to Military training and the afternoons to education and recreation. The Education scheme included classes in English and Arithmetic, Elementary Mathematics, History, Geography and French, the students being classified on the following basis :- (a) Unskilled workers, (b) Technical workers, (c) Commercial Workers, and the instruction given designed to meet their respective requirements. The number of students enrolled is approximately as follows :- Group A.257, Group B. 277 - Group C.125. During the month the Demobilization scheme was commenced, the following being a summary of the groups whose demobilization has so far been ordered :- (a) Coalminers, (b) Demobilizers and Pivotal Men, (c) Certain men who have been longest with the F.F. 104 Men belonging to these groups were demobilized during the month.
			The following is a note of the Honours and Awards received during the month for gallantry displayed in the operations in October and November last.
			    Bleut. E.J.Cuddiford Military Cross. 2/Lieutenant J.H. Gay C.Battery Military Cross.
			                                     M I L I T A R Y M E D A L.
			249556 2/Cpl.J.Murray H.Q. 36164 Sgt.J.Armitage "A"Bty. 645640 Far.Sgt.J.Mc.Dakers "A" Bty.
			635363 Siglr.P.F.Fairlie "A"Bty. L/38067 Sig.R.A.Robson "A"Bty. 224946 Siglr.A.Coupland "A"Bty.
			801750 Gnr. R.H.Lacey "A"Bty. 175381 Dvr.J.Roberston 635887 Cpl.J.McLennan. "B" Bty.
			127532 Gnr. M.Sheldon "B"Bty. 635675 A/Sgt.J.Berry "B"Bty. 635695 Cpl. J.Elder "B" Bty.
			935763 Gnr. T.Young "B"Bty. 635638 Sgt.J.Taylor "B" Bty. 635627 Dvr. C. Rose "B" Bty.
			61646 Cpl. J.W.Laven "C" Bty. 636096 Cpl. D.Summers "C" Bty. 636409 Cpl. W. Dow "C" Bty.
			213870 Bdr. J.H.Spence "C"Bty. 20059 Sgt.A.Cooper "D" Bty. 663032 Sgt.W.McKinnon "D"Bty.
			663092 Dvr.A.Graham "D"Bty. 717410 Cpl.W.Winter "D"Bty. 656469 Sig. S.Simmons "D" Bty.
			169656 Dvr. R.Ross "D"Bty.	

Confidential

War Diary

of

256 (Highland) Brigade R.F.A. T.F.

From 1st January 1919 to 31st January 1919

(Volume No.____)

WD 45
51 Div

301.

Army Form C. 2118.

WAR DIARY
or
INTELLIGENCE SUMMARY.

(Erase heading not required.)

Instructions regarding War Diaries and Intelligence Summaries are contained in F. S. Regs., Part II. and the Staff Manual respectively. Title pages will be prepared in manuscript.

Place	Date	Hour	Summary of Events and Information	Remarks and references to Appendices
FRANCE	JAN. 1919.		The Brigade remained stationed at ROEULX.	
			The Corps Commander (Lt.Gen.Sir A.J.Godley, K.C.B.,K.C.M.G.) inspected the Brigade on 4/1/19.	
			The inspection took the form of a march past in Mounted Drill Order.	
			The M.G.,R.A. First Army inspected the Brigade on 6/1/19. No special parade was held for the inspection which was in the nature of a visit to Batteries while at Stables and in the Gun Park and billets.	
			H.R.H. The Prince of Wales paid a visit to the Brigade on the afternoon of 29/1/19 and watched an inter Brigade Football Match. He spoke to many of the men during the progress of the game.	
			During the month the Education and Training Schemes were continued while Recreation (including Football and Rugby matches, Boxing Tournaments etc.) was carried out.	
			The Demobilization of Men and Horses was continued and the following is a summary of the numbers demobilized during the month :-	
			OFFICERS. O.Rs. HORSES. Major R.R.Will,D.S.O.) 2/Lt.F.C.Jack;) "B" Battery 97. 52. " E.G.Dalziel,M.C.)	
			The following is a note of the Honours and Awards received during the month in connection with the Operations during 1918.:-	

302.

Army Form C. 2118.

WAR DIARY
INTELLIGENCE SUMMARY.
(Erase heading not required.)

Instructions regarding War Diaries and Intelligence Summaries are contained in F. S. Regs. Part II. and the Staff Manual respectively. Title pages will be prepared in manuscript.

Place	Date	Hour	Summary of Events and Information	Remarks and references to Appendices
	JAN. 1919.		NEW YEARS HONOURS.	
			MILITARY CROSS.	
			Captain P.W.JOHNSTON, Adjutant.	
			DISTINGUISHED CONDUCT MEDAL.	
			No.635443 Ftr.Cpl.R.Strachan,M.M. "A" Battery. 635773 Gr.J.Burns, Headquarters.	
			MERITORIOUS SERVICE MEDAL.	
			No.635055 Fitter W.Garvie, "C" Battery.	
			MENTIONED IN DESPATCHES.	
			Major R.R.Will,D.S.O. "B" Bty. Major J.Scott, "D" Bty. Major S.O.Shepherd, "A" Bty. Capt.J.C.D.Mackie, "D" Bty. Capt.J.E.Hanna,M.C.,R.A.V.C. No.935763 Gr.T.Young, "D"Bty.	
			FRENCH DECORATIONS.(FIFTH FRENCH ARMY).	
			CROIX DE GUERRE - GOLD STAR.	
			2/Lt.H.C.Inkson,M.C. "B" Battery. No.178709 Gr.W.Cassimer, "C" "	
			CROIX DE GUERRE - SILVER STAR.	
			No.635443 Ftr.Cpl.R.Strachan,D.C.M.,M.M. "A" Battery.	
			CROIX DE GUERRE - BRONZE STAR.	
			No.41556 B.S.M. C.Dyer, "A" Battery. 630320 B.S.M. W.Morrison, "B" Battery.	

256TH (HIGHLAND) BDE. R.F.A.

Vol 46
51 Div

Confidential

War Diary
of Bde. R.F.A. T.F.
257 (Highland) Bde. R.F.A. T.F.
From 1st February 1919 to 28th February 1919

(Volume No.)

WAR DIARY
INTELLIGENCE-SUMMARY.

(Erase heading not required.)

Army Form C. 2118.

256TH (HIGHLAND) BDE. R.F.A.

Place	Date	Hour	Summary of Events and Information	Remarks and references to Appendices
FRANCE	FEB. 1919.		The Brigade remained stationed at ROEULX.	
			During the month the Education and Training Schemes were continued.	
			The Demobilization of Men and Horses was continued and the following is a summary of the numbers demobilized during the month :-	
			O.Rs. HORSES. 97. 88.	

			OFFICERS.
			   Major.J.B.Meikle, M.C. "C" Battery.
			   Capt.G.A.D.McDowell. " "
			   " R.A.Hunter. " "
			   2/Lt.J.H.Gay, M.C. " "
			   " J.R.Hardern, att. from
			                         T.Ms. " "
			   " A.B.McQueen, M.C. "A" "	

			All battery equipment was checked and stored away.	
			On the 4/2/19 the C.R.A. presented the FRENCH CROIX DE GUERRE MEDAL, to the following, in the presence of the whole Brigade :-	

			CROIX DE GUERRE - GOLD STAR.
			       2/Lt.H.C.Inkson, M.C. "B" Battery.
			       No.178709 Gunner.W.Cassimer. "C" Battery.	

			CROIX DE GUERRE - SILVER STAR. No.635443 Ftr.Cpl. R.STRACHAN, D.C.M., M.M. "A" Battery.	
			CROIX DE GUERRE - BRONZE STAR. No.41556 B.S.M DYER, "A" Battery.	

Army Form C. 2118.

WAR DIARY
or
INTELLIGENCE SUMMARY.

(Erase heading not required.)

Instructions regarding War Diaries and Intelligence Summaries are contained in F. S. Regs., Part II. and the Staff Manual respectively. Title pages will be prepared in manuscript.

256TH (HIGHLAND) BDE. R.F.A.

No. ....
Date 3/3/19

Place	Date	Hour	Summary of Events and Information	Remarks and references to Appendices
FRANCE	FEB. 1919.		On 6/2/19 the R.A. Band (Woolwich) visited ROEULX and played two performances in the Cinema Hall, ROEULX on that date.	

W. Johnston Capt.
Lieut. Col. Commanding 256 Bde R.F.A.T.

256TH (HIGHLAND) BDE. R.F.A.

Confidential

War Diary
of
256 (Highland) Brigade R.F.A.
From 1st March 1919 to 31st March 1919.

(Volume No. 1)

WL 47
6 fm

Army Form C. 2118.

256TH (HIGHLAND) BDE., R.F.A.
No.......
Date 2-4-19

WAR DIARY
or
INTELLIGENCE SUMMARY.
(Erase heading not required.)

Instructions regarding War Diaries and Intelligence Summaries are contained in F.S. Regs., Part II. and the Staff Manual respectively. Title pages will be prepared in manuscript.

Place	Date	Hour	Summary of Events and Information	Remarks and references to Appendices

FRANCE.	MAR. 1919 1st to 25th		A reconnaissance of the area between BRAIN-LE-COMTE - LA CROIX - MANAGE RLY inclusive to the LA LOUVIERE - ROEULX ROAD was carried out with a view to obtaining certain topographical information chiefly with regards to STREAMS, FOREST, MARSHES and other points affecting strategical and tactical operations. The Brigade remained stationed at ROEULX. During this period the demobilization of men and Horses was continued down to Cadre "A" strength. The following is a summary of the numbers demobilized during this period.:-
			
			            O.R's. HORSES. MULES.
			 OFFICERS.
			 Capt.J.C.D.Mackie. "D" Battery.
			 2/Lieut.T.Enstone. "C" Battery.
			            79. 276. 149.
			
			 The following Officers and men were transferred to the Army of Occupation on the RHINE.:-
			
			 OFFICERS.
			 2/Lieut.J.O.Cobham.
			 2/Lieut.H.G.Thorpe.
			        O.R's.
			        115.	

	25th.		All vehicles and Battery equipment etc were transferred to MANAGE STATION to be ready for entrainment for home destinations. Headquarters and Battery Cadre's also moved to MANAGE.	

www.ingramcontent.com/pod-product-compliance
Lightning Source LLC
Chambersburg PA
CBHW080832010526
44112CB00015B/2498